Lavery Library

St. John Fisher
College
Rochester, New York

We Must Have Certainty

We Must Have Certainty

Four Essays on the Detective Story

J. K. Van Dover

SUP

Selinsgrove: Susquehanna University Press

Associated University Presses
2010 Eastpark Boulevard
Cranbury, NJ 08512

The paper used in this publication meets the requirements of the American National Standard for Permanence of Paper for Printed Library Materials Z39.48-1984.

Library of Congress Cataloging-in-Publication Data

Van Dover, J. Kenneth.
    We must have certainty : four essays on the detective story / J. K. Van Dover.
        p.   cm.
    Includes bibliographical references and index.
    ISBN 1-57591-091-8 (alk. paper)
    1. Detective and mystery stories, English—History and criticism.
    2. Detective and mystery stories, American—History and criticism.
    I. Title.
    PR830.D4V36   2005
    823′.087209—dc22   2004028954

For Sarala,
Every Decade

The probability is in favor of my theory; but probability, in such an affair, is not sufficient; we must have certainty.
—M. Lecoq, in Emile Gaboriau's *The Mystery of Orcival*

Contents

Preface

In EARLIER BOOKS I HAVE ATTEMPTED TO LOCATE A SOURCE OF THE appeal of the detective story in plot and in character; in *We Must Have Certainty*, I attempt to locate it in scene. *Murder in the Millions* argued that it was the fairy-tale plotting of Erle Stanley Gardner, Mickey Spillane, and Ian Fleming that made these writers the super-selling phenomena that they became. *You Know My Method* made the case that it was the distinctive character of the detective—his embodiment of a moralized scientific method—that underlay his emergence as a type of the hero in a post–Darwinian world. Now I suggest that it is the special world in which the detective's method infallibly works that makes the detective story such a perennially lively genre.

The first essay lays out a developmental taxonomy of the genre. It began as an introductory section in what is now the second essay; it just grew. I hope it gives to the lay reader who has read only a few dozen (or even a few hundred) detective stories a somewhat larger sense of the dimensions of the genre. It will surely give to the clerisy a sense of the limitations of my sense of the genre. Many of the names I appear to have overlooked were omitted by intention; an essay is not a catalog. Still, far too many important writers, I fear, have been omitted through inattention or ignorance. I have read at least one story by every writer mentioned; I have read scores of stories by many of them.

The four phases in the development of the genre that the essay describes are, I hope, predictable. The first phase, from Poe to Conan Doyle and Chesterton, is one of diversity and experiment. The second phase, beginning around 1920, is one of consolidation, with Holmes casting the long shadow, and writers such as Christie, Sayers, and Carr pressing the form toward the novel: this is the widely recognized Golden Age.

The American hard-boiled revision of the form, which began in the early 1920s, is also widely understood. There is little doubt that the hard-boiled form underwent a decisive softening in the 1970s, producing what I have called the Engaged detective. The label may be disputed, but the shift must be obvious to any reader. Less obvious, I hope, and more original are the implications that I discover in each of the phases.

The second essay began as an attempt to describe the social world of the Hard-boiled detective. At the end of *You Know My Method*, I suggested that the Hard-boiled detective, however Neanderthal he might appear as man and as knower, did still practice a method, and did still know. That suggestion still seems valid to me. The detective, in all his avatars, is essentially a knower. He (or she) is the popular embodiment of a type of knowing that, since the mid-nineteenth century, is the only credible type of knowing: his or her knowledge is based upon an empirically verifiable chain of inferences. As the *ratio sapientia*, secured by faith, lost its apparent power over the world, a *ratio scientia*, based upon experiment, was proving itself to be remarkably effective in interpreting and manipulating the world. But *ratio scientia* is always provisional; it produces hypotheses that, however often confirmed by experiment, are always and inherently vulnerable to refutation by experiment. The *ratio scientia* of the detective, even if it results from a tough guy provoking violent responses with his fists and his wisecracks, always produces certain knowledge, and, moreover, knowledge that separates the sheep from the goats. The main theme of the second essay is that while this knowledge appears to depend upon the distinctive character of the detective, it of course essentially depends upon the detective's world, which must be constructed to yield knowledge, not hypotheses.

But a secondary theme also emerges. Readers of Hard-boiled fiction are attracted to more than the fable of a world fully understood. There is doubtless some satisfaction in following the adventures of a street-wise man or woman using his or her will to impose order on a piece of the big, dark city, as there was in following the ratiocinative man using his (rarely her) intellect to reimpose order in a manor house or a resort hotel. But the portrait of that big, dark city and of the ways of its diverse classes is, surely, also an important attraction. We read the novel not only to discover what really happened, but also to acquire vicariously a sense of what the detective's world is really like: how do con-men and gangsters and corrupt cops and corrupt politicians and corrupt businessmen run the world? (In its later phase, this subsidiary interest lies less in the operation of overt corruption and more in the effects of misguided manners and mores.) Nor is this secondary appeal missing in the Classical forms of the genre. Only in Poe's initial invention is it absent. Poe had virtually no interest in recreating a more than plausible Paris for Dupin, but the Paris of Lecoq and the gaslit London of Sherlock Holmes already clearly have intrinsic appeal beyond their guarantee to provide the detective with certain knowledge. The second essay attempts to explore some dimensions of the special world within which the detective operates.

The third essay plays with the idea of the "mystery." I thought it might be clever to link that label with its etymological origins in the cults of the classical world. There is, after all, an element of ritual in the reading of detective stories. Those who read them tend to read often; we repeat the experience endlessly. W. H. Auden, in "The Guilty Vicarage," has proposed that the typical reader of detective fiction "suffers from a sense of sin," and obtains a "magical satisfaction" when, at the story's end, he or she can identify him or herself with the suspects suddenly relieved of the burden of suspicion. This, I have always thought, is one of the less perceptive observations in an essay whose every observation is enlightening. I, at least, am never conscious of identifying myself with the suspects; I never feel myself vicariously exculpated by their vindication. And while we admire the detective, we do not identify with him; he is clearly what we would, and cannot, be. It seems to me that we are most likely to identify with Dupin's narrator, or Dr. Watson, or Jervis, or Hastings; with, that is, the presumptively innocent, not the suspected. (The outrage over *The Murder of Roger Ackroyd* evidently derives precisely from having this presumption betrayed.) We do not experience relief at being proven not guilty; we experience relief that someone can prove—can prove irrefutably to us—that someone is guilty. It is a disinterested exhilaration, more aesthetic than moral; though the matter is, of course, moral. The detective wonderfully reorders chaos. He demonstrates an efficient cause for every significant effect. This means that he can explain whodunit, but also that he can explain why the housekeeper lied about when she put up the preserves, and why there was a bit of rubber next to the mantelpiece, and why the corpse was thrust upside down in the chimney. We purchase mysteries, I think, because we desire this relief. We purchase them again and again because, in a world of experience where definitive explanation of anything is rare enough, the consolation of formula fiction has replaced the consolation of the catechisms of religion.

The final essay develops this topic, taking up some of the metaphysical implications of this epistemological fable. It struck me, as I was reading a history of Chinese thought which contrasted the characteristic "this-world" metaphysics of China with the characteristic "two-world" metaphysics of the West, that the detective story, with its essential double plot, was in this respect quintessentially Western. If the West is obsessed with "objectivity"—an obsession undeterred by the critiques of Nietzsche, of the Pragmatists, and of others—so is the detective story, which insists that beneath the unhappy and confusing surface narrative of a crime is a retrievable, intelligible, and absolutely certain underplot. Though detectives may be fallible, the genre survives and prospers on the myth that they are infallible; whether ratiocinative or hard-boiled, they always, in the end, reach objective truth. The detective story is a defining fable of Western culture.

Although I have tried to be as comprehensive as possible, my ambition has only been to comprehend the detective story in English. And I must confess that not only are the *roman policier*, the *krimi*, and the *giallo*—not to speak of the *zhen tan xiao shuo*—underrepresented, even the English detective story is viewed with an American eye. American eyes, early in the twenty-first century, are still trained to observe English motes, but doubtless see fewer than English eyes do. As for the American beams that I have missed—I can only hope that my modesty will prove disarming.

Another limitation needs to be acknowledged. When I began to write about the detective story in the early 1980s, it was still possible for a full-time teacher to read everything worthwhile on the subject. In the summer of 2001, I found it necessary to compensate for almost a decade of desultory reading; in catching up on what I had missed, I found I had missed a lot. There has been an explosion of interest in the detective story. Some of it I knew about; the postmodernists had been at play with the conventions, and the explicators of postmodernism had naturally followed. Lacan was a name to conjure with, and Lacan on Poe was talismanic. Feminists had penetrated the hard-boiled world as writers in the 1970s, and as critics in the 1980s. I was prepared for endless incantations of the oracles: Bahktin, Barthes, Baudrillard, Butler, Foucault, Jameson, Gramsci, Kristeva, Said, Todorov. I did encounter them. But, to my dismay, I encountered very few books that could be dismissed as mandarin babble. It was disconcerting to see so many insightful books and articles on the detective story and feminism (or the detective story and masculinity), or the detective and empire, or the detective and ethnicity, or the detective story and forensic science. There were, indeed, a few books, and among them some of the most praised, that demonstrated a vast erudition in matters theoretical and a rather narrow exposure to the detective fiction to which that erudition was applied. But they were the exception. Nonetheless, I have not had much occasion to cite secondary sources in these essays, because they did not address the issues I was interested in.

A final note on pronouns: the editing process has made clear that my use of "he"/"him"/"his" is questionable. It will be noted that I usually use the masculine pronoun when referring to the detectives of the first three phases of the detective story. This is not thoughtless sexism. It reflects the fact that the detectives of the first three phases were exclusively, or nearly exclusively, male. All Hard-boiled detectives are male. One can, if one looks hard, find female detectives in the first, Methodical phase; the best known and most influential of these are Catherine Louisa Pirkis's Loveday Brooke (1894), George Sims's Dorcas Dene (1897), M. McDonnell Bodkin's Dora Myrl (1900), and Baroness Orczy's Lady Molly

(1910). Brooke, Dene, Myrl, and Molly are landmark detectives in their field, but the field is a specialized one. Feminist scholars and others have, in the past decade, made a number of explorations of the territory (see Kestner 2003, Hadley 2002, Jackson 2002, Reynolds 2001, Rowland 2001, Dubose 2000, Nickerson 1998, Klein 1995, and others), and the results have been interesting and provocative. But the practice of Victorian and Edwardian lady detectives simply does not affect the course of the mainstream of male detectives whose pursuits concern me here. And even in the Golden Age, when figures as eminent as Mrs. Marple and Miss Pinkerton can make more substantial claims for attention, I think it would be inaccurate to "he or she," "him or her," "his or her" the detective. Indeed, the typical masculinity of the aggressive detectives of these three phases is itself a point worth examining, but that would be another essay. On the other hand, it is a central point that the detective of the fourth, Engaged phase is as likely to be female as male. If I have carelessly used a solitary masculine pronoun in discussing the Engaged detective, I do apologize.

And then there are people to thank. For good or ill, no institutions contributed to the begetting of this book. I would like to remember a few persons who, in the past, provided occasions for me to think about the detective and other matters. These include the theologian Hans Küng, who long ago encouraged a paper on the detective as god. Professor Küng's colleague, Karl-Josef Kuschel, was also interested and supportive. The historian Robin Winks, who welcomed me to a fruitful NEH summer seminar on the detective and the historian, was a generous scholar as well as master reader of detective fiction. I should also thank the Mystery and Detection section of the Popular Culture Association, who have always received my papers kindly, and have frequently enlightened me about writers with whom I was unfamiliar. Most recently, Bruno Thibault listened and offered encouragement.

But it is the receptive students whom I wish most to thank here. I have never been able to teach the detective story at my own university; Lincoln has properly had other priorities. But through the Fulbright program I was lucky enough to be invited to offer seminars in the subject in Germany (at Tüb-

ingen University and Stuttgart University) and in China (at
Nankai University). All three occasions were very happy
ones. The most recent, my semester at Nankai University in
Tianjin, took place in the spring of 2000, as I began to draft
the essay at the center of this endeavor. It was an extraordinary academic experience. The Fulbright staff (especially
Frank Whitaker and Mindy Kamphausen) in Beijing were ex-
ceptionally supportive, and the English faculty at Nankai (especially Professors Ke, Gu, Cui, and Xiao) were generous
hosts. And the graduate students in my seminar on American
detectives were remarkable: sharp, thoughtful, generous, and
very tolerant of someone who, in July, still mispronounced
their names with the same American vigor with which he
mispronounced them in February. I am grateful that a few of
them have kept in touch with me: Zhang Huifang and Li Xia
especially have continued our East–West dialogue by e-mail.
The undergraduates I met at Nankai were equally inspiring;
some of them have also continued to correspond as they have
moved on in their lives: Lin Lin, Zhang Weilin, Si Qin Gao Wa,
Juan Zhou. And then there were the scholars and teachers
and students who listened to a lecture on Poe and Chandler
and Millhone in Dalian (Ding Xiaoyu), Chongqing (Li Yu-
anhu, Wang Jun, Xiang Chaohong, Lin Xia, Peng Xiaohua,
Fan Dinghang), and Lanzhou (Yang Shihu, Wu Jing). I doubt
they will ever read their names here, but I am grateful to
them all. Students and colleagues like these keep us awake.

Finally, I must, as always, end my preface by acknowledging family. It is, I hope, a forgivable self-indulgence. Students
and colleagues keep us awake; family keep us going. Thanks,
Lara; thanks, Andrew. And Sarala—well, every ten years I get
to say it: you are, certainly, the reality of my world.

List of Abbreviations

IN GENERAL, I HAVE USED AVAILABLE PAPERBACK EDITIONS TO CITE detective stories. The absence of standard editions is inevitable.

In the instance of three major American writers, the Library of America has published well-edited, two-volume texts. All citations to Poe and Hammett are to these editions; most citations to Chandler are as well (the exceptions are references to short stories omitted by the Library of America). The citation short references are:

Poe	*ER Essays and Reviews*
	PT Poetry and Tales
Hammett	*CN Complete Novels*
	CS Crime Stories and Other Writings
Chandler	*SEN Stories and Early Novels*
	LN Later Novels and Other Writings
Doyle	*ASH I, II The Annotated Sherlock Holmes*

We Must Have
Certainty

1

The Development of the Detective Story, 1841–2004

THE MYSTERY/DETECTIVE STORY MADE THE TRANSITION FROM tour de force to genre in 1843, when Edgar Allan Poe published "The Mystery of Marie Rogêt" as the sequel to "The Murders in the Rue Morgue" (1841). There was, of course, a prehistory of stories featuring the study of clues in the investigation of crime, stories that might include *Newgate Calendar* (begun c. 1773), Voltaire's *Zadig* (1747), William Godwin's *Things as They Are; or, The Adventures of Caleb Williams* (1794), and Eugène François Vidocq's *Mémoires de Vidocq* (1828–1829); and, by some lights, Sophocles' *Oedipus Tyrannus* (fifth century BC) and the Apocryphal tales of Daniel and Susanna or Daniel and Bell (fifth/fourth century BC) as well. But it was Poe's hero, M. Auguste Dupin, who established the figure of the detective as a recognizable and reusable icon in the literary marketplace. The first Dupin story had impressed Poe, his editors, and his audience sufficiently to justify a second account of the detective's thoughtful analysis of the circumstances of a murder. "The Mystery of Marie Rogêt" demonstrated not only that Dupin's initial triumph was repeatable, but that the repetition could build economically upon the innovations of the first adventure, reusing the detective, the method, and the narrator, and as well, in a sense, reusing the audience: the initial tale creates the appetite that the second (and seventy-second) tale feeds. The writer could efficiently compose sequels that appealed to a preconditioned audience by offering it both a desired repetition and a desired variation: familiar characters, scenes, and pattern of action; new details.

Although always pressed for marketable material, Poe exploited this approach to composing popular fiction only once more, with a third Dupin tale, "The Purloined Letter." The next step was taken by Emile Gaboriau, who adapted Poe's paradigm to novel-length narrative and to French taste. Gaboriau reused certain motifs in his four Lecoq novels (1865–68), and established a reliable audience both in France and, in translation, in Britain and America. Then, in 1887, Arthur Conan Doyle took up Poe's paradigm, with hints from Gaboriau, as the basis for producing four very popular novels and fifty-six very very popular short stories, and while the repetitiveness of the standard Holmes story came to frustrate Conan Doyle as an artist, it greatly enriched him as manufacturer: the appetite for a detective who could tirelessly repeat his signature performance with undiminished brilliance proved to be insatiable. And, in a market economy of popular literature as in all market economies, where there is demand, there will be supply. Dozens and dozens of variations on the Dupin–Lecoq–Holmes paradigm appeared in the late nineteenth and early twentieth centuries, and dozens were sufficiently appealing to Anglo-American readers (and to the editors and publishers whose livelihoods depended upon the preferences of those readers) to justify repeating their adventures again and again. The mystery/detective genre became what it has been for nearly a century and a half, the preeminent formula in the Anglo-American popular fiction market.

   Though it has remained a readily identifiable genre, easily set apart in bookstores and libraries, the identifying paradigm has undergone significant mutation. While an elaborate taxonomy of the various subspecies can be useful even at the level of precipitating out such categories as the Science Fiction detective story, or the College detective story, or the Ethnic detective story—and each of these categories constitutes a market niche—such a degree of specification sacrifices too much of the forest to the trees. The most useful division is the most obvious one. Two major traditions have defined the genre: that of the Classical detective story and that of the Hard-boiled detective story, the latter emerging through a deliberate revolt against the former. Each of these traditions can be usefully divided into two lines. Further specification serves no purpose here.

*   *   *

In detective stories there are two kinds [of detective], the
Hard-boiled ones who are always drunk and talk out of the
corners of their mouths and do it all by instinct; and the
cold, dry, scientific kind who split hairs under a microscope.

—Laura Hunt, in Vera Caspery's *Laura*

Laura Hunt's division of detective stories into the Hard-
boiled and the Cold, Scientific is widely accepted, though it
points to only one of the key distinctions between the two paradigms. "Cold" and "Scientific" are certainly attributes Sherlock Holmes would embrace; they are the qualities, he
asserted, that underlay his power to analyze successfully
what had gone wrong in the streets and households of his England. His epigones might prefer "detached" or "objective" to
"cold," and "ratiocinative" or "logical" (or "using one's little
grey cells") to "scientific," but in all cases, the basic assumption was that if the detective looked clearly at the physical evidence, listened carefully to what was said, and *thought* about
it, he could infallibly discover whodunit. The world in which
he found himself was essentially a well-ordered place whose
decency had been violated by a criminal whose disruptive
deed had left readable traces in the physical and human environment. Crime was an anomaly, and by correctly tracing the
anomalous evidence that the anomalous deed had left behind,
the detective could apprehend the perpetrator and erase the
disruption. Detectives from Dupin to Poirot and Wimsey followed this method, and inhabited this world.

The Hard-boiled detectives, "who are always drunk and
talk out of the corners of their mouths," disparaged this
method and disowned this world. The world the private eye
inhabits is not naturally well ordered; violations of decency
are commonplace. The detective cannot rely upon inferences
drawn from anomalies; engagement, not detachment, charac-
terizes his emotional state; instead of scientific method, he
applies instinct, toughness, and perseverance. As a result, he
is a quite different man, confronting quite different victims
and criminals, moving in a quite different world. "Hard-
boiled" refers to a style and an ethos that reaches well beyond

the detective story, touching writers such as Hemingway, Dos Passos, Farrell, and Steinbeck. But it is in the detective story that the Hard-boiled vision proved most effective, partly because it could so clearly set itself against the detached, objective, and, to many eyes, effete vision of the Classical paradigm, and partly because the generic paradigm continued to impose a reassuring moral structure on Hard-boiled detective stories: even though the world is as disordered and as tough at the end of a Hard-boiled detective story as it was at the beginning, the Hard-boiled detective always achieves the same victory as his Classical colleagues. He always discovers the truth of the case at hand; he always catches the villain.

The two paradigms, Classical and Hard-boiled, divide the genre, but even a simplified history must recognize that each of these paradigms has emerged in two broad phases. The Classical detective story opens with a long initial period of experimentation from Poe to Chesterton, followed by a sort of reification in the "Golden Age" of the 1920s and 1930s, with the apotheosis of the gentleman-amateur detective conducting extended inquiries at country houses and on Orient Expresses. The Hard-boiled paradigm began as a militant secession in the pulp magazines of the 1920s, but by the 1960s and 1970s was softening all of its edges, and shifting toward a gentler detective working in a more complex world. These four phases might be called those of the Methodical Detective (Classical I), the Golden Age Detective (Classical II), the Hard-boiled Detective (Hard-boiled I), and the Engaged Detective (Hard-boiled II).

Such a division admittedly reflects an Anglo-centric bias, but then so does the genre. Other writers in the genre from Continental Europe, Latin America, Japan, India, and Africa have generally acknowledged, explicitly or implicitly, the priority of the Anglophone tradition. (Students of *le roman policier* may argue that Balzac's *Une Ténébreuse Affaire*, which antedates by three months "The Murders in the Rue Morgue," is actually the seminal work, and that Gaboriau, LeBlanc, Leroux, and Simenon are the *maîtres*; students of the detective story must insist upon the greater claims of Poe, Conan Doyle, Christie, Hammett, Chandler, etc.) Conan

Doyle and Chandler, especially, seem to have inspired imitation and homage around the world. Maigret matters, as does Martin Beck, and Judge Di (Dee). There are innovators outside the Anglo-American tradition, but that tradition has remained, for a century and a half, at least, the central tradition in the genre.

THE METHODICAL DETECTIVE (1841–1920)

The Classical detective story, then, begins with a period of invention and experimentation as the genre defined itself and secured its audience. Writers of this first phase tended to prefer the short story. "The roman policier," wrote Chesterton, "should be on the model of the short story, rather than the novel" ("On Detective Novels," in *Generally Speaking*, 5; Chesterton did allow some "splendid exceptions"). From Poe to Conan Doyle and Chesterton, the focus is upon the detective's forceful intervention in a crisis, ending with his sudden and dramatic solution to the puzzle.

A number of writers played with employing the conventions of the paradigm in full-length novels, but these tended to be novels with detectives in them, rather than detective novels. Works by Wilkie Collins and Charles Dickens fall into this category; Inspector Bucket (1852–53) and Sergeant Cuff (1868) are memorable figures, but they are not protagonists. Even successful novelists who developed series detectives— Anna Katherine Green, with Ebenezer Gryce (1878) and Amelia Butterworth (1897), or Mary Roberts Rinehart, with Miss Pinkerton (1932), for example—produced notable detective novels, rather than notable detectives.[1] The most successful novelist of the first phase was the Frenchman Emile Gaboriau, whose works, translated into English, briefly constituted a reference point: "the modern Gaboriau novel" was a generic rubric in England in the 1880s at a time when the phrase "detective story" was still a novelty to be printed in inverted commas (Kayman, 131). In this first phase, the detective is an eccentric individual with an extraordinary intellect; confronted with a baffling crime, he thinks his way to an infallible reconstruction of the actual events. The emphasis is upon the cleverness of the plot and upon the power of the detective, and for this reason, the short story—which favors plot and discourages characterization—was the preferred form.

As a result, the mystery/detective story presents an intense fable of the power of an uncommon man. The common man— represented by Dupin's companion and Inspector G———, Dr. Watson and Lestrade—is completely baffled by the circumstances of the crime. The natural linkage between appearances and reality has been disrupted; the conventional signs of innocence and guilt have become unreadable. It takes the unconventional intelligence of the detective to read through to the truth, an intelligence that seems a matter of genius, but which, the detective professes, is a matter of method. Sherlock Holmes emerged in the early 1890s as the classic embodiment of this peculiar synthesis of the romantic egoist and the disciplined scientist. His appearances in *The Strand* clearly struck a chord in an audience eager to be told again and again that the world's rubbish—cigarette ashes, abandoned hats, frayed bell cords—was meaningful, and could betray a nefarious plot, unmask a nefarious plotter, vindicate the innocent. It helped that the detritus spoke to a man who was idiosyncratic in his habits as well as singular in his acuity. Dupin was barely more than a ratiocinative method with a dash of arrogance; Holmes, in the course of his many cases and adventures, exposed some of the nooks and crannies of his own individual character. He remained essentially a detective, but he also began to emerge as a man, with a personal past and idiosyncratic tastes. (And he was, in early reviews, criticized for precisely this extension of his humanity. Peter Drexler cites the 1892 *Atheneum* review of the first edition of *The Adventures of Sherlock Holmes:* "The chief defect of the book is the attempt to infuse vitality into Sherlock Holmes. It would have been better to leave him more of a detective machine" [83].)

Sherlock Holmes cast a very long shadow, and there soon appeared the inevitable proliferation of Holmes would-bes— detectives who were noticeably more eccentric in some aspect of their person or character such as M. P. Shiels's decadent Prince Zaleski (1895), Chesterton's Catholic Father

Brown (1911), Ernst Bramah's blind Max Carrados (1914), Melville Davisson Post's frontiersman Uncle Abner (1918); or noticeably more methodical in their approach to detection such as Freeman's Dr. Thorndyke (1907), Jacques Futrelle's Thinking Machine (1907), Arthur B. Reeve's Craig Kennedy (1910). Equally inevitably, there appeared a number of anti-Holmeses: detectives who were noticeably *not* Bohemian in habit or odd in person such as Arthur Morrison's Martin Hewitt (1894) or Freeman's Dr. Thorndyke, or who were explicitly *not* rational or scientific in their method such as Chesterton's Father Brown or Sax Rohmer's Morris Klaw (1920). In virtually all instances, however, the main emphasis remained where Poe put it: upon the detectiveness of the detective. He is created to solve problems; he is expected to attract and retain readers because he can solve problems. Although the central concern of the plot of the detective story is a moral investigation—an act of violence provokes an inquiry into the character of the victim and of that of those who suffer or profit from the victim's misfortune—the moral history of the detective himself (rarely, herself) is generally undefined. Father Brown's childhood, family relations, education, aesthetic tastes, intimate social or sexual relations—all are unknown. Father Brown can penetrate the secrets of others; he is himself impenetrable, except for his key detective qualities: his Catholic faith and his catholic sympathies with victims and with sinners. Dupin, The Thinking Machine, Martin Hewitt, The Old Man in the Corner, and Craig Kennedy exist as comparably complete detectives and incomplete persons.

This is, of course, not the result of incompetence; it is the intended effect: the detective in this first phase is an emblem more than an embodiment: the emblem of the power of methodical thinking (analysis/ratiocination/science/Catholicism/dream detection). This power is the true protagonist; the detective is merely a life-support system for an approach to thinking about the disorder of human affairs. This approach always succeeds in restoring order, and the new order transforms the lives of the individuals affected—the suspects, bystanders, and villains; it does not transform, or even affect, the detective. He begins every investigation as a clean slate, unmarked by prior personal or professional experiences. He even offers his *sang-froid* as proof of his capability: he can detect *because* he is untouched. He is without memory—without *personal* memory: he may recall what sort of mud appears in which districts of Greater London, and he may recall obscure marks at the scene of a crime or subtle phrasings in testimony, but he does not recall his own childhood; he does not recall his intimate relationships; he does not recall himself. He exists as a proof that the events of the past can be recovered; but his own past remains inaccessible.

The three Dupin stories display many of the conventions that would become staples of the detective story: the locked room, narration by the detective's less clever companion, competition with the less clever police, the detective's use of disguise and of ruses, the closing recapitulation of the logical steps that led the detective to his surprising conclusions. Dupin is an amateur; Poe goes to some length to present him as a theoretician, not a technician; he is not a workman, and will take no wages. His primary interest lies in the exercise the crime affords his intellect; his other rewards—redeeming a favor, saving a damsel, winning a bet—are incidental. Financial remuneration, when it is accepted, is fantastic— 50,000 francs for the purloined letter. The Dupin narratives contain some of the flourishes Poe favored in his other fiction—recherché allusions and poses of profundity, but, granting that Dupin's Paris is not meant to be France's Paris, they are realistic enough.

Conan Doyle chose to make Sherlock Holmes's London more than realistic enough; Holmes's first two appearances were in novels (*A Study in Scarlet* [1887] and *The Sign of Four* [1890]), though, in fact, Holmes's investigations occupied novella-length adventures, with the remainder of each novel filled by discrete romances, respectively, of Mormon America and of India. Still, Holmes found space enough to emerge as a character in a credible social world. Emile Gaboriau provided the precedent for this approach. *Monsieur Lecoq* (1869), for example, appeared in two sizable volumes. The first, *L'Enquête* (*The Inquiry*), describes Lecoq's detective work, leading to his identification of the villain Mai (May) with the Duc de Sairmeuse; the second, *L'Honneur du nom* (*The Honor of the Name*), provides the melodramatic history of the families involved in the plot of the first part. This second part has been disparaged, and for readers looking for a detective story, with justice. But these melodramatic family histories were an essential part of Gaboriau's Balzacian project, his effort to depict the state of France in the 1860s.[2] Conan Doyle had no such program, and while there are very interesting implications to his use of America and India as the ultimate sources of moments of disorder in London, it is clear that the brief fables of Holmes's successful endeavors to restore the order in London through methodical investigation constitute the essential appeal of the series. It was with the short stories published in the new *Strand Magazine*, beginning in July 1891 and first collected as the *Adventures of Sherlock Holmes* in 1892, that Holmes became the icon he has, for well over a century, remained.

Urban settings prevailed in the first phase: the Paris of Dupin and Lecoq, the London of Holmes and Hewitt and Thorndyke, the New York of Craig Kennedy, the Boston of The Thinking Machine. The short story form tended to focus attention upon functional details of setting as well as of character, but, as Gaboriau and Conan Doyle saw, the requirements of circumstantial realism invited a measure of extraneous description. And while a single short story could not capture a cityscape, a series could. The natural scene of the detective story was an interior: a middle- to upper-class interior, for these were the homes whose deceased occupants might plausibly justify the expense of a private investigation. But although Holmes's work centers on interiors (including his own famous rooms at 221B Baker Street, where the fable often begins), Conan Doyle sent him ranging through the various microenvironments of Victorian London and the surrounding countryside. In the course of his detective adventures, Sherlock Holmes encounters lascars and monarchs; artists and country squires; sadistic boys, victimized young women, and old men who vainly pursue artificial rejuvenation. Even matters pertaining to the larger world are broached, as Conan Doyle interjects commentaries upon the empire and its peoples, on education, on race, on World War I. Arthur B. Morrison's prior experience as a naturalistic chronicler of the London slums is touched upon in his Martin

Hewitt series. Chesterton's views on finance or on revolution are as visible in the Father Brown stories as are his views on sin and salvation. The center of the Methodical detective story is always the detective's clever unraveling of a web which the author has cleverly raveled, but the form did allow writers to insinuate what might fairly be called a criticism of the world.

THE GOLDEN AGE DETECTIVE (1920–40)

In the second phase of the Classical paradigm, the Golden Age, the novel supplanted the short story, and this had implications for the character of the detective, the crime, and the world in which the crime takes place. The Golden Age writers displayed an inclination to discipline themselves with some strictness, forming clubs and imposing "rules," but inevitably the leisure of the novel encouraged them to develop their diverse talents in diverse directions. The most celebrated— writers such as Agatha Christie, John Dickson Carr, and Ellery Queen—were so good at plotting that the qualities of their characters, settings, and ideas have often been overlooked; other Golden Age writers, less facile in plot-making, assigned a more visible role to other qualities in the narrative as supplemental attractions for the reader.

The social world of the Golden Age detective novel was generally a world of privilege; and, as has often been noted, the detective story was pushed toward comedy of manners. (In part, this push was a response to a conflicting pressure to distill the genre into a set of characterless intellectual puzzles.) The remarkable intelligence of the detective continues to receive emphasis, but its methodological basis is underplayed. A genteel ratiocination replaces the muscular scientism of Sherlock Holmes and Dr. Thorndyke. The complexity of the puzzle that he solves becomes the warrant of the detective's ingenuity. He need not proclaim his bona fides as an analyst through dissertations and exhortations; he performs his analysis, and his invariable success vindicates him. The Golden Age novelists often devised very complex puzzles, frequently requiring the reproduction of maps, diagrams, timetables, and facsimiles. Time and space had to be charted with some precision in order for the truth to be apprehended. The detective of the first phase was often an aggressive investigator, the shortness of the form forcing him into sudden, dramatic assertions of his power to interpret the information, which his examinations and his interrogations provided. The detective of the second phase had to reserve his key interpretations for the final summation, an exposition that often required more than one chapter to complete. Consequently, the detective was obliged to devote much of his attention during the early and middle portions of his investigations to observing character and scene rather than to expounding inferences. The result was at once an increase in artificiality and an increase in realistic texture. The novel appeared to force the mystery story writer toward Byzantine plots and a self-conscious, often openly ironical pose toward this open artifice, but it also forced writers to camouflage the artifice with more extensive views of the social and natural setting and with more sophisticated portraits of the persons who engage in or who are affected by the crimes. Characters in short stories are, by convention, permitted to commit abrupt, revelatory gestures; in a novel, the gestures must be rooted in some larger vision of a character's pattern of action.

The prototypical novel of the Golden Age is E. C. Bentley's *Trent's Last Case* (1913). A. E. W. Mason's *Murder at the Villa Rose* (1910) appeared even earlier, but was less influential, and Mary Roberts Rinehart's *The Circular Staircase* (1908) initiated a sideline in the genre—the "had-I-but-known" model, which was popular, but which was disparaged by purists. Bentley, an intimate of Chesterton, was the commanding figure, though after *Trent's Last Case*, he added to the genre only a collection of Trent short stories and, more than twenty years after the first, a second, co-written novel. He was, in *Trent's Last Case*, deliberately guying the Dupin–Holmes paradigm, presenting a very model of the infallible-amateur-ratiocinative detective, Philip Trent, and setting him on the trail of the murderer of a vulgar American millionaire, Sigsbee Manderson. Trent attends to the detritus overlooked or misinterpreted by the common investigators (Inspector Murch, the reader), especially the dental plate that the victim

left in a bowl by his bedside, and he very cleverly reconstructs a plot of action that would account for physical traces
that he has accumulated. His individual inferences are indeed correct, but his final conclusion is faulty, and he accuses
the wrong man. When his error is made plain, Trent re-
nounces detection in favor of love: it is his last case because
he failed, and because he prefers being a husband to being
a detective, and he knows the two roles are incompatible. A
detective is a detective, not a man; a husband is a man.

Bentley thought that this conclusion would illustrate the fa-
tuity of the paradigm: short fables of investigative power, in
the absence of narrative genius, were degenerating into mechanical tricks performed by flat detectives upon flat suspects in flat settings. Given the generous rope of a novel-
length narrative, Bentley seemed to suggest, the detective
story would hang itself. A host of second-rate writers were,
in the 1910s, proving his first point in countless unreprinted
magazine stories. Arthur B. Reeve, whose remarkably popular and thoroughly flat Craig Kennedy stories were actually
reprinted in a standard edition, represented a nadir of sorts.
But *Trent's Last Case* did not reduce the conventions to ab-
surdity; rather, it pointed toward a new direction, one that
made the detective novel viable. Some of Bentley's gestures
would remain undeveloped. His presentation of a detective
who not only has character, but also has maturing character—reaching ultimately a maturity that disqualifies him for
detection—was generally dismissed (though Dorothy Sayers
would eventually take up the hint, only to discover that it also
disqualified her detective). And it would retreat from Bentley's opening gesture toward linking the world of the crime to
the larger social and economic world of the times. The Golden
Age detective would remain a relatively unbodied ratiocina-
tor, and he would function in a limited sphere of largely domestic violence. But that domestic sphere could acquire the
higher degree of social texture that Bentley introduced, and
the depiction of that world could take on the self-conscious-
ness that Bentley's bemused prose proclaimed. The Golden
Age detective's world would be populated with a larger variety of more fully realized character types. The reader would
be invited not merely to recognize the dramatis personae, but

to grow to know them. They would be types, to be sure; and they would be drawn largely from the middle and upper-middle class, with the lower and the higher orders imagined from that middling perspective. But though it is certainly limited, and, since the 1930s, increasingly discredited as altogether too elitist, that middle-class perspective was a broad one and, admitting its limits, a sane one. In any event, the best writers always *used* the types; they played with—and against—them. One of Agatha Christie's signature devices involves deploying a full cast of stereotypes and then achieving surprise by turning one or more individuals against type. The model secretary would suddenly reveal a very un-secretary-like jealousy; the reprobate cousin from Australia would reveal an unexpected magnanimity.

Christie was the acknowledged mistress of the Golden Age form. She introduced Hercule Poirot in her first novel, *The Mysterious Affair at Styles* (1920), and Miss Marple a decade later in *The Murder at the Vicarage* (1930). She continued regularly to produce best-sellers into the 1970s. Over thirty volumes, mostly novels, featured the retired Belgian policeman, Poirot. Where Dupin offered expansive lectures on his analytic technique, and Holmes offered methodological "axioms" on the "Science of Deduction" ("When you have excluded the impossible, whatever remains, however improbable, must be the truth," *ASH II* 299; see also *I* 613, *II* 446, *II* 720) and little exercises in deducing a wife's disaffection from a husband's dusty hat, Poirot refers to his "little grey cells" and establishes his bona fides by solving the baffling case at hand. Conan Doyle focuses attention on the detective—the disaffected wife plays no part in Holmes's recovery of the Blue Carbuncle; she is there to make Holmes seem powerful. Christie focuses attention on the mystery; Poirot emerges to dominate the narrative only when he has mastered the plot. Indeed, Poirot has no apparent life outside of his inquiries; his mannered vanities are inconsequential. Christie assigned him an amusing mania for neatness and a repertoire of Gallic interjections, but little other substance. Poirot's peculiar excellence lies in the nearly complete subordination of his character to his function.

The paradox of Poirot's combination vainglory and vacuity

is echoed in other detectives of the Golden Age. Philo Vance, who debuted in 1926, is a flamboyant egoist, but S. S. Van Dine's inability (or lack of interest) in developing Vance's character over the course of twelve novels suggests that Vance's vanity, like Poirot's, is merely a mask concealing a vacuum. John Dickson Carr's detectives—Bencolin (first appearance 1930), Fell (1933), and Merivalle (1933)—are also inflated caricatures; Carr, like Christie, works with plot and atmosphere, not with the character of his detective. Philip MacDonald's Anthony Gethryn (1924) and H. C. Bailey's Reggie Fortune (1934) are satisfied to be gentlemen, and distinguish themselves by their detecting, not by their fascinating characters. Freeman Wills Crofts's Inspector French (1925) is an anomaly insofar as he is both a Scotland Yard detective and a married man; but neither his professional connections nor his marriage is developed with much texture; he is not a Maigret.[3] French is a model of the Classical detective in his subordination of his personal life to his function as an investigator.

But not all Golden Age detectives were so essentially vacuous. Earl Derr Biggers's Charlie Chan (1925), the first important ethnic detective, began as a stereotype—an anti-stereotype, to be exact: Biggers posited him as an anti-Fu Manchu—but Charlie Chan did move toward substance as his prematurely terminated series of six novels progressed. Ellery Queen (1929), Albert Campion (1929), and Roderick Alleyn (1934) all eventually acquired degrees of individual depth over the course of their long careers. The Golden Age detective who matured the most was, of course, Lord Peter Wimsey (1923), who began as a fop with an aptitude for detection and ended as a man—a lover and husband and even a father—with an aptitude for detection. In the final novel, *Busman's Holiday*, accurately subtitled "a love story with detective interruptions," Sayers had clearly become more interested in the problem of her detective's manhood and its relation to the detective's wife's womanhood than she was in how his detective aptitude would respond to the problem posed by the death of William Noakes. This focus on Peter and Harriet made *Busman's Holiday* Sayers's valediction to the genre. The readers who loved it and its predecessor,

Gaudy Night, were more lovers of novels (or lovers of Peter and Harriet) than lovers of detective novels.

The Golden Age mystery/detective novel still took plot as the essential matter. The detective may or may not have a character, but he must have a tangled skein to untangle. And in the novel, there was room now for the plot to develop baroque epicycles, in which ancillary characters engage in subplots that coincide with, and drag red herrings across, the main plot. The main plot itself is often a matter of considerable complexity, involving peculiar pathologies and exceedingly complicated devices. Golden Age villains can display marvelous degrees of ingenuity, opportunism, timing, and patience; the mechanisms through which they commit their murders are often highly improbable, though always possible: there *could* be twelve miscellaneous persons (a jury's-worth) each of whom has been personally affected by a child's kidnapping and murder; the twelve *could* agree to execute the kidnapper/murderer; they *could* board the same train as the kidnapper/murderer and Hercule Poirot; they *could* each stab the victim and then, because the train happened to be snowed in, Poirot *could* investigate and discover the truth; the authorities *could* agree to overlook the truth.

The truth is the truth of murder: it is in the Golden Age that "murder mystery" becomes a phrase. One of Dupin's three cases does not involve a murder, and only 38 percent of Sherlock Holmes's adventures (23 of 60) are homicide investigations: robbery (20%), fear of harm or scandal (13%), and disappearances (10%) constitute other major categories. The mystery/detective novel evidently required a capital crime to justify its length. This obsessive focus upon a single form of crime gave the genre a clearer identity; the reiterative scene of the detective examining the corpse became a signature, and has occasioned Freudian speculations about its primal qualities. But the obsession with murder led, as has been often observed, away from horror. The repetition is too mechanical, and the actual homicide is treated lightly: it is the sufficient occasion for two hundred pages of ingenious raveling and unraveling; it is rarely the occasion for emotional response. The victim is usually only lightly sketched, and is often disagreeable. The aloof detective, in any event, has no personal interest in solving the case; he is dispassionate in his pursuit of truth. But it is also rare that anyone has a strong personal interest in pursuing the killer. Though the Golden Age produced thousands of victims and thousands of killers, it produced few avengers. The detective identifies the killer; society, through its judicial system, normally disposes of him or her, and the story usually ends before the disposal takes place. Of course, the killer himself/herself might be motivated by revenge, but that is what marks him/her as unfit for a society in which the truth is discovered and the culprit captured only for the highest, most disinterested of motives. Whatever secondary passions move the characters, vengeance, if it moves anyone to action, moves only the villain.

This elimination of passion from the pursuit of truth fits with the Golden Age's redefinition of the mystery/detective story as a sort of game, a competition in which fair play demands that it be at once possible and extremely unlikely for the reader to draw the conclusions the detective draws. Both S. S. Van Dine and Ronald Knox published "rules" for the game. In the first phase, it had been enough that the reader marveled at the detective's perspicacity; now it was necessary that the reader also be abashed by his or her own obtuseness. (The early novels of Ellery Queen, with their "challenge to the reader" just prior to Ellery explaining it all, ensured that all readers confront their humiliation.) There are many brilliantly plotted Golden Age novels, many that strain for brilliance, and many that are merely strained. Christie and Carr, in their different ways, are surely among the most consistently successful in composing plots that fairly provide and fairly conceal the information the reader needs. At their frequent best, both provide genuine surprises, Christie with a deceptive easiness, Carr with a good deal of rhetorical huffing and grunting.

The insulation of the Golden Age mystery can be overstated, but W. H. Auden's observation that it tends to transpire in a Great Good Place is accurate enough. When, in "Wasp's Nest" (1929), Poirot warns that murder is imminent, the reply from the potential victim is: "This is England. Things like that don't happen here" (*Double Sin*, 28). Wherever the place is, it is a place where murders don't happen.

The preferred scene is the country house, the seaside resort, the train coach, the quadrangle. These contained scenes serve the practical function of limiting the possible suspects; they also imply a nostalgia for a certain sort of innocent place: a place where everyone has a role, and where everyone finds fulfillment within that role. Of course, there are minor discontents, but there is only one radically discontented person: the murderer. The crime, however, exposes all of the minor discontents, and as a result, many are suspected. By identifying the killer, the detective enables the many to resume their normal, relatively contented lives. The country house, resort hotel, sleeper coach, college quadrangle—England—is restored to the innocence which it ought to have.

To be sure, the fable is not quite this simple; those minor discontents are not illusions. The efforts of the killer to conceal his or her motives/means/opportunity had to be complemented by other characters independently attempting to conceal their own, less deadly sins. As Patricia Wentworth's Miss Maud Silver says in *The Brady Collection:* "so many people have something to hide, and an enquiry in a murder case has this in common with the day of judgment, that the secrets of all hearts are apt to be revealed" (102). As a result, the pre-enquiry world is inhabited not merely by a single expellable villain, but also by a number of individuals who are not quite what they seem, and who will be exposed in the course of the enquiry. As a result, the post-enquiry world is actually a better place and everyone is happier, both because the villain is gone and because the minor deceptions have been lifted. Auden is essentially right: the Golden Age mystery asserts that everyone except the villain is innocent, and that the detective can exculpate the innocent many by indicting the guilty one; but it is also true that the innocent are often colored off-white, and need to be purged of venial sins as well as be proven innocent of major sin.

The Golden Age saw the emergence of the mystery writer. Poe, Gaboriau, Conan Doyle, and Chesterton were all writers who wrote, among other things, mystery stories. Conan Doyle was so disturbed by the prospect of becoming a mystery writer that he invented Dr. Moriarty and had him grapple with Holmes at Reichenbach. Agatha Christie was a mystery writer, and a half-dozen romances published under the name of Mary Westmacott do not change her identity. She too felt compelled to write out a narrative of her detective's demise, but though she wrote *Curtain* in 1940, she did not publish it until 1975; she knew that Poirot was her fate. The Golden Age writers were mystery writers, and banked upon being mystery writers.

The mystery writer's product was a branded narrative which promised an engaging, sophisticated escape into a superficially disordered, always re-orderable world, and this clearly appealed to a generation of readers who had experienced the profound and irremediable barbarisms of the First World War. But what, in 1930, was a nostalgia for the social order of one's childhood was, by 1950, a nostalgia for the social order of one's parent's childhood, and while this evidently provided some consolation to a generation that experienced the even greater barbarisms of the Second World War, its credibility was diminishing. A sufficient audience remained, and the Great Good place of Classical mode never entirely vanished. The warhorses of the Golden Age—Christie and Carr, Allingham and Marsh and Queen—all continued to produce and to sell at a consistently high level into the 1960s and 1970s. If the quality of the work of the first two appeared to fall off ever so slightly from its heights, that of the latter three, it has been argued by some, actually rose to a higher level in the 1940s and 1950s.

But the new movement in popular literature was away from escapes to redeemable country houses, resort hotels, sleeper coaches, and college quadrangles, and toward fantasies of engagement with the affairs of the world. Through the 1950s, the James Bond novels were preparing the way for what, in the 1960s, would be an avalanche of espionage fiction. The new writers who took up the Classical model of the detective story would continue to satisfy the need for complex plots and strategically placed trifles which would point to the true story of what happened. But they would also return to the notion that Bentley played with in *Trent's Last Case*, and that Sayers developed and then abandoned: the detective would become himself an object of study and the larger world (now even more than in 1913 dominated by American millionaires).

P. D. James and Ruth Rendell created detectives of sensitivity, capable of growth. Later writers would go even further in developing the biographies of their investigators. In addition to the plot of the crime, which the detective would unravel, there would be the plot of the detective's life and relationships, and these would be developed over the course of a series of novels. Thus, readers of the novels of Colin Dexter or Anne Perry or Elizabeth George are encouraged to read the next novel in the series not only to see how Morse, or Charlotte and Thomas Pitt, or Lynley and Havers solve the crime, but also to see what happens next in the lives of Morse, or Charlotte and Thomas Pitt, or Lynley and Havers. In this way, the Classical tradition accommodated itself to a trend which had made its initial inroads in the American alternative to the Golden Age.

HARD-BOILED DETECTIVE STORY: THE HARD-BOILED DETECTIVE, 1920–60

The Hard-boiled form revolted precisely against the too-civilized artificiality of the Classical detective and his insulated world. The Hard-boiled detective was a tough everyman in a tough, everyman's world, and everyman's world, in America of the 1920s and 1930s, was a brutal place, run with undisguised self-interest by wealthy industrialists, corrupt politicians and police, and gangsters. The crimes are no longer outré, the investigator is no longer intellectual, and the solution, though final, is no longer completely satisfying. The detective still always gets his man, but he does so through dogged persistence, not brilliant inference, and the crime occurs in a big, dark, often rainy city. A number of competent and prolific writers adopted the Hard-boiled style: a number of ambitious writers, like Hammett and Chandler, and a host of two-cents-a-word hack writers filled monthly issues of the pulp magazines with fast-moving tales of tough-guy detectives chasing down quick-triggered villains and easily undressed dames. In the 1950s, the Hard-boiled paradigm began to move toward a somewhat softer mode, leading to the Engaged paradigm of the 1970s in which the detective compromised some of his cynical toughness by shifting from a street-smart accommodation to the injustices of the city to an evangelical embrace of the causes of the disadvantaged.

Upon his initial appearance, however, the Hard-boiled detective was singularly tough. He was in revolt against the niceties and hypocrisies of his genre as well as those of his world. Poe invented the Classical detective as an Olympian figure, detached from and amused by the ways of his world. The Hard-boiled detective is of his world and in his world; he may express himself through wry or bitter laughter, but he is not amused. It is a lousy world. Auden, right as always, calls it the Great Wrong Place. It is irredeemable; the detective has no illusion that he can alter this. In the Hard-boiled detective story, the detective pursues the evildoer because he can and should, not because he believes that expelling an evildoer will restore order and redeem innocence. Expelling evildoers is what he does for a living. As Sam Spade tells Brigid O'-Shaughnessy, "I'm a detective and expecting me to run criminals down and then let them go free is like asking a dog to catch a rabbit and let it go. It can be done, all right, and sometimes it is done, but it's not the natural thing" (*CN*, 582). Sam Spade does not imagine that apprehending Brigid (or apprehending Brigid *and* Casper *and* Wilmer *and* Joel) will measurably reduce crime in San Francisco. The Hard-boiled dick has no illusions about restoring innocence. His task is to solve the case at hand: to do the job of work he has committed himself to; to do the natural thing.

The Hard-boiled world is an urban world, and its city is largely unredeemed by any compensating cultural heritage; not only is the private eye not a habitué of salons and museums and recital halls, these places are largely beyond his frame of reference. His is a world of getting and spending, with success measured by incomes, and large cars, and country club memberships. It is a raw American urban world; a big, tough city—New York, Chicago, San Francisco, above all Los Angeles; cities where what high culture there is exists within gated temples visited by a sheltered elite, and the mean streets down which the detective walks belong to workers and capitalists and organized crime.[4]

The archetypal Hard-boiled world appears in the first great

Hard-boiled novel, Dashiell Hammett's *Red Harvest* (1929): Personville, pronounced "Poisonville" by cognoscenti, is a mining town based upon Butte, Montana, a city with great claims to imperial importance or cultural monuments neither in fiction nor in fact. Hammett portrays it as an abstract of the Great Wrong Place. It is entirely corrupt: capitalists, workers, and organized criminals—all pursue lives of a Hobbesian nature: nasty, poor, solitary, brutish, and short (the only exception being the life of the chief capitalist, the Continental Op's client, Elihu Willsson, whose life is neither poor nor short). At the novel's end, having purged Poisonville through more than two dozen murders by knife, pistol, machine gun, and bomb, the Continental Op tells Willsson that he is returning the city, "all nice and clean and ready to go to the dogs again" (*ASH II*, 176). No Hard-boiled detective can even pretend that he has restored New York or Chicago or Los Angeles to a pristine niceness and cleanness—not even a block, not even for a moment. Both the Golden Age and Hard-boiled forms adopt an a–b–a structure, but the content is reversed: in the Golden Age world, the crime constitutes a brief interval of discord between the normal happy rhythms of life; in the Hard-boiled world, the successful investigation constitutes a brief interval of justice in a normally unjust world.

Like the Classical form, the Hard-boiled paradigm also emerged first in short fiction. But the chief vehicle for the short stories was not a middle-class journal like the *Strand*; it was the decidedly working-class medium of the pulp magazine. Preceded by *Detective Magazine*, and followed by *Dime Detective, Dime Mystery, Spicy Detective, Hollywood Detective*, and others, the chief vehicle was *Black Mask*, founded in 1920.[5] In 1923 it began to publish the Race Williams stories of Carroll John Daly and the Continental Op stories of Dashiell Hammett. In the course of the decade, it built its reputation (and inspired imitators) by publishing stories by Erle Stanley Gardner, Cleve Adams, Norbert Davis, Frederick Nebel, and George Harmon Coxe, and it was marketed specifically to a male audience (see Erin A. Smith, *Hard-Boiled: Working-Class Readers and Pulp Magazines*). The new paradigm quickly took shape: the stories were usually narrated by a tough, tough-talking detective, usually working alone; usually carrying and usually using a gun: He would usually be threatened and usually beaten up; he would usually encounter at least one dame/twist/frail/jane with bedroom eyes. The investigation would move forward through a series of confrontations in which the detective and his antagonists would assert their sexual identity—their manliness or their womanliness—and the antagonists would incidentally reveal a bit more of who they really were. By assembling these forced revelations, and without any pretense of ratiocination, the detective would realize who must have committed the crime.

One effect of this new approach was to diminish the distance between the short story and novel. The novelist in the Classical mode had to design a significantly more complicated plot, with a proliferation of clues and subplots, all of which must come to a satisfactory resolution in the final chapters. The novelist in the Hard-boiled mode simply inserts more collisions, the collision often being very nearly an end in itself. Thus, Hammett's *Red Harvest* was published first as four separate "novelettes" in *Black Mask* (November 1927–February 1928) and then, with some revision, published as a novel in 1929. In a slightly different fashion, Raymond Chandler could splice two *Black Mask* short stories ("The Curtain" [September 1936] and "Killer in the Rain" [January 1935]) plus parts of two other stories to create his first novel, *The Big Sleep* (1939). For Chandler especially, the integration of several short Hard-boiled narratives into a single, relatively coherent larger one was challenging, but he did it again twice (*Farewell, My Lovely* and *The Lady in the Lake*). As the market for pulp magazines shrank in the late 1930s and 1940s and the market for paperbacks exploded, the Hard-boiled detective story had already accommodated itself to the dimensions of the novel. The Hard-boiled form antedates the fashion of the film noir, which flourished in the 1940s, but there is a natural connection between the two, in style as well as in matter. The Hard-boiled affinity for a succession of collisions correlates with the cinema's quick-paced cutting from scene to scene.

The Hard-boiled story is still a fable of an individual who possesses the power to know with certainty who has (and who has not) committed a crime. But the character of the individual, of the power, and of the crime have all been radically altered. Though still an isolated individual, with little personal history, the detective is a working man, with a working man's habits and a working man's prejudices. The Classical detective was always conscious of class distinctions; the private eye is always contemptuous of class distinctions. The rich, Philip Marlowe remarks in *The Big Sleep*, make him sick. The private eye has an edge, an attitude. The Classical detective condemns individuals, and often condemns only the actions of individuals, excusing crimes committed by decent men unnaturally provoked. The Hard-boiled detective condemns individuals, and often condemns their lives, their livelihoods, their families, their ethnic backgrounds, their sexual preferences. He condemns professions, and whole classes of society; he condemns social institutions; he condemns his city.

And his success as a detective depends upon this capacity to judge and condemn, rather than upon any intellectual capacity to analyze physical clues. Street-smarts—intimate and accurate knowledge of the ways that the corrupt city works—not any "science of deduction"—enables the detective to survive, and by surviving to win his passage through the confrontations that lead to revelation. He is, like the Classical detective, self-reliant: the Hard-boiled detective story remains a fable of individualism. Its problems cannot be solved by the community, only by the diligence of a single man. But whereas the Classical detective tended to express his individuality through the cultivation of elite eccentricities—he *chose* a nocturnal (Dupin), or a bohemian (Holmes), or an aristocratic (Vance) lifestyle—the Hard-boiled detective's individualism expresses itself through ascetic renunciations: he works in a bare office—"There was nothing there but an old red davenport, two odd chairs, a bit of carpet, and a library table with a few old magazines on it" (Chandler, "Finger Man" *SEN*, 95), and lives in "a single apartment with a pull-down bed" (Chandler, Letter, *LN*, 1046). These chosen privations mark his separation from the power and the wealth of the corrupt city.[6]

The isolation of the Hard-boiled dick is not Olympian; he is not above the passions that wreck lives, but that do not influence detectives in the Classical stories. He cares, sometimes a great deal, about who has been killed and about pursuing and punishing the killer. He belongs to the world he condemns, and is moved by the same drives that move everyone else, including the villain. His distinction lies in reserving enough of his integrity to outlast—to out-man—antagonists who yield too easily to temptation. The Classical detective, for example, was unmoved by sexual passion. He was either an untempted bachelor (Dupin, Holmes, Thorndyke, Kennedy, Abner, Poirot, Vance, Queen, Merrivale, Wolfe), or, in some of his later incarnations, a placidly monogamous husband (Alleyn, Campion, Fell). The Hard-boiled detectives renounce marriage and the social commitment that it implies, but they do not renounce sexual desire or sexual activity. The Hard-boiled detective takes his pleasures as he finds them— he also drinks and gambles—but he never trusts that happiness can be institutionalized or made to last. He trusts no one. His ultimate value is self-preservation, and this requires, as Sam Spade famously put it, that he play the sap for no one.

The private eye is, in a sense, more realistic than his amateur counterparts in the Classical mode. Dupin and Holmes, Vance and Wimsey must all have been extraordinarily well tutored in childhood; they easily discourse on arcane topics (nebular hypotheses, the polyphonic motets of Lassus, Egyptian dynasties, incunabulae). The Hard-boiled detective went to American public schools, and only because he was obliged to. He speaks the language real working men might speak (articulate working men, to be sure); he acts and he suffers the way real working men might act and suffer. Classical detectives act; they never suffer. The Hard-boiled detective suffers physically, of course; but he also suffers emotionally, and he cares. Holmes, Wimsey, Queen are not given cause to seek revenge, and would not seek it were they given cause. When, in a late Holmes story, Watson is wounded, Holmes admonishes the villain, "If you had killed Watson, you would not have got out of this room alive" (*ASH II*, 645). But the wound is superficial not fatal; it could not be otherwise in a Classical story; and Holmes would never have carried out his threat anyway. But the Hard-boiled dick does lose his friends and his partners and his lovers, and he does exact revenge. Mickey Spillane's *I, the Jury* is the quintessential Hard-boiled story in this respect.

The crimes in Hard-boiled stories are also realistic; at least more realistic than the murders-by-obscure-poison and the murders-by-a-conspiracy-of-twelve-fellow-travelers which the Classical form seemed to favor. As Chandler wrote: "Hammett gave murder back to the kind of people who commit it for reasons, and not just to provide a corpse; and with the means at hand, not with hand-wrought dueling pistols, curare, and tropical fish" (*LN*, 989). Of course, the Hard-boiled form has its own special artifices and conventions, beyond those essential to all art. Hammett's caution is appropriate: "'Realistic' is one of those words when it comes up in conversation, sensible people put on their hats and go home" (qtd. in Forter, 19–20). Still, there is a clear truth to Chandler's observation. The crimes in Hard-boiled fiction cease to constitute Rube Goldberg contraptions calling for remarkable coincidences and extraordinary ingenuities. They cease to be aesthetic occasions; they are fairly brutal affairs, committed by brutal means for brutal motives.

But however realistically one portrayed the private eye and his world, private eyes were inherently romantic figures. Chandler's famous encomium makes the point: the man who goes untarnished down the mean streets is a hero, not a real detective: "He must be a complete man and a common man and yet an unusual man. He must be, to use a rather weathered phrase, a man of honor. . . . He must be the best man in his world and a good enough man for any world" (*LN*, 992). This is Chandler's conclusion to a polemical essay, which took as its premise the ambition of writers like Hammett to bring realism to the genre of detective fiction. But real private detectives do not solve many murders; real private detectives, like real men and women in any profession, are not the best in their world. They are not heroes; they are not everything.

The real men and women who solve murders are the police, and this led to the emergence of the police procedural. The police procedural is not intrinsically Hard-boiled; its practitioners include a range of talents—John Creasy (as J. J. Marric), Peter Dickinson, Colin Watson, Ruth Rendell, Ed McBain, Dorothy Uhnak, J. A. Jance, Georges Simenon, Maj

Sjöwall, and Per Wahlöö—but it was as an annex to the Hard-boiled impulse toward realism that the procedural made its claim to a place in the genre in the 1950s and 1960s. Laurence Treat's *V as in Victim* (1945) and Hilary Waugh's *Last Seen Wearing* (1952) are taken as the starting points of the new movement; it reached its fullest embodiments in the 87th Precinct novels of Ed McBain (1956). (The peculiar programmatic Martin Beck novels of Maj Sjöwall and Per Wahlöö (1965–75), in part an homage to McBain, may be the highest achievement in the subgenre, but they are in crucial ways sui generis). Tough, organized cops systematically do what needs to be done: they conduct interviews, trace ownerships, study autopsies, fill out forms; they deal with the bureaucracy of investigation. In a sense, the procedural attempts to return the central appeal of the narrative to where Poe originally claimed to place it: detecting, not the romantic figure of the detective, is what matters. Poe assumed that the methodology of detecting would be most attractive if it were exercised ingeniously by a distinctive hero; the procedural assumes it will be attractive if exercised realistically by a team of professionals. That the procedural has remained a strong, but minor, tradition suggests that ingenuity and individualism still trump collective realism.[7]

Carroll John Daly is generally acknowledged to be the initiator of the Hard-boiled paradigm. Race Williams's first adventure was published in *Black Mask* in June 1923, four months before the debut of Hammett's Continental Op. Though Race Williams did not grow as a character and Daly did not grow as a writer, Race Williams remained a very popular figure in *Black Mask*. The greatest writers in the Hard-boiled tradition are undisputed: they are Dashiell Hammett and Raymond Chandler; the only debate is over which of the two is the greater. Hammett is favored by those who prefer authenticity, Chandler by those who prefer art; but Hammett is far from artless, and Chandler certainly claims a kind of authenticity. James M. Cain and W. R. Burnett were also masters of the Hard-boiled, but did not write detective stories. Erle Stanley Gardner wrote what were by far the most popular stories and novels in the form, producing them with a remarkable efficiency (John Creasy was his efficient counterpart in the Classical vein). Bret Halliday's Mike Shayne (1939) is perhaps the best example of the standard-issue Hard-boiled dick: he embodies all of the necessary qualities, and all of them in creditable form, without ever pressing far beyond the paradigm. Other reliable producers in the early phase include George Harmon Coxe (1937) and Cleve Adams (1940). Mickey Spillane is usually cited as the example of the form at its discreditable worst: in the Mike Hammer novels (1947), he conscientiously removed all pretensions to art (though he by no means removed all art) and reduced the fable of the Hard-boiled to its most brutal elements: a tough guy uses toughness to beat the truth out of less tough men and women. Spillane's soufflés of revenge, self-righteousness, violence, and lust were enormously popular, and much imitated (e.g., Frank Kane [1947], Henry Kane [1947], and Richard S. Prather [1950]).

After Hammett and Chandler came Macdonald and Mac-Donald. Ross Macdonald is often identified as the son to Hammett's father and Chandler's holy spirit. Even the major writers in the Classical vein were modest about their ambitions—Willard Wright (S. S. Van Dine) explicitly disparaged his excursions into detective fiction ("I Used to be a Highbrow, But Look at Me Now"), and Dorothy Sayers acknowledged that the form was inherently inimical to artistic achievement. The Hard-boiled writers could be equally modest—Gardner referred to himself as a fiction factory. But Hammett certainly had ambitions, and Chandler was a very self-conscious artist. Ross Macdonald earned a doctoral degree in English with a dissertation on Coleridge's psychological criticism, and he came to the detective story with the studied intention of elevating its range. He began as an imitator of Hammett and Chandler, but by The Galton Case (1959) he had turned his Lew Archer novels into vehicles for subtle explorations of human relationships. His fascination with parent–child relations becomes almost obsessive in his later novels, but in his writing and his plotting (and his critical respectability), Ross Macdonald made a major contribution.

John D. MacDonald brought a somewhat more varied background to his writing. He worked an apprenticeship in the final days of the pulps, and through the 1950s wrote prolifically in the Hard-boiled genre. In 1964 he introduced Travis McGee. McGee began as a peculiar hero: a Hard-boiled detective, but not a private eye. Living on a Fort Lauderdale houseboat, he made his occasional investigations for personal reasons, or to finance his unusual lifestyle. MacDonald's training enabled him to write eventful stories in a flexible prose, but it was his experience (and his curiosity) that gave distinction to the series: the McGee series becomes an anatomy of American enterprise in the last quarter of the century. MacDonald knows (or seems to) how people run businesses and how businesses run the country. Above all, he has his heroes show that they know how modern American things— boats, banks, cartels, stock markets—work. MacDonald's men are masters of the material and social technologies of America in the third quarter of the twentieth century. They are also masterful critics of these technologies. The line of detectives that includes Emma Lathen's John Putnam Thatcher (1961), Jonathan Gash's Lovejoy (1977), and Nevada Barr's Anna Pigeon (1993) continues to exploit the extra authority acquired by a detective who knows the inside story of how things work—how various businesses are run (Thatcher), how to distinguish true antiques from fake (Lovejoy), how divers explore wrecks or how forest fires are fought (Pigeon).

Sherlock Holmes might incidentally exploit the authority invested in him by his successful investigation of crime to comment upon boarding schools or upon the significance of an alliance between Britain and the United States, but Mac-Donald uses Travis McGee for regular and broad social commentary. Having shown that he knows how things work, McGee becomes, in effect, a credentialed critic of his world, not merely a private observer. MacDonald used the detective story as a soapbox in the best sense of "soapbox." And finally, by placing Travis McGee in Fort Lauderdale, not New York–Chicago–Los Angeles, MacDonald contributed to the development of the detective as the citizen of his region. McGee can eulogize the Florida that is passing as he excoriates the Florida that is emerging. MacDonald is always, as his heirs have not always been, a storyteller first, but his inclination to educate his readers about the way things really work, about morality, and about his region would be imitated by the deluge of Engaged writers who followed him.

MacDonald adopted another innovation, one that also antic- ipated the shift into the Engaged phase of the Hard-boiled form. Though distinctly alienated in some respects—what better sign of alienation than withdrawal from the American continent into a houseboat moored in Fort Lauderdale?— Travis McGee acquires an evolving life of his own. The Bus- ted Flush, with all its detailed accommodations, resembles 221B Baker Street, more than it does the empty apartment of Philip Marlowe. McGee possesses a best friend, maintains friendly relations with his community of Bahia Mar house- boaters, and develops extended relationships with other char- acters. If on the one hand, he delivers jeremiads upon the extravagances of American consumer culture, he is himself a creature of that culture; he develops bonds. In the later nov- els, characters from the earlier novels begin to reappear; in the final novel, *The Lonely Silver Rain* (1985), he discovers that he has actually had a daughter from a relationship in *Pale Gray for Guilt* (1968). Travis McGee accumulates a per- sonal history. And this changes things.

SOFTENING THE HARD-BOILED: THE ENGAGED DETECTIVE, 1970–

The Engaged paradigm emerged most directly from the Hard-boiled model of detective, with its polemical commit- ments to realism and to social commentary, though there were certainly antecedents in the Classical tradition as well: by the late 1940s Classical detectives such as Roderick Alleyn and Nero Wolfe were moving significantly toward expanded private lives and, in Wolfe's case, toward extended social and political commentary. And new Classical detectives, like Amanda Cross's Kate Fansler (1964), were being endowed with complex lives and active social concerns which set them clearly against the Classical Olympians. But it was the Hard- boiled writers—above all Chandler—that gave the detective an emotional responsiveness to other people (a responsive- ness he might, on principle, repress) and a sensibility and an

attitude that fitted him for the role of social critic. Philip Marlowe only began to acquire a life in his final appearances, but
he was from the start a voice through which Chandler could—
and did—anatomize his world. The Engaged model clearly
builds on this precedent: detectives after 1970 are still outsid-
ers, but they are not alone. They attach themselves to significant others, but also to identity-granting groups with social
agendas: many are women; some are gay; some are Black, or
Hispanic, Navaho, or Scottish, or belong to some other ethnic
group; some are intensely Catholic, or intensely Jewish; some
are linked to a particular region.

The popularity of the Hard-boiled detective had lasted well
into the 1950s, but was diminishing in the 1960s as the readership became a full generation removed from the conditions
that inspired the original revolt. Mickey Spillane's toughest
of tough-guys, Mike Hammer, appeared first in 1947, and
through the 1950s he enjoyed an unprecedented popularity
with his fellow ex-GIs. Other versions of the private dick also
prospered in paperback originals. Brett Halliday's Mike
Shayne continued his steady appeal in annual volumes. Bart
Spicer's Carney Wilde debuted in 1949, Richard S. Prather's
Shell Scott in 1950, Stephen Marlowe's Chester Drum in 1955.
All are lonely men pursuing justice in dark cities. Even Chester Himes's team of Grave Digger Jones and Coffin Ed John-
son (1957), though they are distinctive in their teamwork and
in their uneasy bond with the community of Harlem, remain
dark, violent, alienated heroes.

But in the 1970s the genre shifted. The private eye remains
the hero, but he is less alone, he is more apt to possess (and to
proclaim) views on issues of national concern, and he is often
female. Although he always remains in some measure isolated from his world, the Classical accent of the alienated
aristocrat and the original Hard-boiled accent of the alienated proletarian vanish as the detective acquires a circle of
intimates: friends, and lovers, and kin. Prior detectives might
have a comrade, a guy who could be trusted. But in the Classical tradition, comradeship was governed by Victorian conventions of masculine friendship, and was, in any event, to
some degree dictated by the utility of an obtuse narrator like
Watson, Jervis, Hastings, Van Dine, or even Goodwin. Com-

rades appear less often in the Hard-boiled model—Sam
Spade's contempt for his partner is a core issue in the novel,
and detectives like Marlowe and Lew Archer have no continuous friendships at all. Those Hard-boiled detectives who do
admit comrades—Mike Shayne and Timothy Rourke, Mike
Hammer and Pat Chambers, Travis McGee and Meyer—
regard the relationship as exceptional. (The comrade remains a minor motif in the Engaged manner. A characteristic
twist involves making the comrade a more violent, less moral
shadow to the detective: Spenser's Hawk, Robicheaux's Clete
Purcell, Easy Rawlins's Mouse. This shadow adds a touch of
chiaroscuro to the portrait of the detective. The detective's
manliness is appreciated not only by those whose weaknesses
call upon his strength, but also by those whose unrestrained
manliness acknowledge him as, in Clete Purcell's phrase, a
"noble mon.")

When, in his fifth novel, Lord Peter Wimsey began to acquire a larger private life (meeting the woman who would, in
his ninth novel, accept his proposal of marriage), he began
what Sayers knew at the time was a movement toward extinc-
tion as a detective. When, in his first novel, Mike Shayne met
the woman who would become his wife, the author, Brett Halliday, had to rescue him for the detective profession by sched-
uling her death in childbirth between the seventh and eighth
novels: wives and children were as inimical to the Hard-
boiled detective as to the Classical. Sam Spade keeps a playful distance from Effie Perrine. Perry Mason retains Della
Street as a perpetually loyal secretary, but never advances
their intimacy (Gardner actually makes Della insist upon the
more distant relationship; Mason proposes marriage, she de-
murs). Hammer holds his secretary, Velda, at arm's length,
as a sort of perpetual virgin. In their different manners, the
Hard-boiled dicks reject the intimacies of masculine or femi-
nine companionship. The exceptions prove the rule. Nick and
Nora Charles are sports; Hollywood might make them serial
characters, but Hammett did not. *The Thin Man*, in any event,
marks Hammett's move away from the Hard-boiled. The Pam
and Jerry North novels (1940) of Richard and Frances Lockridge are not Hard-boiled at all. The Bertha Cool/Donald Lam
novels of Erle Stanley Gardner play the partnership for

laughs, and even in his D.A. series, where sentimental attachment is a motif, Gardner could not bring his detective to make a commitment.

The Engaged detective, by contrast, possesses a surfeit of committedness. He (or she) almost always acquires family. By 1970, in deference either to realism or to ideology, "family" no longer signifies the nuclear household. Rather, it means a circle of intimates, and almost always an inclusive circle. Sarah Paretsky's V. I. Warshawski's parents are dead (though they remain important influences); she was only briefly married, and has no children. Her most pleasant blood relative, her cousin Boom Boom, dies in the second novel in the series. But Warshawski does have an evolving intimate relationship with the psychiatrist Lotty Hershel, and includes in her family two dogs, an elderly neighbor, and an old police comrade of her father.

Engaged detectives, unlike any of their predecessors, thus explore their own origins and the traditional families that formed them, often acknowledging, as Warshawski does, their positive influences, but in their own lives they construct nontraditional (and often antitraditional) families of their own. They have intense relationships with adoptive children and with senior citizens; with men and with women; with homosexuals and with heterosexuals; with Blacks and with whites (and, as appropriate, with Asians, Hispanics, Native Americans, Bantus); with Christians, Jews, animists, and Wiccans; with the living and with the dead (Jeremiah Cuddy communes with his dead wife; Dave Robicheaux with his dead wife and his dead father). The Classical detective often, especially in the Golden Age, appeared to have no inner life; the Hard-boiled detective usually strained to withhold his inner life; Engaged detectives thrust their inner lives upon their intimates and upon their readers. Indeed, reader interest in the detective's life sometimes seems to surpass interest in his or her detection. A 1992 paperback edition of Robert B. Parker's *Pastime* (1991) gives equal billing to two attractions on its cover: on the left, *Kirkus Review*'s description of the story ("Emotionally tense . . . Gripping . . . vintage hard-core Spenser!"); on the right, the appeal: "The secrets of Spenser's past—revealed at last!" Readers are expected to be as interested in Spenser's autobiographical revelations as in his emotionally tense and gripping investigation into the disappearance of Paul Giacomin's mother.

The Engaged detective acquires a place of his own. The post-1970 private eye still occasionally finds himself in the megalopolis (New York or Chicago or Los Angeles) of his Hard-boiled ancestors, but if he does, he is more attentive to neighborhoods and ethnicities. Increasingly he inhabits lesser cities (Boston, Indianapolis, St. Louis, Cincinnati, New Orleans, Detroit, Seattle), small towns (Rocksburg, Pennsylvania; Maggody, Arkansas; New Iberia, Louisiana), or even rural districts of Montana, Arizona, Alaska. Though he frequently made excursions into the countryside—especially to seaside resorts and to manor houses with libraries, butlers, and nearby vicarages—the Classical detective was a creature of London, and occasionally of New York, and Paris. He was at home in his bohemian (Holmes) or very neat (Poirot) flat; he was at ease in his city. The private eye was uneasy in his city, and at home nowhere. The Engaged detective is at home in his community; he not only knows his place, he loves it. Local color becomes a primary motive for the writer and the reader: the desire to explore one's native region seems second only to the desire to criticize society in the production of Engaged novels. There is a measure of sentimentality in detective story local color, as in all local color, and this fits nicely with the softened edges of the Engaged private eyes. Their alternative to the hypocrisies and corruptions of the world is not a barren apartment, but a homeland full of odd and interesting local characters.

Most importantly, the new private eye acquires sensitivity: the original Hard-boiled hero, even when he was not guilty of prejudice against women, Blacks, Latinos, Jews, Orientals, homosexuals, often spoke in the language of prejudice. Often enough, he was indeed prejudiced.[8] The post-1970 writers regularly contrive opportunities for their detectives to express their disapproval of and distaste for such prejudices. They act to achieve justice in the case at hand, and they speak for justice in society at large. The Hard-boiled detective knew that he could never expunge the liquor–gambling–drug syndicates which made his world fundamentally a wrong place; the softer post-1970s detectives believe that what makes their world a wrong place are the race-gender-sexual-orientation biases which infect their unenlightened contemporaries. The Hard-boiled detective made the pragmatic gesture of accepting and even, in a degree, respecting the syndicates and their codes of behavior. The Engaged detective never compromises with bigotry.

As a result, while the latter-day private eye continues to inhabit a Great Wrong Place, the quality of Wrongness has shifted. In the first phase of the Hard-boiled, wrongness seemed structural, built into the economic and political system. There was a radical divide between the usually corrupt elite who ran the industries, the newspapers, the gangs, and the local governments, and the sometimes corrupt middle and lower classes who labored. The divide is still there in the world of the Engaged detective, but it is based less on class and more on morals. There are the victimizers, who still include the rich, but more frequently include the inconsiderate middle class; and there are the victims, whose poverty, race, sex or sexual orientation, or religion mark them as vulnerable. The Hard-boiled enemy was embodied in the tycoon and the gangster; the Engaged enemy is more often the military-industrial complex. It is one thing to condemn a venal mayor or cop; it is another to condemn hegemonic foreign policies and heartless domestic policies. The former evils are immediate and concrete and can be traced directly to personal greed or lust; the evils of the latter type are more abstract, derived from racism and capitalism and sexism. The Hard-boiled villains wanted power: through money, or muscle, or sexuality, they had achieved some control over a piece of the urban jungle, and they struggled to achieve more. The Engaged villains are more complacent; they have achieved (and often inherited) a high place in the Establishment, and they act to maintain it. Even when they are psychopaths, they tend to be textbook psychopaths (the detective often works with a psychiatrist/psychologist who can, with authority, cite the textbook that diagnoses the relevant psychopathology).

The Engaged detective novel becomes self-consciously a didactic work, at a moral as well as at an informational level.[9] There is certainly the impulse to educate readers about the topography and the customs of the writer's region. There is also the ambition to introduce the reader to the workings of a particular institution—a hospital, a hotel, a retail electronics store. But above all, there is the desire to reform the reader's political incorrectness (or, if preaching to the choir, to reinforce the reader's political correctness). The Classical detective story was, superficially, playful, though it too could teach lessons about the way things work, and it certainly was dedicated to reinforcing those attitudes which it, conservatively, took to be correct. The initial Hard-boiled detective story was sober in its realism; it claimed to portray the truth of human relations in the city and it argued that the truth was often—usually—not pretty, but it was cynical about instituting correctness. The post-1970 detective story tends to be uncommonly earnest and implicitly optimistic in its exhortations. What in the Travis McGee novels appeared as occasional jeremiads against environmental degradation and racial injustice now become raisons d'être. Writers take up the popular form in order to proselytize on behalf of their vision of humane social relations. The Hard-boiled detective was sure only of himself; he had a full measure of the post–World War I disillusionment with moral and patriotic abstractions. The Engaged detective is always confident in his abstract principles (tolerance, equality, harmony), never in himself. He is not sure if he is acting properly, especially if he is white and male and Protestant; but he knows what constitutes proper action. He has an agenda.

Many Engaged series start with a polemical premise: the author has his or her detective investigate cases that involve a particular identifiable group of citizens who are oppressed in some degree by the inhuman prejudices of the racist, sexist, capitalist majority of society. The identity may be racial or ethnic or sexual or religious or economic. Although a few of the good writers become openly polemical in their outrage against the immoral majority (Sjöwall and Wahlöö led the way in this respect), the general result is an affirmative and often complex portrait of the group being advocated. Engaged detective novels tend to feature Detectives with a Point of View: the woman's point of view—Marcia Muller (Sharon McCone, 1977), Sue Grafton (Kinsey Millhone, 1982), Sharon

Paretsky (V. I. Warshawski, 1982), Linda Barnes (Carlotta Carlyle, 1987), Patricia Cornwell (Kay Scarpetta, 1990); the homosexual point of view—Joseph Hansen (David Brandstetter, 1970), Katherine V. Forrest (Kate Delafeld, 1984); the Black point of view—Walter Moseley (Easy Rawlins, 1990), Barbara Neely (Blanche White, 1992); the Native American point of view—Tony Hillerman (Joe Leaphorn, Jim Chee, 1970), Kirk Mitchell (Emmett Quanah Parker, Anna Turnipseed, 1999). These series are inspired in some measure by the desire to convey a hitherto silenced perspective on the world, and are thus linked to such experiments as Earl Derr Biggers's series featuring Charlie Chan (1925), Arthur Upfield's Australian aborigine, Napoleon Bonaparte (1929), Baynard Kendrick's blind Captain Maclain (1937), Robert van Gulik's Judge Dee (1958), or H. R. F. Keating's Inspector Ghote of Bombay (1964). But the post-1970s writers create their detectives as advocates for their party, not merely representatives. They are meant to persuade the reader of the virtue of their party, not merely to enlighten the reader regarding the party's history and character. There is a sense of grievance.

Some of the more popular series—those of Paretsky and Moseley, for instance—place the grievances at the center of the narrative; in other very popular series—Hillerman's and Cornwall's—they are peripheral. Probably the most popular have been Sue Grafton's Kinsey Millhone novels, which have been the best-sellers in hardcover as well as in paperback. Grafton is a fluent and versatile writer. Kinsey Millhone debuts in *'A' is for Alibi* as a thirty-two-year-old woman whose parents died in an automobile accident when she was five, who has been married and divorced twice, who has no pets and keeps no houseplants. No one knows when or how the parents of Sherlock Holmes died, or the parents of Poirot, or Spade, or Marlowe, or Archer. Kinsey Millhone continues to reveal additional facets of her personal history in the course of the series of novels. Indeed, the events that transpire in the novels themselves become part of her history: characters reappear, and Kinsey is concretely altered by what has happened to her in past investigations. Philip Marlowe, like Raymond Chandler, may grow older and wiser or more tired; he never deepens his relationship with Ann Riordan or Red

Norgaard by connecting with them again.[10] Engaged private eyes have lives as well as attitudes. They accumulate experience; their memories function; they are altered by experiences that dedicated readers have shared with them. Kinsey Millhone kills a man at the end of *"A" Is for Alibi*, and the trauma echoes through her later novels. Philip Marlowe kills a man in *The Big Sleep*, and never refers to the event again. (And this is not because his first homicide is buried beneath the corpses of later homicides: Marlowe only kills once.)

This development of the detective's life changes in a significant way the essential appeal of the series hero. Devotees of detectives from Dupin to Lew Archer purchased successive adventures expecting to see the hero do what he does; the detective's immunity from personal growth focused attention upon the defining action of the investigation. Fans of Kinsey Millhone attend to her active function as a detective, but they also expect to learn more about the woman who she is. They follow her introduction to Robert Dietz in *"G" Is for Gumshoe*, and then they observe the affair as it works its uneven course through later novels. In *"J" Is for Judgment*, Kinsey discovers she has a hitherto unsuspected set of relations, and in succeeding novels, readers note the way Kinsey connects to her grandmother and her three new-found cousins. The detective's biography becomes an object of interest.

This is true of Engaged male detectives as well; they too have lives. Robert B. Parker's consistently popular Spenser begins his career in *The Godwulf Manuscript* (1973) as a clear homage to Philip Marlowe, but the orphaned Spenser, over the course of more than twenty-five novels, acquires an adopted son, a tough Black sidekick, an independent Jewish girlfriend, and a dog. The diversity of Spenser's "family" indicates the special strain placed upon white, heterosexual, gentile, hominid male detectives: their new engagements compete with their inherited toughness. Spenser is far freer with his gun than Spade or Marlowe or Archer or McGee; only Mike Hammer's career is comparably homicidal. But Spenser is also far gentler than any of his predecessors. In fact, he tends toward a bipolarity: toward those who are intolerant and possessed of power, he is remorselessly judgmental; toward oppressed women, children, and minorities, he is unremittingly deferential. Other white, heterosexual, gentile male detectives of the second phase, such as Lawrence Block's Matthew Scudder (1976), Jonathan Valin's Harry Stoner (1980), Loren D. Estleman's Amos Walker (1982), and Jeremiah Healy's John Francis Cuddy (1984), may be somewhat less violent, and somewhat less deferential, but they too declare themselves on the side of the angels, and they too develop complicated biographies. The most interesting may be James Lee Burke's Dave Robicheaux (1987), whose intensity is sometimes reminiscent of the toughest of the first-generation Hard-boiled detectives. But Robicheaux's engagement with issues of race and class and gender in the local setting of Cajun Louisiana marks him distinctly as a man of the second phase.

The Hard-boiledness of the Hard-boiled detective had a largely parochial appeal: readers and writers were primarily American (and, presumably, male Americans of lower than average brow), though the artful voice of a writer like Chandler might actually receive greater respect abroad than at home. British writers made little use of the Hard-boiled paradigm in its first phase. Peter Cheyney attempted with some success to exploit the manner in his Lemmy Caution and Slim Callaghan series (both 1938), but it was not until the paradigm was radically softened that it was more widely adopted in Britain and around the world. Occasionally a good writer such as William McIlvanney will exploit the fully tough rhetoric; McIlvanney's Jack Laidlaw (1977) walks down Glasgow streets as mean as any in Los Angeles. But generally it has been the softened version of the private eye—the Engaged detective—that has inspired imitation. The British Golden Age had itself been independently evolving the Detective toward the Man (or Woman) Detecting. While Agatha Christie's hegemony in the Classical form lasted to her death in 1975 and Christie never felt obliged to expand Poirot's humanity, gestures toward Man Detecting could be discovered in the later novels of Margery Allingham's Albert Campion series or Ngaio Marsh's Roderick Alleyn series. John Dickson Carr kept Gideon Fell innocent of real relationships in a real world until his death in 1977, but Ellery Queen began in 1942 a series of Wrightsville novels which, while retaining a Classical emphasis upon plot puzzles, moved toward realistic social observation. The evolution of Wimsey, Alleyn, Queen, and other Classical detectives surely contributed to the development of the Engaged detective. In *An Unsuitable Job for a Woman* (1972), P. D. James, continuing (and modifying) the Golden Age style, introduced Cordelia Gray, clearly a Woman Detecting; James certainly influenced some of the writers who inundated the genre with female detectives in the later 1970s and 1980s. Dick Francis's Sid Halley (1965) can embody the same clubland virtues as John Buchan's Richard Hannay, just as James Lee Burke's Dave Robicheaux can enact the same extreme violence as Mickey Spillane's Mike Hammer, yet both Sid Halley and Dave Robicheaux inhabit worlds that are more socially and psychologically sophisticated than those inhabited by Hannay and Hammer, and both detectives lead more complex personal lives.

In the end, then, there is a confluence, rather than an articulated dialectic. There is a definite moment when the Hard-boiled revolted against the Classical, and relatively definite moments when the Classical contracted into the Golden Age and the Hard-boiled softened into the Engaged. But, especially after 1970, there has been a great deal of interpenetration of the two paradigms, and it becomes pointless to demark subgenres, or even to ascribe definite influences. A writer such as Peter Robinson, writing clearly in an English tradition, with an English detective (Alan Banks) operating in an English scene (Yorkshire), can acknowledge Chandler as an inspiration; Sara Paretsky, clearly writing in the Hard-boiled, private eye tradition, can admit the influence of P. D. James and Ruth Rendell.

Colin Dexter's Inspector Morse (1975), for example, has considerably more interior life than M. Poirot or Inspector French, and his Oxford is considerably more naturalistic than the Oxford of John Masterman's *An Oxford Tragedy* (1933) or Sayers's *Gaudy Night* (1935): it extends well beyond quadrangles and senior common rooms of the university. Dexter's novels remain Classical in their emphasis upon plot as a principal source of appeal, but they have moved significantly from the Golden Age allegory of the Great Good Place Restored. Dexter's novels are not as overtly polemical as many of those directly in the Engaged vein, but neither do they take place in a carriage of a train immobilized by the snows of the Balkans.

Anne Perry, in her Thomas and Charlotte Pitt series, shows the influence of the Hard-boiled mode in other ways. The Pitt novels are written in the Classical tradition. Their nine-teenth-century setting harks directly back to Holmes's gaslight and hansom cabs. The normal world is firmly well-ordered by Victorian proprieties. (In the true Classical mode, these proprieties are violated by the murder; in the modern Engaged mode, they are also questioned by the detectives. Still, however advanced their sensibilities, the Pitts are not revolutionaries.) The detectives work in the Classical manner by diligently collecting evidence and interrogating witnesses. Or, rather, by interrogating witnesses and collecting evidence: the Classical privileging of the analysis of trifles—tufts of hair, bits of glass, muddy footprints—has yielded to the Hard-boiled preference for reading spoken and unspoken reactions to the inquiries. As a result, the rewards of the Pitt novels lie in character and setting, not in plotting.

The Engaged manner tolerates bad plotting. If the hero's ideological bona fides and personal development are princi-pal sources of appeal, the final identification of the villain need only be acceptable, not persuasive. The detective must still detect; he or she still must exhibit the power to know what has happened. But that power is no longer an end in it-self. It is, rather, the warrant that validates the detective's various judgments and behaviors, judgments and behaviors the writer wishes to advocate.

CONCLUSION

The Engaged detective is, at the beginning of the twenty-first century, in a healthy state. Each new novel featuring Spenser, Kinsey Millhone, Kay Scarpetta, Alex Delaware can expect at least a short run on the best-seller list. The qualities that distinguish the Engaged detectives have made them widely attractive figures beyond the American and English markets. Because he or she is by nature a thoughtful examiner of his or her own life, a principled critic of society, and a close observer of local customs, he or she functions in Gaborone, Botswana or Barcelona, Spain as effectively as in New Iberia or Glasgow (for Botswana, see Precious Ramotswe, featured in Alexander McCall Smith's *The No. 1 Ladies Detective Agency* [1998]; for Barcelona, see Appolònia Lònià Guiu, featured in Maria-Antonia Oliver's *A Study in Lilac* [1987] or José (Pepe) Carvalho, featured in Manuel Vásquez Montalbán's Pepe Carvalho series [1977]). Paris is still the Mecca of the polars, but Jean-Claude Izzo's highly regarded Fabio Montale series is set in Marseilles. (Izzo's homage to Raymond Chandler exemplifies Chandler's influence in the non-Anglophone world. See also the Uruguayan Hiber Conteris's *Ten Percent of Life* [1985, 1987].)

The fashion will eventually exhaust itself, and perhaps the genre as well. The emphasis upon the detective's biography, upon his/her region/ethnicity/religion, and upon his/her social and political views may suggest that Poe's paradigmatic fable of the infallible secular knower has lost its essential appeal, and that the reiteration of the paradigm has become a vestigial remain, with the real interest lying elsewhere. If the detective ceases to be someone who knows, and becomes merely someone who inquires, the paradigm will have truly shifted. Writers interested in biography, region/ethnicity/religion, and social and political views may well decide that "knowing" is a passé patriarchalism, and that an open-ended investigation is a "truer" one. And readers may well agree. And then the detective story will go the way of the sonnet, or, better, the triolet. It will be a curiosity.

But perhaps knowing exactly what happened will continue to a desideratum, and whatever other subsidiary attractions graft themselves to the form, the detective story will persist as a form of popular fiction, in the Anglo-American world and elsewhere.

2

The World of the Detective Story

THE PECULIAR QUALITIES OF THE DETECTIVE'S WORLD ARE AS ES-
sential to the appeal of the detective story as is the peculiar
character of the detective himself. It is, indeed, his world
which empowers him as a detective: it is because his world
has been manufactured to yield truth to his method of inquiry
that he can be the successful inquirer that he is. There are
two necessary and distinctive aspects of the detective's
world: its visible present must contain signs that, properly
read, point infallibly to the true narrative of the singular, invisible past that led to this present; and both past and present
must be, in some degree, realistic. The first aspect is a distinctive feature which has far-reaching implications. It implies that time's forward arrow can never entirely erase the
backward trail of effect and cause; the past is always recon-
stitutable. Most of the story describes effects, usually traumatic effects, but the story's end always describes causes.
And because the reader's surprise at the causes must be accompanied by a sense that "I should have (or, at least, could
have) known," the narrative must be realistic: it must be governed by the probabilities that apply in the experience of the
reader, and its mise-en-scène must evoke the texture of the
quotidian world.

The real attraction of the genre may lie in this knowability
of the world. The cleverness of the detective, or his willfulness, or even his idiosyncrasies will be the obvious attraction
readers can cite as the principal reason for purchasing additional adventures in which the hero repeats his struggle and
repeats his success. He (or, since the 1970s, she) is the active
and noticeable feature which defines the genre. His presence
on the cover—"A Spenser Novel," "A Kinsey Millhone Mys-

tery"—announces that the reader will encounter a narrative that begins with exciting confusions, moves through a deliberate investigation, and culminates with irrefutable clarity, all presided over by the reassuringly familiar voice of the detective. Using empirical means, the detective discovers all that needs to be known; he does not arrive at an 80 percent certainty, or even a 99 percent certainty. He may, though he usually does not, leave the reader wondering how much sympathy to feel for a killer, but he never leaves the reader wondering who the killer is. He always wrestles truth from doubtful circumstances, and readers always admire his performance. But he always performs on a special stage. His world is predestined to be comprehensible; the real world, and the world of much fiction, offers no such guarantee: the wrestlers often strain to no avail; circumstances often yield only doubts. The contract of the detective story stipulates that here some details, some pieces of experience, will tell the true story. As a result, readers are promised a world that superficially resembles the ambiguous one of their experience, but which will eventually yield the truths that matter. The social landscape that they are about to enter will be troubled, and so interesting; and the troubles will be understood, and so satisfying. The troubles may be sensational, and the understanding simplistic, but promise is always kept. An unknown villain causes the trouble; it is the unknown-ness rather than the villainy that receives the main emphasis in the detective story. Highbrow novels may explore the morality, or aesthetics, or pathology of evil. The detective story may include, as an element, a meditation on the nature of evil, but it is never a primary element. The detective's principal drive is to eliminate the uncertainty, and his world always enables him to do so.

The World of the Methodical Detective

A snapper-up of unconsidered trifles.
—Shakespeare, *Winter's Tale*

Edgar Allan Poe understood that the real source of the detective's appeal lay in the construction of his world. Writing to the friendly poet Philip P. Cooke in 1846, after publishing the third Dupin story, Poe declared:

> You are right about the hair-splitting of my French Friend:—that is all done for effect. These tales of ratiocination owe most of their popularity to being something in a new key. I do not mean to say they are not ingenious—but people think them more ingenious than they are—on account of their method and air of method. In the "Murders in the Rue Morgue," for instance, where is the ingenuity of unraveling a web which you yourself (the author) have woven for the express purpose of unraveling? The reader is made to confound the ingenuity of the suppositious Dupin with that of the writer of the story. (*Letters* 2.238)

The detective's factitious ingenuity lies in solving the crime, given the misdirections present in the scene of the crime. The author's authentic ingenuity lies in giving those misdirections, in designing a scene of the crime that appears to lead to one conclusion (the murderer was Adolphe Le Bon), but to the analytic eye leads to another (the murderer was an orangutang). Readers think they appreciate the cleverness of the detective who solves the problem; what they really appreciate is the cleverness of the author, who has contrived a world of windows and locked doors and scattered gold, slaughtered women and contradictory witness.[1]

This structural web dictates what characters, settings, and styles are possible; the web defines the parameters of the reality in the world of the detective story. On top of this core web-reality, the author must then lay a cloak of distracting circumstances, the red herrings of misleading detail that, until the final exposition, obscure the web-reality. Finally, he must set both the core and cloak in a recognizably real location. Once he has woven his web, the author has, effectively, created his detective: the detective, essentially, *is* the unweaving of the web. He may also be a "young gentleman of an excellent—indeed of an illustrious family" who has been reduced to poverty and prefers to live in "a time-eaten and grotesque mansion" (*PT* 400), but he *is* the ingenuity ("the suppositious ingenuity") that infers from the lightning rod and shutters, from the overheard voices, from the tuft of hair—from all of the strands of the web that the author wove for him to unravel—that the murderer must have been an orangutang.

But this is precisely what the detective story must conceal. It does so in part by endowing the detective with a flamboyant character which occupies the reader's attention.[2] The detective impresses the reader by reviewing the events that have transpired and highlighting the significant moments. The significant moments are, of course, those with which the author began his initial, backward construction. But the detective's final, forward exposition which highlights these moments is dramatic—ingenious—only if the narrative itself has lowlit them. And the narrative achieves the lowlighting by presenting the detective's world—the significant details and the insignificant—under a common cloak of circumstantial realism as described by a narrative eye that is sharp enough to render the detail and dull enough to mismeasure significance—the eye of a Dr. Watson, or of the reader. The author must construct a complex world of objects and voices that to a common eye signify nothing, but which, to the eye of the detective signify what really happened. This superficial chaos of disconnected things and testimonies constitutes the disordered world in which the detective, his narrator, his fellow citizens, and the reader find themselves. By showing that chaos, carefully analyzed, points to order overlooked, the detective restores everyone's confidence that the world makes sense.

This can only be done, and only matters if it is done, in a recognizable place. Poe placed his detective stories in the real world, not in "some large, old, decaying city near the Rhine." A degree of realism was useful to make the crime—the murder of two women in "The Murders in the Rue Morgue"—a credible outrage and, more importantly, to make the detective's inferences persuasive. "Ligeia" opened in that nameless and decaying Rhenish city and moved to an abbey "in one of the wildest and least frequented portions of fair England" (269), where the narrator created a fantastically furnished setting for the phantasmagoric climax of the story. "The Murders in the Rue Morgue" is set in one of the capitals of the world, and while the recovered plot of action is fantastic—an orangutang, attempting to shave an old woman, nearly beheads her, then strangles the woman's daughter and thrusts her corpse up a chimney—there is no element of phantasmagoria. Indeed, the atmosphere is antiphantasmagoric: the emphasis is upon the detective's sober reconstruction of the realistic sequence of necessary actions that have caused the horrific result found in the apartment of Mme and Mlle L'Espanaye.

The L'Espanaye apartment must, therefore, be set in with some firmness in the world of the reader's experience. Paris belongs to that world in a way that an abbey "in one of the wildest and least frequented portions of fair England" does not. And Poe concretizes the Paris of his story by references to actual Parisian streets and districts (Rue Montmartre, Rue St. Denis), buildings (Palais Royale, Théâtre des Variétés), parks (Bois de Boulogne, Jardin des Plantes), and persons (Crébillon, Chantilly). For the same reason, Poe concretizes the immediate scene of the crime, providing journalistic descriptions of "the wildest disorder" (*PT*, 405) which has been discovered in the apartment: broken furniture, blood-smeared razor, tresses of hair, "four Napoleons, an ear-ring of topaz, three silver spoons, three smaller of *métal d'Alger*, and two bags containing nearly four thousand francs in gold" (*PT*, 405). This is a degree of circumstantial realism that recalls Defoe: the three hats, one cap, "and two Shoes that were not Fellows" which washed up from his ship and which Robinson Crusoe finds on the shore after a storm (Defoe, 46).[3]

There are at least three aspects to this primal scene of disorder: it signifies the radical disruption of normalcy which the crime represents; it anchors the disruption in a concrete, realistic scene; and—as readers soon learn—it always contains some items that are merely accidental (though only accidental as regards the present investigation; were other truths being pursued, other items might be significant: were all truths being pursued, all items would be significant), and some items which, read properly, reveal the intentional actions of the villain (and thus reveal the identity of the villain). These primal scenes of chaos are repeated throughout the early phase of the detective story. In Gaboriau's *Le Crime d'Orcival* (1867; *The Mystery of Orcival*, 1871), Lecoq enters a bedchamber:

A frightful disorder appeared in this room. There was not an arti-
cle of furniture, not an ornament, which did not betray that a ter-
rible, enraged and merciless struggle had taken place between
the assassins and their victims. In the middle of the chamber a
small table was overturned, and all about it were scattered lumps
of sugar, vermilion cups, and pieces of porcelain. (14)

Conan Doyle concentrated attention more upon the disrupted
person—the corpse—than upon the disrupted scene, but the
sense of disorder is still there. The room at 3 Lauriston Gardens in which he and Watson encounter the body of Enoch
Drebber is mildewed and dusty, but not frightfully disordered; the body is: "His hands were clenched and his arms
thrown abroad, while his lower limbs were interlocked, as
though his death struggle had been a grievous one. On his
face there stood an expression of horror, such as I have never
seen before on human features" (*A Study in Scarlet*, *ASH I*,
168). Inspector Gregson itemizes the contents of Drebber's
pockets: "A gold watch, No. 97163 by Barraud, of London.
Gold Albert chain, very heavy and solid. Gold ring, with ma-
sonic device. . . ." (*ASH II*, 169). Again, some of these concrete
details are accidental, and contribute to realism; some are,
as well, revealing. When a few anomalies from the bare
room—a wedding ring, the dust (some of which Holmes collects in an envelope), "Rache" scrawled in blood on a bare
wall—are added to this inventory of the corpse, the evocation
of a realistic, frightening, and portentous primal scene has
been achieved.

The realism matters. The movement of European taste in
mainstream literature moving from the aesthetic of early
nineteenth-century romanticism to that of mid-nineteenth-
century realism reinforced the use of realism in detective
fiction. It became more than a cloak for concealing clues and
a signal that the probabilities of ordinary life were applicable.
It became an intrinsic value. Gaboriau and Conan Doyle set
their stories in a more fully realized physical and social world
in part because it enabled them to promise readers the excitement of observing the behavior of actions that were credible
as well as extreme (a homicidal orangutang with a razor attempting to shave an old woman in a locked upper story flat is,

after all, merely extreme), and in part because it could offer readers the additional voyeuristic pleasure of observing the intimate details of the way others, more or less like themselves, were living their lives.

A comparison of Dupin's Paris to Holmes's London illustrates the point. Dupin's Paris is just real enough; Holmes's gaslit London is real. Dupin's Paris may be a real city, and the specified furniture of the L'Espanaye apartment may resemble that of real apartments, but "Rue Morgue" is not real or realistic; there is no Rue Morgue in Paris, and Poe does not bother to describe its pavements or its facades or its street-life. Nor is there a high precipice called "Bishop's Hostel" (or "Bessop's Castle") near Sullivan's Island, where Poe set "The Gold-Bug" (nor is there such an insect as a gold-bug). In the second Dupin story, "The Mystery of Marie Rogêt," Poe translated New York locations and institutions into "Parisian" locations and institutions by giving them French names, without modifying their character in any way. He even provided footnotes translating the names back into their New York equivalents, lest readers think that he thought he was actually writing about Paris. These outrages against realism had consequences. When the Dupin stories were translated into French, there were objections raised against Poe's faux Paris, as, in Charleston, there were decriers of the false topography of "The Gold-Bug." But these contretemps only prove the point: readers took—and were meant to take—the world of Dupin as real, and those who could not take it as real, took offense. The entomologists who sneer that no scarabaeus in nature resembles the gold-bug discovered by Legrand, like the herpetologists who sneer that no viper in nature resembles the swamp adder that killed Julia Roylott and her stepfather in Sherlock Holmes's "The Adventure of the Speckled Band," and all the close readers who catch a detective story writer in a mistake, have a fair complaint. The point is that the genre has trained them to complain; readers of detective stories expect to encounter a world consisting largely of familiar objects interacting in familiar ways. It will, of course, include some unfamiliar objects—corpses, certainly, and perhaps even orangutangs and gold-bugs. But it must represent the ways and the things of the world as they are. This imperative has only increased as the genre has passed through its various phases. The acknowledgment notes which preface so many late twentieth-century detective novels are, in a way, an attempt to preempt objections: the author advertises the research he or she has executed in order to give accurate texture to the world of the crime and the investigation. Detective story writers, since the mid-nineteenth century, know that there are topographers, entomologists, and herpetologists just waiting to pounce on errors.

*   *   *

Dupin's power lies in his ability to draw from the concrete surfaces of that familiar world the moral story which lay beneath them. When Dupin and the narrator visit the scene, they examine the exterior and then, permitted inside, Dupin "scrutinized every thing" (*PT*, 413), including the corpses. This scrutiny is exhaustive enough that, for example, when he reviews his analysis at the end of the story, Dupin can cite specific details:

> [T]he shutters of the fourth story were of the peculiar kind called by Parisian carpenters *ferrades*—a kind rarely employed at the present day, but frequently seen upon very old mansions at Lyons and Bordeaux. They are in the form of an ordinary door, (a single, not a folding door) except that the upper half is latticed or worked in open trellis. (*PT*, 419)

These details insist that these must be real French shutters; they must have been there. There must have been a there. A complicated plot that requires an improbable ape to commit an incredible double murder in a room and then to escape through an incredibly self-sealing window is rendered plausible (more plausible) by the accumulation of credible detail about the building: the ferrades effect.

The ferrades are also functional in the web of the plot. They are, Dupin decides, ideally constructed to afford "an excellent hold for the hands" and thus become a key link in his explanation of how the locked room of the crime scene was entered and exited. The gendarmes see a locked room and two murdered women, and they see what might have happened: a greedy clerk—the last man known to have been in the room—might have killed the women; Dupin observes the ferrades and other objective details, realizes what they signify, and infers what *did* happen—an escaped ape clinging to the shutter had swung himself into the room.

The detective thus duplicates the action of his author. He recreates the reality of his world in the same way the author created that world, moving backward from significant effect to necessary cause. The Classical detective, like Dupin, will concentrate upon discovering the physical causes of physical effects; the Hard-boiled detective will concentrate upon the causes of moral and psychological effects. But both find themselves in worlds carefully designed to appear full of effects which are realistic and which matter, but which have no apparent cause. The detective story always promises to present the reader with a world that is, up to the last chapter, characterized by incomprehensible things and actions. It is a melodramatically heightened version of the world the reader lives in: the minor bafflements of life—where did *that* come from? why did she say *that?*—become keys to a major puzzle. In the last chapter every thing and every action is comprehended in the detective's reconstruction of what happened.

The methodical detectives of the early Classical phase build directly upon Poe's model of unweaving. Their eyes are always focused upon crucial things—tufts of hair, cigarette ashes, missing umbrellas—which, in their final expositions, will constitute the effects for which their narratives of causes will account. Included among the "things" that are noticed are scraps of conversation; the detective analyzes these scraps as objects in the same way he analyzes footprints or cigarette ashes. This preoccupation with precise enumeration and description of objects becomes a defining characteristic of the genre. It lies behind Sherlock Holmes's repeated maxims—"It has long been an axiom of mine that the little things are infinitely the most important" ("A Case of Identity," *ASH I*, 409); "You know my method. It is founded upon the observance of trifles" ("The Boscombe Valley Mystery," *ASH II*, 148); "There is nothing so important as trifles" ("The Man with the Twisted Lip," *ASH I*, 379). It is this method of the Classical detective that determines a key quality of his world—it is a world of trifles. "The great detective story," wrote Chesterton, "deals with small things" ("The Domesticity of the Detective," in *The Uses of Diversity*, 27).

As a result of this generic attention to detail, the Classical detective story came to provide an important incidental pleasure: it promised an attention to the texture of ordinary life which other genres of fiction might underrate. Small things come to be valued for two contradictory reasons: because they mean something and because they do not. The details that are *not* clues are not merely red herrings, or if they are red herrings, their very redness and herringness become ends in themselves. The detective story thus naturally adopted what might be called a style of "trifle realism," noticing in descriptive prose those details—shutters of the peculiar kind called by Parisian carpenters *ferrades*—that other realisms might overlook. Malcolm Warren, the amateur detective in C. H. B. Kitchin's novel, *Death of His Uncle* (1939), expresses the point nicely: what he likes about detective stories

> isn't so much the puzzle of the plot, still less sensational hair-breadth escapes, but precisely the element you would least expect to find in such stories—the humdrum background, tea at the Vicarage, a morning in the office, a trip to Brighton pier—that microscopic study of ordinary life which is foil to the extraordinary event which interrupts it. (36)

There are many who read, or reread, the Holmes stories for their evocation of the humdrum background—the fogs and hansom cabs and domestic interiors—of gaslit Victorian London. And, as Malcolm Warren says, the microscopic physical details of ordinary life serve as an effective setting for the extraordinary event that constitutes the crime.

The rich minutiae of the detective story provide pleasure; they give the reader a point of reference, indicators that the detective's world is genuinely their own; and they act to camouflage those trifles that constitute the crucial web of action. The Classical detective's apparent genius lies in his ability to winnow the web details from the decorative details. And despite the celebrated immobility of detectives such as The Old

Man in the Corner or Nero Wolfe, and the languid pose assumed by others like Dupin and Philo Vance, the Classical detective always exhibits an active intelligence and, more often than might be expected, a considerable amount of corresponding physical activity as well. Though the heroic knower may be less visibly athletic than the heroic warrior, he is not, in fact, less active.[4] His world is full of trifles; he must seize the significant ones. In the second Dupin story, Poe attempts the tour de force of a genuinely armchair detective; his conceit is that Dupin can infer truth merely by reading the reports of journalists. Seizing facts from newspapers lacks dramatic force, and "The Mystery of Marie Rogêt" is uniformly regarded as the least of Dupin's three achievements in detection. In the first and third stories, the detective is more physically active in his collection of data. In "The Murders in the Rue Morgue," Dupin travels to the scene of the crime, making a close inspection of everything inside and outside the apartment of the L'Espanayes. In the third story, Dupin makes two sorties to the apartment where Minister G——— conceals the purloined letter. Although his reference to "a three-pipe problem" in "The Red-Headed League" has become one of his signatures, Sherlock Holmes was, of course, vigorous in his pursuit of the cigar ashes and footprints which litter the scenes of crime. Nero Wolfe himself can, when necessary, exert himself (*The Black Mountain*; the Zeck novels), and Archie Goodwin always adds mobility to the investigation. The Classical detective is, despite his occasional pose of intellectual ennui, an aggressive reader of the trifles of his world, not at all a passive observer.

*   *   *

But if the Classical detective story needs to be set in a detailed realistic physical environment, a comparably textured social matrix is not obligatory. There needs to be a motive for the crime, but it may be quite conventional—greed, revenge, escape from blackmail—and, if the murderer is an orangutang, even motive may be dispensed with. It is by examining the inert detritus that the Classical detective can discover what happened, and that is the main point. The human relations that lead to the crime and then to the solution of the crime are secondary, and in Poe's initial version of the paradigm, even ornamental. In "The Murders in the Rue Morgue," there are no human relations between the villain and his victims; the villain is entirely inhuman. But even the victims are given virtually no character. Mme et Mlle L'Espanaye, and, as well, such ancillaries as Inspector G———, Alfred Le Bon, and the Maltese sailor who owns the ape—all are equally intangible as persons with human backgrounds or human associations; they might as well be orangutangs. They exist solely as actors in the plot. Dupin's Paris is a world of things and of actions, but it is largely stripped of any human dimensions.

This is, of course, in part, a condition of the short story form. But "The Murders in the Rue Morgue" shows that there is another factor at work. The murder of Madame L'Espanaye and her daughter Mademoiselle Camille L'Espanaye took place in a fourth floor apartment of a rooming house on the Rue Morgue, the first three floors of which are vacant. This location is a functional part of the web: it makes the locked room dramatically inaccessible to all but an energetic orangutang. But it also strikes a note which echoes through the genre: the detective story works best in the anonymous metropolis in which individuals exist as isolated monads. Dupin reads the *Gazette des Tribunaux* account of what was known of the victims. Two witnesses testified to the characters of the deceased: a laundress who had worked for them for three years, and a tobacconist who had sold the old lady snuff for the six years that the two women had occupied the apartment. The tobacconist reported that they had lived "an exceedingly retired life." In fact, other than a porter who had entered the apartment once or twice, the only visitor had been a doctor, and he had called but "some eight or ten times" in the six years. The laundress reported that Mme. L'Espanaye told fortunes for a living; the tobacconist reported that she was "childish." Over a period of eight years she had made frequent small deposits. These bits of information are the L'Espanaye epitaph; this is what their lives amounted to. Paris did not notice their existence, and, but for its bizarre circumstances, would never have noted their deaths.

The detective story generally wastes little sympathy for the

victim; sympathy would inevitably shift the narrative toward
tragedy, and neither pity nor fear are appropriate in a drama
where the principal effect should be awe at the brilliance of
an analyst. And had the L'Espanayes lived with an extended
family, or had they had a lifetime's commerce with neighbors, the murder might not have been committed—the orangutang might have been deterred by a roomful of relatives, or
the crime might not have required Dupinian analysis for its
solution—neighbors would have noticed its ascent or descent.
But the L'Espanaye women lived very much alone; they are
mere ciphers; neither their neighbors nor the reader ever
knows who they are. Their deaths are horrible, but their lives
are empty.

It is not just the victims who appear as monads in the story.
It is remarkable how alienated everyone is in "The Murders
in the Rue Morgue." Dupin's isolation is, in some measure,
the conventional alienation of the Romantic hero. Philo Vance
is perhaps more supercilious than romantic when he insists,
"I can not say with Terence, '*Homo sum, humani nihil a me
alienum puto*', because I regard most things that are called
human as decidedly alien to myself" (Van Dine, *The Benson
Murder Case*, 66), but he is repeating the theme: he is cast of a
different metal; his tastes and his ethics certainly differ from
those of supplicants who appeal to him for knowledge, but so
is his nature different. He is a special sort of human.

But the detective's alienation is not on the scale of the Byronic or Faustian hero (and so he could survive the passing
of the Byronic vogue). Manfred and Faust posit themselves
against the universe; Dupin and Vance posit themselves
against society, and even then the rebellion is half-hearted:
they invariably rescue those to whom they condescend. Their
egoism is real, but qualified. They withdraw from the street,
but not too far: the seventeen steps from Baker Street to the
files and scientific apparatus (and the violin and the seven
percent solution) in 221B measure the distance. Ennui and
lethargy become the detective's hallmarks: when Dupin (or
Holmes or Vance) works (investigates), he works intensely;
his normal state is one of retirement. Poirot is literally retired
when he first appears; Wimsey is a fop and a bibliophile when
he is not detecting. All are, in essence, disconnected individu-

als, self-sufficient in their private worlds. Dupin is a young man of good family—"indeed of an illustrious family"—who had suffered financial reverses and now chooses to live in perfect seclusion in the midst of Paris with a friend who could afford to rent "a time-eaten and grotesque mansion . . . in a retired and desolate portion of the Faubourg St. Germain." The two kept the location secret from all their associates and "existed within ourselves alone" (*PT*, 400–401). Their Paris is no one else's Paris.

The victims are alone in the city; the detective is alone in the city; *everyone* is alone in the city. It is a modern, urban world of strangers. Because the murders of the L'Espanayes took place inside the locked apartment, there were only ear-witnesses to the crime itself. They all heard two voices, and all agreed that one voice spoke in French. They could not agree about the second voice. The French gendarme, Isidore Muset, thought it spoke in Spanish; Henri Duval, a neighbor, thought Italian; Odenheimer, a Dutchman, thought French; William Bird, an Englishman, thought German; Alfonzo Garcio, a Spaniard, thought English; Alberto Montani, an Italian, thought Russian. The contradictions constitute an important clue, which Dupin reads to indicate that one of the perpetrators was speaking no human language at all, and was, in fact, an Ourang-Outang (*sic*) from Borneo. But such a collection of mutually incomprehensible human beings—a Frenchman, a Dutchman, an Englishman, a Spaniard, and an Italian—occurs only in a metropolis where everyone is profoundly unknown to everyone else. As a result, the detective who has abandoned his world is called upon to solve the murder of two women who have lived their lives without being known by anyone, and he achieves success in part because he understands why none of his witnesses can understand what they have heard. After he has succeeded, the Prefect of Police mutters "a sarcasm or two, about the propriety of every person minding his own business" (*PT*, 431). The prefect is expressing his resentment of Dupin's triumph, but he is also advocating what constitutes the normalcy of the detective's world, a normalcy which the crime violates. It is because every person minded his own business that the L'Espanayes could be murdered, and their murderer escape.

The essential strangeness of the detective's urban world is indicated by a similar device in the Sherlock Holmes saga. *A Study in Scarlet* opens with Watson returning from the Afghan war to a London which he describes as "that great cesspool into which all the loungers and idlers of the Empire are irresistibly drained" (*ASH I*, 145). Watson, with no apparent family to receive him, escapes from the cesspool when he agrees to share lodgings with the equally alone Sherlock Holmes. In the crime that occupies the novel, foreigners are again the emblems of the unattached isolatoes who need detectives. The newspapers suggest that the murder of Enoch Drebber can be attributed to the flood of foreigners who have, for various reasons, sought refuge in London. And, in fact, both victim and his murderer are Americans. In the second Holmes novel, the villain is a denatured Englishman, and his accomplice is a very un-English Andaman islander. In the first Holmes short story, the villain is again an American. Not until "The Red-Headed League" does an English villain prey upon an English victim, and even then Conan Doyle inserts the spectacle of London's Fleet Street "choked with red-headed men": "from north, south, east, and west every man who had a shade of red in his hair had tramped into the City" (*ASH I*, 423). This riot of unrelated red-headed men is the epitome of the detective's city. Each man jostles the others in the effort to obtain the advertised job. As it happens, no one is killed; but if, when the crowd cleared, there had been a red-headed corpse, it would have taken a Holmes to identify the killer.

The estrangement of Dupin's Parisians is, of course, extreme, and Conan Doyle's broader interest in the anatomy of Victorian society leads him to further moderate the air of alienation in Holmes's London. If there is a strong element of the foreign in the second Holmes novel, there is also a strong domestic element, as Watson ends the novel by proposing marriage to Miss Mary Morstan. Watson has served in Afghanistan, and Miss Morstan's father had served in India, but the Watson–Morstan marriage is a thoroughly English affirmation of intimate human connection. Throughout the saga, Holmes does encounter problems whose sources and contexts are entirely insular, but the number of adventures that involve alienated foreigners or foreign-influenced Britons remains disproportionately large.

*   *   *

Poe also set the fashion for detaching his fables of analysis from the history of his time. If he was obligated to make his narratives realistic in trifling matters, he was not obligated to set them in an actual time and place. He had to anchor them in recognizable circumstances, but not in a recognizable decade or, as noted above, in a fully recognizable city. In "The Mystery of Marie Rogêt," Poe flaunts the Parislessness of Dupin's Paris. He takes an actual New York crime, recognizable in circumstances and time—the body of the cigar girl, Mary Rogers, had been discovered floating in the Hudson River on July 28, 1841—, and deliberately estranged it by transferring it to Dupin's faux Paris. He might easily have had Dupin make a visit to the States and avoided the necessity of footnotes correlating the Barrière du Roule with Weehawken and *L'Etoile* with the *N. Y. Brother Jonathan*; or, with a bit more effort, he might have created a Parisian variation on the New York theme. Too much historical reality, Poe clearly felt, would ruin his fable. When, in "The Purloined Letter," Dupin undertakes a case that affects affairs of state, Poe remains entirely vague about the state. The person to whom the purloined letter was written is described by Inspector G—— as "a personage of most exalted station" and as a woman who occupies "the royal boudoir" (*PT*, 682). From these hints, it can be inferred that she is the queen of France. But knowing that the queen of France between 1830 and 1848 was Maria Amelia, consort of Louis Philippe, adds nothing at all to the understanding of the story. The queen is a cipher signifying "noble object of pity and protection." Dupin's actions on behalf of his queen are surely a sign of his chivalrous character, but they hardly justify conclusions about his approval of the policies of the court of the citizen-king.

"The Gold-Bug" makes a similar point. It is rare among Poe's works in being definitely set in a scene with which Poe and a portion of the paying audience were familiar, and the presence of his manumitted slave, Jupiter, ties William Legrand definitely to the world of the antebellum South which

Poe and his readers knew. But the main action of the story depends upon events that occurred in the legendary past: Captain Kidd (1645?-1701) was a historical figure, but one shrouded in Romantic fiction. His treasure was, in fact, being actively sought in the 1830s and 1840s—but in the vicinity of New York's Long Island, not near Charleston, South Carolina. Just as erecting a cliff called "Bishop's Hostel" or "Bessop's Castle" shifts the topography toward fantasy, the seventeenth-century legend of Captain Kidd shifts the history toward romance.

Conan Doyle again was more moderate in detaching his fables from their times. On the one hand, he would invent a factitious king of Bohemia ("A Scandal in Bohemia") or Prime Minister Lord Bellinger ("The Adventure of the Second Stain"); on the other hand, Holmes attends concerts of Wilhelmina Norman-Néruda (*A Study in Scarlet*) and Pablo de Sarasate ("The Red Circle"), and Watson acquires portraits of General Gordon and Henry Ward Beecher ("The Cardboard Box"), and these were all authentic Victorians. The legendary enters Holmes's world only *as* legend (the Legend of the Hound of the Baskervilles). When vampirism is introduced, it is only to be dismissed: "Are we to give attention to such things? This Agency stands flat-footed upon the ground, and there it must remain. The world is big enough for us. No ghosts need apply" ("The Adventure of the Sussex Vampire," *ASH II*, 463). The flat-footed world of Victorian England constitutes the mise-en-scène of the Holmes saga; Conan Doyle feels obligated to insert no arch allusions to the fictionality of his narratives.

Nonetheless, except in the special instance of "His Last Bow," in which Holmes takes on the agents of the Kaiser during the First World War, Holmes's cases are not set directly in historical circumstances; that is, the larger events of the time do not seem to have directly influenced any of the crimes he investigates and neither Holmes nor his clients express partisan views about changes in ministries or the conduct of the Boer War, or the depredations of Jack the Ripper. As Watson reports in "The Adventure of the Bruce-Partington Plans," "I was aware that by anything of interest, Holmes meant anything of criminal interest. There was news of a revolution, of a possible war, and of an impending change of Government; but these did not come within the horizon of my companion" (*ASH II*, 432). As the Baker Street exegetes have shown at one level and scholars, especially since the 1980s have shown at another level, the Holmes saga is in some respects a valuable seismograph of social realities in late Victorian and Edwardian England, but the evidence tends to be indirect.

Holmes's world is fundamentally built upon the generic requirement that it be knowable, that there be a crime committed by an individual and that the crime leave behind a web of traces which can be read by the detective. But where Poe was satisfied to provide world enough to make that web credible, and no more, and even to undercut that world's plausibility with gestures such as escaped orangutangs, Bessop's Castle, and Hoboken-on-the-Seine, Conan Doyle chose to seize the opportunity, so far as the essential web permitted, to enrich the realism and to make the detective story become a brief yet concrete chronicle of its time. Conan Doyle gained much by this commitment to a flat-footed world; he also lost a bit of the edge of Poe's invention: in Poe's stories, the appeal of the detective's world never competed with the appeal of the detective's process of knowing that world. The center of the Dupin stories remains how Dupin comprehends and manipulates things and events; everything in his world is subject to comprehension and manipulation simply because if it were not, it would not be in the world. Conan Doyle's plots are often very clever, but even the cleverest contain things and events—"the humdrum background"—that are not there to be comprehended, but to add realism. Holmes does not, consequently, dominate his world with the completeness of Dupin. As a compensation, Conan Doyle developed a technique he described as "Sherlockholmitos": "clever little deductions, which often have nothing to do with the matter at hand, but impress the reader with a general sense of power" (*Memories and Adventures*, 107). If the matter at hand contained extraneous details over which the detective had no control, the author could insert extraneous matters over which the detective had total control. Thus, "The Blue Carbuncle" opens with Holmes's examination of a hat. He draws numerous inferences about the owner of the hat, all of which are verified when the owner, Henry Baker, appears. But Henry Baker has nothing directly to do with the mystery of the Blue Carbuncle. He is merely the accidental vehicle through which the stone comes to Holmes's attention. Baker's domestic arrangements, which have left their marks on his hat, are utterly irrelevant to the solution of the mystery. But they have enabled Conan Doyle to establish Holmes's power to know his world before he sends the detective off on a colorful chase through Bloomsbury and Covent Garden Market.

The main line of British heirs to Holmes—Martin Hewitt, The Old Man in the Corner, Max Carrados, Dr. Thorndyke— followed in his more realistic footsteps, but, perhaps because they did not achieve anything approaching Sherlockholmitos, they did not achieve his renown. It could be argued that R. Austin Freeman did create a sort of Johnthorndykitos, and the Dr. Thorndyke stories do achieve excellence in one sort of realism: no detective in the Classical tradition approaches the diligence with which Thorndyke and his technician, Polton, follow actual scientific procedures for eliciting information from trifles. The principal American successors to Dupin were, like Poe, more inclined to sacrifice verisimilitude to dramatic effect. Jacques Futrelle's Professor Augustus F. X. Van Dusen and Arthur B. Reeve's Craig Kennedy seem to breathe the thinner air of romance, though they lack in some measure (in the instance of Craig Kennedy, in considerable measure) the compensatory rewards of Poe's wit and originality. The one oddity is the English writer who turned away from realism and back toward the romance of Poe: G. K. Chesterton's Father Brown dominates his world in much the manner of Dupin; there is a slightly unreal quality to the streets of Father Brown's London. Poe and Chesterton share this willingness to slight the world in order to empower the detective; for Poe, this makes the detective the more powerful; for Chesterton, it makes the world slighter. Father Brown is, after all, a militantly drab, unindividualized priest. What he does to the traces of a crime is what any one—any thoughtful Christian—can do to all the things and events of the world: tangible reality is only a divinely constructed set of signs which must be read by right-minded (not ratiocinative) readers.

THE WORLD OF THE GOLDEN AGE DETECTIVE: *ET IN ARCADIA EGO*

The first phase of the detective story thus offered a spectrum of worlds to the reader. There were sober worlds and playful worlds, pedestrian worlds and fantastic worlds, urban worlds and village worlds. The Golden Age consolidated these into the Great Good Place, and while the consolidation certainly meant a narrowing, it also encouraged a deepening. The Great Good Place would eventually appear to be a stifling hothouse against which Raymond Chandler could compose a diatribe, but it was not, in fact, such an effete artifice as he made it out to be.

That the Golden Age consolidation and the Hard-boiled revolution both secured their identities in the 1920s is surely related to that watershed in Western culture, World War I. The detective story's indifference to historical events prior to 1914 was relatively uncomplicated: a form based on crime by individuals in domestic settings was not obligated to comment upon national and international conflicts. But when the larger conflict thrust a generation into muddy trenches, and left a large portion of it interred in dedicated fields of Flanders, it took a concerted effort to remain oblivious. The disillusionment of the postwar era was a pervasive phenomenon; the Golden Age detective story was a conscientiously anti-disillusionment model of fiction. It took the inherently confident fable of the detective story and made it an almost ritualistic statement: there *is* truth, and it *can* be discovered. The disorder beneath which order is concealed may be complex indeed, and may be the result of byzantine machinations by the evildoer, but the disorder is always illusory, always resolvable into a clear and true account of what really happened.

The war is often there in the early Golden Age novels, but always on the periphery. In Agatha Christie's first novel, *The Mysterious Affair at Styles* (1920, written—and set—in 1916), the war is what brings Hercule Poirot as a refugee to Styles Court. Captain Hastings, Poirot's narrator, is, like Dr. Watson, a disabled veteran, though his experiences at "the Front" are even less well defined than Watson's briefly chronicled debacle in Afghanistan. World War I, like the Second Afghan War, plays no further significant role in the novel. In the second Poirot novel, *Murder on the Links* (1923), Hastings experiences a reflective moment as he passes by the cemeteries at Amiens on the train, but the moment passes. Lord Peter Wimsey was wounded in the war, and in his first appearance (*Whose Body?* 1923), he is himself the victim of flashbacks to the horror of the trenches (again, Sayers, for all her insistence upon formula, stretches the conventions), but even here the war is not a factor in the crime or its investigation.

There is, of course, no reason why the war should have motivated murders or influenced investigations, and obvious reasons why, after such a traumatic conflict, a writer of popular fiction would not strain to bring it in. Nonetheless, the absence of the war points to the Golden Age's steadfast withdrawal from engagement with the social, political, and economic struggles that took place during the time. The world of the detective becomes, by consensus, a quieter, safer place. On the one hand, there is always a murder; on the other hand, there is only a murder. One-third of Dupin's cases involved theft, not murder; fewer than half of Holmes's adventures involve homicide. The Golden Age insisted upon murder, but it also insisted that the murder was an aberration, that tranquillity was normal.

To this end, it preferred Auden's Great Good Place. This is, above all, confined space; "a closed society so that the possibility of an outside murderer . . . is excluded" (Auden, 17). It is, in this respect, a paradise (from the Greek, and ultimately from the Persian, for "enclosed garden"). By the end of the nineteenth century, a literal walled garden was too remote an ideal. Auden suggests four modern substitutes: a Christmas party at a country house, an Old World village, a theatrical company, and a Pullman car; and later he adds a college to the list. In addition to enclosure, the Great Good Place evokes the Christian sense of "paradise": it must, says Auden, "appear to be an innocent society in a state of grace" (18). The shock of the crime shifts the society's covenant to one of law; the detective's task is to restore grace.

The worlds of the first phase of the Classical paradigm met these criteria, but roughly. Holmes frequently finds himself in country estates, and even the London homes of some of his clients have a detachment and an innocence that might qualify them as modern paradises, but the detective also frequently visits markets, and wharves, and opium dens which are neither detached nor innocent. The novels to which Auden confessed himself addicted were the Golden Age mysteries which insisted with some rigor on the closed and innocent world in which the detective operated. Sherlock Holmes, Lecoq, Dr. Thorndyke, and Father Brown were great perambulators, and even Dupin was introduced as a nocturnal flaneur. Auden is speaking of the immediate scene of the crime, but the effort that the early authors took to set their protagonists in the streets of the great cities militated against the enclosure effect Auden desires. The great detectives of the Golden Age are houseplants by contrast: a record of the perambulations of Hercule Poirot or Philo Vance would be a thin one. (They certainly appear in different places; Poirot investigates in Mesopotamia and in Egypt, as well as in dozens of English communities. He travels from Istanbul to Calais. But he functions entirely within the few hundred square feet of the train's coach. The Golden Age detective confines himself to the scene of the crime.) And while the Classical model did encourage the early writers as well to limit the casts of characters and settings in which those characters appeared, the writers of the first phase, especially when they essayed a novel, were careless in this regard. *A Study in Scarlet* brings American victims and an American killer with an American motive to London, and actually installs the killer as a cab driver who commits his crimes opportunistically in various locations. The second half of the novel leaps across one ocean and more than half a continent to explain the origins of the crime in the deserts of Utah. Narratives like these are weedy indeed.

The Golden Age trimmed the lawn. *Trent's Last Case* opens with the international repercussions of the death of the industrial magnate Sigsbee Manderson. These prove to be tremendous, but short-lived; the great man was less important than he seemed. The scene then shifts to the world of the daily press, with its appetite for new sensations. Not until chapter Four does the detective, Philip Trent, reach the scene of the crime, and at that point the narrative moves from the Great World of business and finance and journalism, to the bucolic world of Manderson's country estate, White Gables, where it will remain until the crime is solved. Trent notes "a spacious lawn and shrubbery" and a house that is "beautifully kept, with that air of opulent peace that clothes even the smallest houses of the well-to-do in an English countryside."

> Before it, beyond the road, the rich meadow land ran down to the edge of the cliffs; behind it a woody landscape stretched away across a broad vale to the moors. That such a place could be the scene of a crime of violence seemed fantastic; it lay so quiet and well ordered, so eloquent of disciplined service and gentle living. (41)

This is Auden's Great Good Place, with the discordant note of the murder shattering the natural harmony of the scene. "The corpse must shock," Auden wrote, "not only because it is a corpse, but because, even for a corpse, it is shockingly out of place, as when a dog makes a mess on a drawing room carpet" (19).

The identical contrast is employed, and more quickly, in the first Poirot novel. When Hastings descends from his train at Styles St. Mary, Essex, in 1916, he notices first the "green fields and country lanes": "As one looked out over the flat Essex country, lying so green and peaceful under the after-noon sun, it seemed almost impossible to believe that not so very far away, a great war was running its appointed course. I felt I had suddenly strayed into another world" (3). He has: in one world, the appointed course includes cataclysms such as the Great War; in the other, the Essex countryside is as green and peaceful as it has always been and always will be. Once he passes into Styles Court, with its matriarch, Mrs. In-glethorp, and her variety of dependents, the world of the war is forgotten (though it does provide the background for a red herring), and the contrast is not between Arcadian Essex and the trenches of Flanders, but between Essex and the corpse. Poirot, called to Styles Court upon the murder of Mrs. Inglethorp, pauses at the gate to make the point:

> Poirot stopped for a moment, and gazed sorrowfully over the beautiful expanse of park, still glittering with morning dew.
> "So beautiful, so beautiful, and yet, the poor family, plunged in sorrow, prostrated with grief." (33)

A final instance: A. A. Milne's *The Red House Mystery* (1922) was taken by Raymond Chandler as the epitome of the unrealistic puzzle mystery which Chandler affected to despise. It does illustrate the subordination of probability to the necessity of weaving a byzantine web for the detective to unravel. It also illustrates the Golden Age impulse to make the murder a striking aberration. The novel opens:

> In the drowsy heat of the summer afternoon the Red House was taking its siesta. There was a lazy murmur of bees in the flower-borders, a gentle cooing of pigeons in the tops of the elms, and from distant lawns came the whir of a mowing-machine, that most restful of sounds; making ease the sweeter in that it is taken while others are working. (13)

This is a Good Place than which no greater could be. The scene is reiterated fifteen pages later, as the gentleman who will be the amateur detective strolls toward the house, and murder is announced:

> As he came down the drive and approached the old red-brick front of the house, there was a lazy murmur of bees in the flower-borders, a gentle cooing of pigeons in the tops of the elms, and from distant lawns came the whir of a mowing-machine, that most restful of sounds . . .
> And in the hall a man was banging at a locked door, and shouting, "Open the *door*, I say; open the *door!*" (28)

There has been a shot fired, and the body of Robert Ablett is discovered in the locked living room. The gunfire and the corpse are in extreme juxtaposition to the murmur, the cooing, the whir; the violent termination of a life juxtaposed to the rhythms of the pastoral world.

*   *   *

There are three clear marks of time in the world of the Golden Age detective. There is the end of time. The victim has passed out of time into eternity. This memento mori, for whom time has abruptly ended, is never emphasized in the detective story, but it is never absent either. Then there is the linear, forward-moving time of the detective's investigation (with its linear, backward-moving reconstruction of the past). This is the narrative time of the detective story; it begins with the commission of the murder, and ends with the identification of the killer (the *proof* of the identity of the killer). And finally, there are the endless (and beginless) cyclic rhythms of the natural environment. It is this last mode of timelessness that distinguishes the Golden Age detective story. The time-sensitive investigation is set against the victim's liberation from time's winged chariot, and, as well, against the frame of the world's unchanging changes.

Even when Holmes ventures into the countryside, he is rarely impressed by bucolic scenes. Traveling through the Hampshire countryside in "The Adventure of the Copper Beeches," Watson remarks upon the scenery: "It was an ideal spring day, a light blue sky, flecked with little fleecy white clouds, drifting across from east to west. The sun was shining brightly . . ." (*ASH II*, 121). There is an "exhilarating nip in the air," and Watson admires the farmsteads and the new foliage. Holmes, however, deflates the pastoral: "You look at these scattered houses, and you are impressed by their beauty. I look at them, and the only thought which comes to me is a feeling of their isolation, and of the impunity with which crime may be committed there. . . . It is my belief, Watson, founded upon my experience, that the lowest and vilest alleys in London do not present a more dreadful record of sin than does the smiling and beautiful country-side" (*ASH II*, 122–23). Holmes is also, on occasion, capable of extolling the restorative powers of nature—in his account of his retirement to Sussex to keep bees in "The Adventure of the Lion's Mane," Holmes extolls "that soothing life of Nature for which I had so often yearned during the long years spent amid the gloom of London" (*ASH II*, 776), yet even here there is an intrinsic qualification: the murderer in the story is nature's creature—a poisonous jellyfish called Cyanea capillata, "The Lion's Mane." In Holmes's last story as in Dupin's first, a genuine beast proves to be the villain. These instances do not prove that Nature in the first phase of the Classical detective story is invariably red in tooth and claw, but it does suggest that it was not painted in pastoral innocence either. Its goodness is not great.

Auden's examples of Great Good Places illustrate the sorts of cyclic times which the Golden Age mystery naturally adopted. The country house is, of course, the acme of English arcadia. It is set amidst the annual rhythms of nature, and it operates according to what, by the beginning of the twentieth century at least, appear to be timeless social relations: there is the gardener, the maid, the housekeeper, the butler, each with his or her appointed rounds. However artificial these statuses may actually be, they seem to be—to the gardener, maid, et al. as well as to the reader—natural and inevitable. And, Auden adds, *a Christmas party* at a country house. There are many Golden Age novels set at that annual moment when Christians celebrate the renewal of the year and of the ages. There are Easter novels, and midsummer novels, and Halloween novels as well, all signifying notches on the yearly cycle of life.

The Old World village—especially as opposed to a New World village—clearly signifies a place governed by immemorial rituals. The theatrical company has its revolving seasons and its rituals and traditions. The Pullman car is, admittedly, an exception: it is new; it is rationalized; it is linear. It does institutionalize social status in one respect—the Pullman porter was a visible addition to the servant class. The Pullman car (or the airplane, or the ship) satisfied the first of Auden's criteria—it provided an environment that was very definitely closed—but it did not provide for much in the way of ceremonies of innocence. Auden's fifth exemplary scene, the college, provided both enclosure and ceremony in solid portions, and became one of the standard scenes for Golden Age mysteries. The college, especially one constructed on the Oxbridge model, offered a place of enclosed green spaces governed by traditions and rituals measured by regular, cyclical holidays. Its primary inhabitants are eternally young; its governors are, by convention, preternaturally old: there are few young dons in Golden Age colleges. It is a place dedicated to endless nonviolent contests between minds and between minds and disciplines. The violent crime and definitive solution of the detective story are antithetical to the university spirit, and thus are perfectly set within a college quadrangle. Other popular scenes for Golden Age novels include the Inns of Court, with their enclosures and rituals, and seaside resorts, where the tides measure a natural cycle and where individuals go precisely to escape from the business of modern working life to the less goal-oriented customs of the resort. All of these scenes constitute the modern Arcadia.

The original Arcadia was Virgil's escape from the historical destiny of Rome. *The Aeneid* was his response to that Roman burden; his *Bucolics* he set in the Greek district of Arcadia, a district he never visited, but which had long been associated with pastoral simplicity (or, pejoratively, pastoral savagery). Virgil imagined Arcadia as possessing "luxuriant vegetation, eternal spring, and inexhaustible leisure for love" (Panofsky, 299). His immediate models were the Sicilian idylls of Theocritus, another urban poet (of Alexandria); both were sophisticated artists who used the conventional ease and simplicity of the shepherd's existence to depict what a civilized man imagined man's life might be if he were freed from the decadent pressures of civilization. Humor, freedom, equanimity, simplicity, and otium (leisure); community, harmony, acceptance: these are the qualities which the Theocritan and Virgilian Arcadias proposed as happy, simplified alternatives to the complexities of civilization (Haber, 13, 20). The Golden Age detective story writers wrote from a similar sophistication, with something of a similar purpose, and with a comparably self-conscious artifice.[5]

As a result, Great Good Place precludes treatment of matters of state and empire. In this respect, it marks a retreat from the wider compass of the first phase of the Classical paradigm. The political Holmes may have dealt with factitious prime ministers like "Lord Bellinger," but he did deal with prime ministers, and kings and popes, too. Naval treaties, and plans for submarines, and letters from foreign potentates are central matters in Holmes's investigations of "The Adventure of the Naval Treaty," "The Bruce-Partington Plans," and "The Adventure of the Second Stain." Even that utterly alienated individual, Dupin, acts in "The Purloined Letter" partly as a partisan of a royal personage.

The Golden Age largely proscribed such matters. When the political content of the thriller or the espionage was permitted to infiltrate the murder mystery, it usually proved an embarrassment. Agatha Christie's Bolsheviks are among her least credible or creditable stereotypes. The political interest of the Great Good Place lies in the suppression of overt politics. Its Arcadias are insulated from national or international issues. (The Nero Wolfe saga represents a telling exception, but Rex Stout's insertion of Wolfe into the political affairs of his time becomes most notable in the later decades (1950–75) of Wolfe's career.) Its world tends to be patriarchal or matriarchal in a literal sense: the highest authority is often a domineering father or mother, or else a father-figure/mother-figure such as a headmaster or a director. It is under this local regime that the individuals, homogenous by nature but divided by circumstance, struggle with one another. What has often been identified as the essential conservatism of the Golden Age mystery expresses itself in the premise that the hierarchical family constitutes the natural and complete order of social relations.

The Golden Age Arcadia thus defines itself as a physically confined space governed by tradition and by cyclical rhythms. It often incorporates a pastoral element—a lawn, at least, though almost never actually sheep herding. But it also exists as a purely urban pastoral. There is nothing green about the penthouses of Philo Vance's New York, but they too constitute gardens insulated from the city around them (Van Dine, *The Bishop Murder Case*). A chief difference between the detective's Arcadia and the shepherd's is a thematic one: the Classical pastoral is essentially about love; the Classical detective story pastoral is essentially about death. Theocritus and Virgil do not completely exclude mortality—that is the point of *Et in Arcadia ego*, but the Golden Age detective story makes mortality the premise of the fiction. (It also anathematizes love—Van Dine's third rule: "There must be no love interest"—but more in theory than in practice.) It is death which interrupts the happy rhythms of the country-house/Old World village/Pullman car/theatrical group/college/Inns of Court/resort. Everyone is touched by the reality that the life of an individual can be terminated, that, indeed, every life will be terminated.

But death is not a familiar feature of the Great Good Place; it would not be an Arcadia if it were. The premise of the genre is that death occurs not by accident, or by disease, or by famine. Death is introduced by a definite malign intelligence. The villain produces in the corpse of the victim a memento mori which is, as Auden says, radically out of place, "as when a dog makes a mess on a drawing room carpet." The corpse asserts the terminal linearity of man's life, and this jars with the sense of permanence which the scene evokes. The detective cannot restore the victim to the cycle of life, but he can expose and expel the malign intelligence, and through this catharsis can restore the Place's Great Goodness. Death is like history: it does not belong in Styles Court, or in the Benson mansion, or in the village of Fenchurch St. Paul. It breaks the rhythm; it disturbs the peace. It suggests that there are unalterable changes, and that these changes may have unalterable effects upon relations between the survivors. The victim is rarely missed in any emotional way in a Golden Age mystery, but he or she is often resented— resented while alive, and even more, resented for the impact that his or her dying has on the lives of others. That the crux of so many detective stories turns upon a will or testament reinforces the point: even in death, the dead insist upon power over the lives of the family, preventing the natural renewal of the seasons of life.

The Golden Age Arcadia stays the same by changing according to a changeless cycle of renewed seasons and renewed generations. Wills and testaments represent a malign attempt to halt the cycle and hold lives in a sterile stasis. An even more telling obstruction is represented in the convention of the sleeping murder: the crime that was committed years, even decades, ago yet still grips and strangles the present. In order to discover whodunit now, the detective must discover who did it then. The exercise is, of course, a bravura demonstration of the detective's power. His analysis is not timebound, and can reach backward indefinitely. It is also a statement about the world: no matter when the web was woven, sufficient traces and trifles will remain to allow the human mind to recover the truth: the world never loses signs of what has really happened. But, finally, it is a reminder that a death that is not understood, and thus integrated into the innocent rhythm of the Great Good Place, will remain a fatal obstacle to Arcadian happiness.

The detective can only understand and integrate death; he cannot undo it, but, as noted, the Golden Age mystery discourages sympathy with the victim as an individual. The detective *can* undo the resented effects, and these do matter: he can clarify the relations which the death obscured, rejoining mutually suspicious lovers, kin, and friends. He can see that the proper will is properly administered (and the author can see that the proper will, properly administered, leads to a satisfactory result). The novel can end with the survivors returning to Arcadia—resuming the rituals of the country-house, Old World village, Pullman car, theatrical group. There has been a singular event which threatened to dissociate the members of the community from the closed social world which gave them an identity—as lovers, or sisters, or friends, or servants. A remarkable individual from the outside enters that shattered world and re-encloses by expelling the one person who is false at heart, who never belonged in Arcadia.

The detective, who enters the world from the outside, identifies and expels the villain, and starts the rhythm beating again. He himself inhabits a peculiar dimension of time. He is prescriptively unaffected by the crises he investigates. The detective must always begin each adventure with an unflagging freshness. He does not bring his past cases into his present case (except for mock-scholarly footnotes which are more advertisements for previously published adventures than felt recollections of prior involvements). But more than this: he never brings his past life into his present life; dedicated to exposing the pasts of others, he is himself a creature virtually without a personal past of any sort. Father Brown, who barely possesses a given name, is the extreme example; the general rule is to provide as little personal history as realism will permit. Poirot is a retired Belgian policeman; the rest is silence. Conan Doyle could not resist filling in some elements of Holmes's history as the saga proceeded, attaching him to the squirearchy, bestowing a brother upon him, recounting a college case ("The Gloria Scott") and an early, pre-Watson case ("The Musgrave Ritual"). But to the frustration of the Baker Street Irregulars, vast portions of Holmes's life are left blank.

If his past is thin to nonexistent, the detective's present is decidedly elastic. The famous example is Poirot, who has retired, presumably in his late fifties at the earliest, prior to his first published case, which is dated 1916. When Poirot finally dies more than half a century later in *Curtain* (1975), he must thus be well over 115 years old, still in full possession of his faculties, though physically enfeebled. Few detectives age naturally, and for obvious reasons. His immunity to time's ravages thus sets the detective in antithesis to the victim and to the villain: they bring time's arrow into the Great Good Place; he uses a patch of time—the duration of his investigation—to make the present comprehend the past. He demonstrates that the past is, in fact, never past: from present traces past actions can be inferred. By moving backward from effects to causes, he masters time. At the narrative's end, in his final recapitulation, he moves forward, from causes to effects. And in so doing, he restarts the rhythms; the college can resume its next semester, the Orient Express can resume its schedule. Time does not control the detective; the detective controls time.

This becomes the peculiar gospel of the Golden Age detective story. It assured postwar readers that the prewar world had not, in fact, been obliterated. The old places were still there, still the same. Bees still hummed, doves still cooed, mowers still whirred. Death might appear to untune the traditional harmony, but a special hero—the detective—could, by observing trifles, reverse time and expose and eliminate the source of the cacophony, allowing the concert to proceed.

CARPE DIEM: THE WORLD OF THE
HARD-BOILED DETECTIVE

It has been observed that the Bible begins in a garden, and ends in a city. There is, as Auden pointed out, a connection between the Edenic paradise in which man first found himself and the Great Good Place of the Golden Age detective. The relation between the city of Revelation and the Great Wrong Place of the Hard-boiled detective story is less definite, though there may be some point in connecting the Los Angeles of Philip Marlowe with the fallen Babylon—"She has become a dwelling for demons, a haunt for every unclean spirit and loathsome bird" (Rev. 18:2). Dashiell Hammett's first novel, *Red Harvest* (1929), reflects in its title and in its content—the bloody purging of the thoroughly corrupt city of Personville (Poisonville)—something of an apocalyptic spirit, and his second novel, *The Dain Curse* (1929), includes a long episode involving the Temple of the Holy Grail, in some respects a dwelling for demons. But the Hard-boiled vision is more about describing Babylon than denouncing it, more about admiring the spirits that endure and prevail than about the imminent collapse of civilization as we—we Americans of the second quarter of the twentieth century—knew it. Chandler's Marlowe may deliver himself of philippics against the vacuity of California culture, but even the Marlowe novels are primarily romances about the strong men who rise to the challenges posed by the barbarians who have rushed in to fill the void—the pornographers and gangsters, the soulless rich and the egoists of Hollywood. Marlowe's remembrances of California past—like Travis McGee's later recollections of Florida before its development—are exceptional. The Hard-boiled novel concentrates its energies upon the present, upon how a tough man can cope with tough times in a tough place.

The Great Wrong Place is, above all, an American place. It is the modern American city that, by the 1920s, had pretty much bulldozed whatever history it might have boasted, and erected in its place tall, efficient office buildings for the new industrial and financial corporations and extensive tenements for the wave of multilingual immigrants from Europe, Asia, and the American South. It was not a city governed by tradition or rituals. It was not, it sometimes seemed, a city governed by elected officials. Plutocrats often appeared to have more influence than voters; gangsters often appeared to possess more authority than mayors. Women, who had been appointed keepers of the home virtues by earlier generations, now trimmed their costumes by a third and their hair by more than a third, took up smoking and drinking, and generally began to narrow the chasm that had seemed naturally to divide the sexes.

The rhythms of nature are largely abolished in the Hard-boiled city, though an elegist like Philip Marlowe will occasionally remark upon seasons past. The tough detective usually only notices today's weather, usually today's tough weather—the rain, the Santa Ana wind, the dirty snow. There are no murmuring bees, cooing doves, or whirring mowers. There is the din of traffic, the smoldering tones of a torch-singer, the whirr of the roulette wheel. Mostly there is traffic: the emblem of the Hard-boiled is the gun, which can be opposed to the Classical magnifying lens; but the more central contrast is between the Hard-boiled roadster and the Golden Age country house. Where the Golden Age narrative functioned centripetally, drawing the cast of characters into the confines of the country house/village/Pullman car/theatrical troupe and producing the crisis, the investigation, and the resolution within those limits, the Hard-boiled narrative is centrifugal, pushing the detective into a variety of milieus, and compelling him to elicit from each encounter a hint which will send him back to his car and on to his next encounter.

And these encounters often occur in distinctly transient sites. Motels figure frequently in Hard-boiled stories. Sometimes the detective moves upscale, to hotels; frequently he moves downscale to flophouses. The mansions of the very wealthy are always there—it is the mansion owner who can afford to hire the private eye, and the story may begin and end there, as in Chandler's *The Big Sleep*. But where Poirot's investigation in his first case (and in his last) is conducted entirely at Styles Court, Philip Marlowe, in *The Big Sleep*, leaves the Sternwood estate to visit a pornographic bookshop, the pornographer's house, the Lido fish pier, his own office, Joe Brody's apartment, the District Attorney's house, the Missing Person's Bureau, the Cypress Club, his own apartment, the Fulwider Building, and Art Huck's garage out in the foothills, before he returns to the Sternwood estate to wrap up his case. Each of these locations provides Marlowe with another essential portion of the case he is trying to assemble. All are occupied by tough men and tough women, most of them not quite as tough as they think they are. Marlowe may not be the toughest, but he is as tough as he thinks he is, and it is his ability to accurately measure his own toughness and the toughness of others that underlies his success.

The focus is entirely upon social relations between men and between men and women, and these tend to become unmediated exercises in using whatever resources they possess to dominate others. It is the men with the money, or the connections, or the guns who give the orders. The women who give orders are the women with the sex. The detective who opposes these powerful men and women has no money, and no connections, and only one gun, which is often taken from him. He also has a susceptibility to sex. He has, therefore, no hope of restoring Arcadia; there is no Arcadia. The city remains as savage a place at the end as it was in the beginning. All he can do is seize the day; he can commit himself to the job of work at hand, and see that the innocent (the relatively innocent) are correctly distinguished from the guilty (the relatively guilty). It is a limited and temporary victory. Even Personville, which has been purged through a holocaust, is, as the Continental Op admits, "ready to go to the dogs again" (CN, 176). Personville never was and never will be the Athens of Montana, and its rhythm—corruption, purgation, corruption again—is not Arcadian. But although it cannot release the city from its radical disharmonies, the Op's knowledge is nonetheless certain and his investigation is nonetheless significant. He does achieve something on the day that he seizes.

Personville is introduced on the first page of what is generally recognized as the first important Hard-boiled detective novel:

The city wasn't pretty. Most of its builders had gone in for gaudiness. Maybe they had been successful at first. Since then the smelters whose brick stacks stuck up tall against a gloomy mountain to the south had yellow-smoked everything into uniform dinginess. The result was an ugly city of forty thousand people, set in an ugly notch between two ugly mountains that had been all dirtied up by mining. Spread over this was a grimy sky that looked as if it had come out of the smelters' stacks. (*CN*, 5)

Personville's environment has been irreversibly degraded by man's work. The degradation of most Hard-boiled cities— New York, Chicago, San Francisco, Los Angeles—is less ornamental, but no less real. They may lack the mountains and the smelters, but they retain all the ugliness. No one trusts anyone in Personville, and this is the prevailing attitude in the Hard-boiled novel. Mistrust is, of course, endemic to the detective story in all its forms. That is the inevitable consequence of an unsolved murder. But the mistrust becomes radical in the Great Wrong Place. People mistrust each other before the murder and after the resolution. At the end of *The Maltese Falcon*, Sam Spade knows what Brigid O'Shaughnessy has done; what he does not know is whether he loves her, whether he can trust her. He can't trust her on the final page, and didn't trust her on the first. Early in the novel he tells her that he and his partner, Miles Archer, never believed the story she told when she hired them; they believed the two hundred-dollar bills she left as a retainer. The lives of Mme L'Espanaye and her daughter were mysteries to the police and to their neighbors because, as isolatoes in the city, they had only commercial transactions with their fellow citizens. The lives of the inhabitants of the Great Wrong Place remain closed because no one knows even his comrades or his lovers. Spade is as much a stranger to his partner, Miles Archer, with whose wife he sleeps, as he is to Brigid. Even Spade's admirable secretary, Effie Perrine, in the end, doesn't know Sam, and rejects his touch. Loyalty is one of the highest values in the Hard-boiled world because it is one of the rarest. It is almost never based on intimacy: Spade regards Archer with contempt and betrays him while he is alive; it is when Archer is unreachably dead that Spade's sense of loyalty obliges him to hunt down Archer's killer: "When a man's partner is killed he's supposed to do something about it. It doesn't make any difference what you thought of him" (*CN*, 582). Doing matters; thinking doesn't: people must be known and judged upon their actions, not their motives or emotions. Maybe Brigid loves Spade and maybe Spade loves Brigid, but Brigid certainly killed Miles Archer, and for that action, she takes the fall. Similarly, Caspar Guttman may love his gunsel, Wilmer—"I couldn't be any fonder of you if you were my own son" (*CN*, 563), but what matters is that he agrees to betray Wilmer to the police. His "son" kills him: "He ought to have expected that," says Spade (*CN*, 584).

*   *   *

Knowledge, in the Hard-boiled world, is thus based upon action and reaction. The Hard-boiled dick rarely considers trifles. The burden of Chandler's indictment of the Classical mystery novel in "The Simple Art of Murder" is precisely that it pretends that trifles matter. Poor writers, he declares, think that "a complicated murder scheme which baffles the lazy reader, who won't be bothered itemizing the details, will also baffle the police, whose business is with details. The boys with their feet on the desks know that the easiest murder case in the world to break is the one somebody tried to get very cute with; the one that really bothers them is the murder somebody only thought of two minutes before he pulled it off" (*LN*, 986). Chandler's chief charge is that the Classical mystery is unrealistic: it is unrealistic in the baroque schemes that its murderers perpetrate, and it is unrealistic in the way these schemes are detected. Hammett's essay, "Suggestions to Detective Story Writers," lists twenty-four trifles which, he says, detective story writers get wrong: (2) The Colt .45 automatic pistol has no chambers. The cartridges are put in a magazine. . . . (9) The pupils of many drug-addicts' eyes are apparently normal. . . . (21) Fingerprints are fragile affairs. Wrapping a pistol or other small object up in a handkerchief is much more likely to obliterate than to preserve any prints it may have" (*CS*, 910–12). Physical evidence, in the Hard-boiled world, explains little of what has happened.

What explains what has happened is how people respond to

stress. The Classical world assumes that the crime disturbs the environment, and that from the residue of this disturbance—the fingerprints, cut bell-ropes, cigarette ashes, shifted sculptures, scratched keyholes, unwashed teacups—its cause can be detected. The metaphysic of the Hard-boiled world assumes that the crime disturbs the psyche, and that by observing the way people act—and by instigating additional tensions which will stimulate latent stresses—the detective will be bumped toward the discovery of the killer. Thus, to the surprise of Tom Polhaus, Spade has no interest in climbing down to examine Miles Archer's corpse where it has fallen. The police can attend to those details, those trifles. Spade *is* interested in the subsequent behavior of his client, Miss Wonderly/Brigid O'Shaughnessy, and in that of those who are associated with her: Guttman, Cairo, Thursby, and Wilmer. How they respond to developments will be determined in part by their prior experience with Archer or with Archer's murder. Instead of leaving inert traces at the scene of the crime, the murder in Hard-boiled fiction leaves dynamic traces in the behavior of those touched by the crime, and it is these that the private eye must read. He must be a provocative reader of actions, not a meditative reader of things. He studies people's actions, and whenever the opportunity arises, he challenges people, forcing them occasionally to reveal information and always to reveal how they react to challenges. The information and the reactions guide him as unerringly as the trifles guided Holmes or Poirot.[6] The Classical detective appears to exercise a remarkable power to run time backward, recovering particular causes from particular effects. The Hard-boiled detective runs time forward, pressing reactions—frequently violent reactions—from a large number of people, and using these reactions, in a manner that is more improvisatory than ratiocinative, to lead him to the next step in his investigation.

This Hard-boiled method is a deliberate one. Spade explains to Brigid: "My way of learning is to heave a wild and unpredictable monkey-wrench into the machinery. It's all right with me, if you're sure none of the flying pieces will hurt you" (*CN*, 465). The flying pieces will hurt her, and Caspar Guttman, and Joel Cairo, and Wilmer, and they even hurt

Spade, but he is tough enough to be hurt the least. He survives. Classical detectives assumed that cerebral logic—ratiocinative, scientific, "little grey cells"—would unravel the web of crime. The Hard-boiled detective employs the "wild and unpredictable monkey-wrench," a proletarian tool, and an uncerebral one. And the metaphor for the world in which he operates is "machine," not "web." "Web" implies a weaver, the criminal or the author. "Machine" is impersonal; the world of the Hard-boiled functions like Hobbes's Leviathan: machines turn within machines, and the result is a Great Wrong Place of egoists pursuing their own interests, and making the fewest possible concessions to the necessary social contract.

The Hard-boiled detective does not attempt to apply the wrench systematically to dismantle the machine bolt by bolt; rather, he heaves it. Aggressive action, not analytic thought, is his forte. And strength—toughness—is his virtue. Hammett's Continental Op had earlier made the same profession of technique, also to a woman: "'Plans are all right sometimes,' I said. 'And sometimes just stirring things up is all right—if you're strong enough to survive, and keep your eyes open so you'll see what you want when it comes to the top'" (CN, 79). Stirring things up and being strong: these are what it takes to force the Hard-boiled machines to yield their secrets. Cleve Adams's Rex McBride declares: "When you don't know what you are doing, you light a fire under everybody and sort of hope something happens" (qtd. in Geherin, 79). The Hard-boiled detective doesn't think; he *does*; and doing brings knowledge.

That truth must be forced in this manner, and not inferred through esoteric processes of analysis, was, for Hammett, realism. Hammett, as a practicing Pinkerton, saw this as the way of the world as the world is. And Erle Stanley Gardner, a practicing lawyer and one of the workhorses of *Black Mask*, came to a similar conclusion: stirring things up and being strong fairly describes the method of Perry Mason as well. Mason is, of course, endlessly throwing legal monkey wrenches into the machines of malefactors (and, as well, into the machines of the police and district attorney). Indeed, Mason epitomizes the Hard-boiled detective's antipathy toward machines. The villain in the Classical detective story was, at his best, a mechanic: his crime was an artful construction designed to commit a murder, leave himself with an alibi, and direct suspicion toward an innocent. From Minister D———— in "The Purloined Letter" on, the villain prides himself on the complex gearing of his plot. And, as Poe observed, the wonderfulness of the detective lies in his ability to dismantle the villain's wonderful machine, demonstrating gear by gear how the police and the readers have been misdirected. The Hard-boiled detective's key tools, his gun and his car, are actual machines (the sort of machines which Classical detectives are utterly baffled by; Dupin, Vance, Van Dusen, Fell, Wolfe are, at most, minimally competent with these devices). But the social machines that function in the Hard-boiled world are almost always engines of malign influence. Political "machines" were a ubiquitous and, from the militantly individualist Hard-boiled perspective, thoroughly malignant feature of big American cities in the 1920s and 1930s. The underworld's notorious machine—the mob—was, of course, abhorrent to everyone. But even the machinery of decency is disparaged. Perry Mason's invariable embarrassment of the police and the district attorney reflect the same Hard-boiled luddite response to organization men. Hamilton Burger and Lieutenant Tragg are certainly well-intentioned pursuers of criminals (Sgt. Holcomb in the early novels is less clearly well-intentioned), but Burger and Tragg are bureaucrats; they are part of an establishment machine. And the machine always gets humanity wrong. Mason is the individual who can push the levers of the judicial system to set things right.

Mason is not just a clever manipulator of the law. Especially in the first few dozen novels, Gardner also emphasized Mason's physical combativeness, his toughness. Mason is portrayed as a pugilist in the opening of the first novel, *The Case of the Velvet Claws:* "He gave the impression of being a thinker and a fighter, a man who could work with infinite patience to jockey an adversary into just the right position, and then finish him with one terrific punch" (1). Gardner would eventually downplay this physical toughness, as he relied more upon Mason's legal ingenuity and loyalty to his clients as the chief components of the lawyer's ability to detect what really happened. But Mason is always a dexterous thrower of monkey wrenches.

The greatest of the Hard-boiled writers, Raymond Chandler, acquired some sense of the realities of the Hard-boiled world through his experiences as an oil company executive in California in the 1920s, but he was not a detective or a lawyer. Like most writers of Hard-boiled fiction, he combined some direct knowledge of the roughness of the world with a picture of that roughness derived from his reading. Hammett and Gardner were a key part of that reading. Chandler's measure of distance from the actual Hard-boiled world, and his English public school education, and his genius, enabled him to imagine a hero who could be at once a working stiff asking for twenty-five dollars a day plus expenses, and also a player of solitaire chess games against Capablanca; a hero who can trade wisecracks with a cop or a bindlestiff and still plausibly evoke an image from beyond a distant hill. "He has a range of awareness that startles you, but it belongs to him by right, because it belongs to the world he lives in" ("The Simple Art of Murder," *LN*, 992). That range may make Philip Marlowe less realistic than the Continental Op, but Chandler's romantic streak enabled him to create a detective capable of comprehending more dimensions of the Great Wrong Place.

*   *   *

Thus, when Marlowe describes his method for pursuing the hidden truths of his world, he declares his values as well as his technique. "I'm selling what I have to sell to make a living. What little guts and intelligence the Lord gave me and a willingness to get pushed around in order to protect a client" (*SEN*, 674). Guts comes before intelligence; in second-rate Hard-boiled fiction, it comes way before intelligence. Marlowe is intelligent enough; he has read T. S. Eliot and Ernest Hemingway. But his guts are his signature virtue; he investigates by asking everyone the tough questions, and he usually receives hard words and hard blows and sometimes bullets in response. Guts, intelligence, and loyalty: first he heaves the monkey wrench with the confidence that he is strong enough to survive; then he reviews the results; and always he retains his commitment to his client and his code. He is a working man, who affirms the integrity of his work. What in Dupin and Holmes and Poirot was a splendid, chosen isolation has become a minimalist assertion: the private eye just does his job, and is proud of doing his job.

Sam Spade and the Continental Op operate with exactly the same priorities—guts, intelligence, loyalty; they may not possess Marlowe's sensibility, but if Marlowe is a cynical romantic, Spade and the Op are romantic cynics. Spade wants Brigid; he wants an unconditional relationship; he just knows that there are always conditions when men engage with women—or with partners, or with partners' wives, or with fat men. The private eye's relationship with his client is the only unconditional relationship in the Hard-boiled world. This absolute commitment to protecting the client—a commitment which Perry Mason endlessly reiterates—is probably the single most important value linking the rough first generation of the private eye to the more sensitive generation since 1970. Personal loyalty is rarely a factor in the Classical world, where the detective's allegiance is to the truth; the truth, it is assumed, will clarify all genuine relationships, blessing the good ones and dissolving the unwise ones. Dupin acts for Adolphe Le Bon and against Minister D———, but personal motives are generally disparaged in Classical detectives; the detective examines objects objectively. In the Hobbesian world of the Hard-boiled, clarity only brings disillusionment. Greed and lust underlie all endeavors. In a pervasive environment of self-seeking and corruption, the detective posits loyalty as a value worth being beaten for. Two of the most complex Hard-boiled detective novels are Hammett's *The Glass Key* and Chandler's *The Long Good-bye,* and both are essentially meditations on meaning of one man's loyalty to another.

Loyalty to the client is the professional standard of the Hard-boiled world; loyalty to the partner or friend is the personal standard. Loyalty to the female beloved appears conspicuous by its absence. The Classical detective was either apparently asexual (Dupin, Holmes, Thorndyke, Van Dusen, Vance, Queen, Poirot, Marple, Wolfe) or properly monogamous (Fell, Wimsey, Alleyn, Campion). The Hard-boiled detective is a philanderer. He desires women and he mistrusts women, which makes him a misogynist: he hates them for being desirable. He disparages them as janes and frails and twists. This is partly the Hard-boiled response to all of the classes of people who, in the 1920s and 1930s, were challenging the prerogatives of white, heterosexual Christian males: the generic disparagement of women, Blacks, Latinos, Asians, homosexuals, and Jews has distressed many readers, and constitutes one of the defining issues that divides the first phase of the Hard-boiled from the Engaged model which emerged in the last third of the twentieth century. But where the private eye's relations with Blacks, Latinos, Asians, homosexuals, and Jews are almost always incidental, his relations with women are almost always central. His uneasiness with them is intense.

The nineteenth-century stereotype of the woman as homemaker has little place in the Hard-boiled world. She appears occasionally as a witness, but even then usually as the sharp-eyed biddy—a widow or a spinster—who expresses thin-lipped disapproval of the neighbor's activities. Women occasionally appear as plucky working girls—Gardner's novels are full of the type; Effie Perrine in *The Maltese Falcon* and Anne Riordan in *Farewell, My Lovely* are other examples. They occasionally appear as neurotic types—Gabrielle Dain in *The Dain Curse*, Carmen Sternwood in *The Big Sleep*. But mostly they appear as temptresses, women endowed with a lot of this and a lot of that, and willing to use this and that to get their way in the world. And if honesty and integrity are the private eye's ultimate virtues, deceit and disloyalty are the endemic vices of women. Brigid O'Shaughnessy is only the best known of these lying, scheming females; there is at least one, and often more than two, in almost every Hard-boiled novel.

On the one hand, the temptress is a libel on the gentle sex; on the other, it is an admission that "the gentle sex" is a libel on women. To accuse women of sexual appetite and greed and a capacity for homicidal violence is also to acknowledge that they are human, and in precisely the ways that men in the Hard-boiled world are human. Brigid O'Shaughnessy is a great deal like Sam Spade; Velma Valento is a great deal like

Philip Marlowe (even to the ambiguous sentimentality of her final gesture). To be sure, the women always come off second-best to the men, but that is because the Hard-boiled detectives are always men, and everyone comes off second-best to them.

The sexual, racial, and ethnic prejudices of the Hard-boiled detective are the unhappy by-products of the paradigm's determination to engage with its times. Instead of escaping the social realities of the Roaring Twenties and the Depression Thirties into encapsulated worlds of idyllic timelessness, the Hard-boiled paradigm thrust the detective (and the reader) into the raw issues and conflicts of the time. These included the divide between the rich who ran things and the new multi-ethnic working poor who were run upon; the moralism which imposed Prohibition, and the Gangsterism which Prohibition promoted; the movement of women into the voting booth and the workplace; the rise and fall of eccentric religious cults; the emergence of the cinema as a mass producer of fantasy (Robert Leslie Bellem's Dan Turner, Hollywood detective, debuted in *Spicy Detective* in 1934 and remained a popular figure until 1950). What the Classical detective ignored, the Hard-boiled detective observed and commented upon: he was cynical about the cinema (*The Little Sister*); he exposed the chicanery of the cults (*The Dain Curse*; *Farewell, My Lovely*); he manhandled women; he was opposed to Prohibition and moralism; he hated the rich (*The Big Sleep*); and he made free with the usual epithets for nonwhite, non-Christian, non-heterosexual men.

The Hard-boiled detective was articulate about what he opposed; like the common man he represented, he was less articulate about what he was for: integrity, certainly; finishing a job; often a chivalrous impulse to rescue the distressed, usually the female distressed, though this impulse was often undercut by the distressed female's aversion to rescue. It is not clear that there was a Hard-boiled program for repairing the problems that the detectives observed and commented upon. Hammett was moving toward his commitment to Communism in the 1920s, but efforts to read a socialist message even into his most politically explicit novel, *Red Harvest*, have been largely unpersuasive. The private eye knows how to solve a crime; he does not know how to solve a criminal state.

And so it is not surprising that while the Hard-boiled detective faces his time, he does not face the larger politics of his time. He will, of course, often confront local politics: corrupt cops are legion, and corrupt councilmen and mayors are not rare. But he ignores the national issues on which he might have taken a position: he does not mention Sacco and Vanzetti, or the Scottsboro boys, or the coal-miners or the auto workers; he does not refer to the New Deal, or Father Coughlin, or Huey Long; he does not notice Bolshevism, or Fascism, or the Spanish Civil War. (When he does notice these things, the result is no less embarrassing than the Golden Age's flirtation with Bolshevik conspiracies: Chandler's "No Crime in the Mountains," with its cartoonish Nazi and Japanese agents, is the most foolish of all his narratives.) The unblinking eye of the private investigator usually exhibits tunnel vision; in any event, it shuts at the edge of town; it does not scrutinize any larger political units.

*   *   *

There is an atmosphere of improvisation in the Hard-boiled world that is missing in the Classical mode. Incidental persiflage and whimsy are present, sometimes in excess, in the Golden Age, but, following Poe's lead, the action is always disciplined by the backward construction which enables the detective so brilliantly to deconstruct the mystery that chance, unwitting accomplices, and the villain had manufactured. A few Hard-boiled novelists employed plot as a central bearer of meaning—Ross Macdonald is an example; most operated on the principle that Chandler proclaimed in the "Introduction to *The Simple Art of Murder*": "When in doubt have a man come through a door with a gun in his hand" (*LN*, 1017). In the end, the detective must propound a credible sequence of actions, but the reader often has the impression that the writer is only just ahead of his detective in comprehending this sequence. Where in the Classical version, the final chapter prescribed the content of the early and middle chapters; in the Hard-boiled version, the early and middle chapters are more autonomous units of experience, tending, certainly, toward a preconceived end, but capable of seizing the reins and altering the course. Plot, Chandler acknowledged, was secondary to vivid scenes of confrontation: "[m]y plot problem invariably ends up as a desperate attempt to justify a lot of material that, for me at least, has come alive and insists on staying alive" (*Selected Letters*, 130). Hard-boiled detective stories are detective stories, and the material must, as Chandler admits, be justified. The novel must end with the fundamental message that there is some order amidst the disorder of experience, and that this order can be articulated by a man with guts, intelligence, and integrity.

This improvisatory quality of many Hard-boiled novels alters a basic aspect of the detective's world. The premise of the Classical detective story is that evil is the result of the machinations of an intelligent and perverse evildoer. Evil that has been plotted can be unplotted; the detective unweaves the web which the villain (or the author) had woven. But Evil is systemic in the Great Wrong Place; that is why there is always another man with a gun ready to walk through the door. Everyone has an eye to the main chance, from gangster to grifter; sometimes even the detective. Even those who do not aim at wrong, often achieve it: Hamilton Burger does so infallibly. As a result, there is no need to plot a complex web of wrong, which then is concealed beneath a cloak of circumstances and misinterpretations. Artful plotting is not needed in the Great Wrong Place. Wrong is in the warp and the woof of the Hard-boiled world; the detective's challenge is to separate the deceit and violence which points to the villain in the case at hand, from the deceit and violence which is endemic to the city.

Raymond Chandler assigned a statement of the implications of this reality to Lt. Gregory, a tired Missing Persons policeman:

> "I'm a copper," he said. "Just a plain ordinary copper. Reasonably honest. As honest as you could expect a man to be in a world where it's out of style. . . . Being a copper I like to see the law win. I'd like to see the flashy well-dressed mugs like Eddie Mars spoiling their manicures in the rock quarry at Folsom, alongside of the poor little slum-bred guys that got knocked over on their

first caper and never had a break since. That's what I'd like. You and me both lived too long to think I'm likely to see it happen. Not in this town, not in any town half this size, in any part of this wide, green and beautiful U.S.A. We just don't run our country that way." (*SEN*, 743–44)

Wide, green, and beautiful, but no Arcadia.[7] This is the Hard-boiled world.

THE WORLD OF THE ENGAGED DETECTIVE

The world of the Engaged detective is in its essential aspects similar to that of the first phase of the Hard-boiled detective: a private eye faces a realistic, urban environment in which provocative confrontation, not reflective thought, produces the truth. The detective continues to carry a gun, to engage in physical conflicts, and is forever driving to a new encounter. He (or now often she) continues to value integrity and continues to pride himself (herself) on finishing a job. But there is a new emphasis upon the complexity of individuals in the Engaged world: they are often seen to have been molded for good or for ill by their particular environments. The two new aspects of the environment which appear most influential are family and region. Engaged detectives often discover that family pathologies lie behind the crimes; they often assert that healthy families (which are often not the nuclear married-couple-with-children) are the salvation. The detective also often discovers that local color, while it rarely influences the plot of the crime directly, provides a substantial element of the texture of the narrative.

The Hard-boiled detective shared with the Classical detective the fundamental belief that the world consisted of individuals whose behaviors could, when the true nature of those behaviors had been exposed by the detective, be fitted fairly directly into conventional moral categories. The conventions operating in the Great Good Place might differ from those operating in the Great Wrong Place, but whether he exculpated an avenging lover (Holmes, "The Adventure of the Devil's Foot") or convicted a killer of a crime he did not commit

(Continental Op, "The Golden Horseshoe"), the detective expected even his peculiar judgments to be ratified by the reader. The Engaged detective is more willing to challenge social conventions, not because he or she must deal with a unique exception to convention, but because he or she rejects conventions and the society that imposes them. He or she finds that individuals are complicated creatures, molded by a variety of influences to which a measure of responsibility may be attached, and that when their behavior has been fully laid out, its irregularities prevent it from being neatly slotted into any moral category.

Some of the Golden Age writers had moved in the direction of psychological complexity (Sayers, Allingham, Queen), and some of the Hard-boiled writers had played with psychopathologies. But they had continued to assume that fundamentally, the individual was simply responsible for his or her actions. It is generally less simple in the Engaged world. Individuals find themselves in a social matrix which has defined their opportunities and conditioned their responses, and instead of indicting the individual, the detective indicts the matrix. Where the Hard-boiled style implied that bad men and women had corrupted society, the Engaged style implies that bad societies have corrupted men and women. The Hard-boiled tone was cynical: only a society of whores could so easily be seduced; the Engaged tone is earnest: if only it would reform itself—reform its chauvinism, or its racism, or its capitalism, or its patriarchalism—society would breed fewer criminals, and detectives could beat their .38 police specials into ploughshares. This underlying premise that social structures are the true villains is perhaps the feature that has most encouraged detective story writers worldwide to adopt the Engaged style. Maj Sjöwall and Per Wahlöö were the prophets of this international Engaged movement.

At the core of the Engaged vision of the world is the sense that the family is the key element in the deforming social matrix: individuals in the Engaged world are not isolatoes like Mme and Mlle L'Espanaye and the Maltese sailor, like Enoch Drebber and Jefferson Hope, like Miles Archer and Brigid O'Shaughnessy. In Engaged stories, victims and villains and detectives all belong to families. The nuclear family had always provided a context for crime in both the Classical and the Hard-boiled paradigms: it is an inescapable fixture of bourgeois life. But the detective story had never emphasized the formative influence of the emotional relationships which develop in a family; it had tended to regard the family as it regarded all social entities: as a cooperative unit of autonomous individuals. A husband might love or fear or hate his wife (or his mother or his uncle), but he was not *made* by his wife/mother/uncle; nor was a woman made by her husband or her parents. Relationships might provide motives for crime (jealousy, envy, resentment, etc.); they did not define a person's nature or condition a person's proclivities. With its presumption of the moral responsibility of the individual, the detective story had always underplayed family. It had, for example, almost no room for dependents: small children, who are always being formed by familial influences and who are thus not legally or morally responsible for their actions, appear only as accessories. Even in the Hard-boiled revolt against the Classical presumption that patriarchy was natural, there is little interest in children. There is an interest in the rebellion of young adults, and there is especially an interest in the failure of patriarchs. General Sternwood, wrapped in blankets in his hothouse while his daughters run wild, is an icon of this failure. But Elihu Wilsson, who clings desperately to his power, in Hammett's *Red Harvest* is as well. All of Hammett's novels include failed patriarchs (or would-be patriarchs): Edgar Leggett, Caspar Guttman, Paul Madvig and Senator Henry, Clyde Wynant. Chandler adds Lewin Lockridge Grayle in *Farewell, My Lovely*, and the corrupt matriarch Elizabeth Bright Murdock in *The High Window*. The old governors have been emasculated in the Hard-boiled world, and no replacements have emerged. In the first phase, this condition tends to yield a Hobbesian wilderness. But as early as the 1950s, Hard-boiled writers like Ross Macdonald were beginning to explore the social and psychological causes and effects of the collapse of traditional parental authority. Macdonald's novels, especially the late novels, are full of children and adolescents, and they are forever suffering the consequences of the misdeeds of their parents (and grandparents).

Macdonald came almost obsessively to locate the source of

crime in Oedipal conflicts rooted in familial pasts. His Freudian perspective was not universally accepted, but this focus
upon generational conflict appealed to a number of the new
writers of the 1970s and 1980s. Dysfunctional families prolif-
erate in the Engaged world; immature and incompetent
fathers and neurotic and incompetent mothers are frequently
identified as the source of the delinquencies of their offspring
(the immature and incompetent fathers are sometimes also
identified as the source of the mothers' neuroses and incompetence). Two archetypal villains of the Engaged world are
the businessman and the psychopath: the man who soullessly
pursues profit instead of humane (familial) relationships, and
the man or woman who has been so malformed by his or her
familial experience—often in a family headed by a man who
soullessly pursues profit instead of humane (familial) relationships—that he or she is unable to make healthy connections with other people. The villains are alienated, and family
is what they are alienated from.

Family badly done is the generator of crime, but family
well done is the hope for redemption, and the Engaged detective does family well. The detective becomes a pater (or
mater) familias. The detective's own menage becomes the
paragon of virtue. The bachelor's quarters at 221B Baker
Street and the private eye's spartan apartment also functioned as paragons: Holmes's flat bespoke a man who could
pursue an eccentric variety of personal interests—music, artificial stimulants, archiving, chemistry; Marlowe's apartment represented the beleaguered bit of cleanness that a man
could hold against the corruption and the vulgarity of the society of the mean streets. The Engaged detective's collection
of very intimate friends models a quite different vision of how
a hero centers his or her life. The hero no longer is a hero because he takes care of himself as he solves someone else's
problems; he is a hero because he takes advice from others as
he solves someone else's problems. (Here it is John D. Mac-
Donald, not Ross Macdonald, who supplies the prototype:
Travis McGee's colloquies with the wise Meyer set the example). The detective takes this advice not from a traditional
family which is, by definition, homogeneous, but from an em-
phatically heterogeneous "family": an elderly neighbor (Kin-

sey Millhone, V. I. Warshawski), a psychologist/psychiatrist girlfriend (Spenser, V. I. Warshawski), a male comrade, especially a Black comrade (Spenser, Dave Robicheaux, Easy Rawlins), a gay man (Sunny Randall, Skip Langdon, Alex Delaware), an adopted child (Spenser, Carlotta Carlyle, Dave Robecheaux, Easy Rawlins). He or she will even commune with the dead: Jeremiah Healey's Francis X. Cuddy talks to his dead wife; Dave Robicheaux and V. I. Warshawski to dead parents. From this melange of supporters and advisors, living and dead, the detective fashions a spiritually sustaining community. Kat Colorado, at the end of Karen Kijewski's *Alley Kat Blues* (1995), offers this encouragement to a girl whose character has been deformed by the experience of having been raped and by having been raised in an oppressively religious family: "I wanted you to meet my family. I wanted you to know that there are many definitions of family and community. Alma, my grandmother, and I are not related. She adopted me informally. Lindy, whom you'll meet soon calls me her cousin. We're not related, either. She was a discarded child, a teenage runaway and prostitute when I found her" (361). Conventional nuclear families corrupt; unconventional, "not related" families save.

The Classical detective had belonged to a community of two, in which he was in all respects the senior partner: good old Watson serves Holmes by getting everything wrong, and thus stimulating the Master to get things right. The Hardboiled detective belonged to a community of one: his dialogues were usually with himself ("Marlowe, you're not human tonight"). The Engaged detective is still an individual hero: ultimately, he or she finds within him or herself what it takes to get to the truth: his or her own guts, intelligence, and integrity. But while detecting the true cause of crime remains the detective's signature action, his or her character, as expressed in relationships with family, "family," friends, antagonists, bureaucracies, institutions, ideologies, etc., becomes increasingly the point of the story: the reason why the author writes another novel, the reason why the reader reads another novel. The detective's world is still obligated to provide him with a plot that will justify his power to know what happened, but it is also obligated to provide him with a cast of foils—victims and victimizers—which will enable him to strike poses of goodness and decency and benevolence. He is no longer a hero merely because he has the genius or the will to detect truth; he is a hero because he lives a moral, politically correct lifestyle. The role of family exemplifies this new component of heroism. Family members may help, though never decisively, in the investigation, but they are crucial in helping the detective become the man or woman he or she wants to be.

*   *   *

The second major innovation made by writers in the Engaged mode was the attention to local environment. If some of the Engaged writers took up the genre in order to hector readers about the injustices a particular category of humanity is suffering in the modern world, another group of writers seem to have been motivated by a desire to depict a beloved region's social and natural beauties and deformities: southern Louisiana, the sunshine coast of British Columbia, eastern Montana, the four corners area of the Southwest—or Bengal, India; Ystad, Sweden; Yorkshire, England; Barcelona, Spain; Gaborone, Botswana; Trekkersburg, South Africa. There were differences between the metropolises in which earlier detectives detected: Holmes's London and Marlowe's Los Angeles were more than half a world apart. And Marlowe's mean-streeted Los Angeles was significantly different from Mike Shayne's contemporary mean-streeted Miami. But the differences between Thomas Black's Seattle, Dave Robicheaux's New Orleans/New Iberia, Joe Leaphorn and Jim Chee's Four Corners, and Mario Balzic's Rocksberg, Pennsylvania are, one suspects, why there *is* a Thomas Black's Seattle, a Dave Robicheaux's New Orleans/New Iberia, a Joe Leaphorn and Jim Chee's Four Corners, and a Mario Balzic's Rocksberg, Pennsylvania. Earl Emerson, James Lee Burke, Tony Hillerman, and K. C. Constantine each had a place which he knew and loved, and which he wanted to get into fiction. The detective story gave them a form of fiction which, one, sold, and two, featured a hero whose profession obligates him or her to travel through all the social and natural ecosystems peculiar to that place.

Faulkner was dedicated to representing his postage stamp of delta Mississippi before commercial considerations encouraged him to use Uncle Gavin Stevens to extend his representation; commercial considerations probably come a bit earlier in the creative process with the later writers, but the impulse is the same.

Some of the regions are rural or semirural, but there is little Arcadian about them. They are not retreats from reality, they are reality. Except in the humorous vein exemplified in the Maggody novels of Joan Hess, the regional writer aims at the gritty realism proclaimed by the initial Hard-boiled writers. Because the detectives are placed in regional capitals, or even regional countrysides, not in dark megalopolises, they are usually not the angry Isaiahs that Marlowe and Hammer sometimes, in their very different ways, appear to be. But they are not uncritical: they portray the regional customs and the regional landscapes with a close observation for defects as well as beauties.

An additional implication of the Engaged impulse toward regionalism is linguistic. The writer is often sensitive to the idiom and dialect of the region. This was a key element of the regionalist—Local Color—movement of the late nineteenth century as well. The writer who was most influential in this attention to the language world of the detective did not actually write detective stories: George V. Higgins, beginning with *The Friends of Eddie Coyle* in 1972, demonstrated brilliantly how the vernacular of a region—for him that of Boston and its environs—could serve as a vehicle for popular crime fiction. Higgins's influence can be seen in the fiction of Elmore Leonard, K. C. Constantine, George Pelecanos, and others. The vigor of James Lee Burke's dialogue surely owes something to Higgins. The usefulness of underworld slang had been exploited by the Hard-boiled realists, but the Engaged writers—and many of the best of them—use local phrasings to evoke an even stronger sense of the quiddity of the detective's world.

The two impulses of the writer of Engaged detective stories—to promote a social agenda and to anatomize a region—are both signs of the didacticism that prevails in so many of the post-1970 detective novels. The initial realism of the

Hard-boiled was a didactic response to the artificiality of the Golden Age: the *Black Mask* boys insisted upon educating the reader in the ways the urban world of the Great Wrong Place really worked, while entertaining him with fantasies about how a manly man could make those ways work to serve both justice and his own advantage. Writers in the Engaged mode are more liberal in dispensing the education (and, as well, less masculinist in the entertainment). The essential lesson of the Hard-boiled was universal: life is tough in all cities, and it takes a tough man to survive in the mean streets. Diversity is the key to the Engaged world: places are different, and so are people. This is an aesthetic truth, illustrated by close observation of local topography, history, dialect, etc., and it is a moral truth, embodied in a creed of tolerance. Everything must be accepted on its own terms; heroes must be open-minded. They, like detectives before them, need intelligence and toughness, but they also need forbearance, and sympathy, and a willingness to accept help.

As a result, the Engaged detectives find themselves in a dual relation to their world. They must still treat it as an object to be worked upon; they must still manipulate whatever instruments of investigation they possess to elicit a true plot of causes and effects from the physical evidence, spoken words, and observed actions which they encounter. But they must also treat it with a sympathy that recognizes their own involvement with the lives of others. From Dupin to Spade, the detectives present themselves as islands unto themselves. The bell is always tolling for someone else. The Engaged detectives know—feel—that they are not islands; they are attached to lovers, to families, to regions. They have tears for the world; their minds are touched by mortality.

For good and for ill, the world of the detective has become less simple. The puzzle which Dupin agrees to solve may be complex, but the decision to agree is not. Dupin chooses to investigate, and thus can do so on his terms. It does not matter that Paris has no Rue Morgue—and London no 221B Baker Street. These places exist because the author, who makes the world for the detective, will have it so. The author of Engaged detective stories makes the detective for the world. Or, more precisely, makes the character of the detective for the world.

The action of the detective still requires a made world. Plot still stipulates much, and stipulates all of the essential. The detective must succeed, and must still do so by reading a text of the world the author has constructed so as to be legible. But who the detective *is*—his or her home, family, language, social and political views, aesthetic and sexual preferences—is now conditioned by the world which the author wishes to depict and promote. This development has enhanced the reader's ability to identify with the detective and with the world, but at the cost of reducing the illusion of the detective's almost magical command over the affairs of the world. There is certainly less mystery in the world of the Engaged detective story, and more ambiguity. This, clearly, is the sort of world that the common reader of the late twentieth century preferred.

3

Classic Mystery

"I'm not Christ," he said irritably. "I can't work miracles
out of thin air."
— Sam Spade, in Dashiell Hammett's *The Maltese Falcon*

In ITS ORIGINAL, GREEK USAGE, A MYSTERY (*MUSTERION*) MEANT A
cult experience in which initiates (*mustai*) acquired esoteric
knowledge by passing through ordeals, secret rites, and ec-
stasies. In its most common modern English usage, a mystery
means a mass-produced narrative, composed according to
certain conventions involving crime and its detection which
guarantee the narrative a prepared readership and its author
and its publisher a predictable profit. Although religious cults
and paperbacked novels are different in some respects, they
both do share a fundamental premise: what matters is what
you know in the end.

The mystery religions were, by and large, successful in
sealing the lips of their initiates (the Greek root *myo* means
to close the lips or eyes); we do not know exactly what arcane
knowledge was imparted to the worshippers of Demeter, or
Orpheus, or Dionysus, or Mithras, but it certainly had to do
with final things. "We only know . . . that these mysteries were
a favorite means of assuring oneself, by means of certain
ceremonies and magic arts, against misfortunes in earthly
life, against an unhappy existence in the beyond, or against
total annihilation after death" (Burckhardt, 160). The theme
of death and resurrection is certainly evident in the traces of
the myths that survive; evidently those inducted into the rites
and rituals of the cults were empowered by the sense that
they had penetrated to some esoteric truth about the significance of man's brief pilgrimage on earth: they knew what the

116

destination was, and they knew that knowing this gave them some considerable advantage when they arrived at that destination, and perhaps on the passage as well. It is doubtful that initiation brought specific knowledge about specific fates: oracles are always a bit fuzzy about details (a great empire will fall, but *which* empire?). What the initiate knew was that specific knowledge existed; someone knows what has happened, is happening, will happen. Through the exact repetition of ceremonies prescribed in the immemorial past, initiates were assured that life—their lives—meant something. There was an order to the cosmos that was thoroughly real and at least partially knowable. The events of one's lifetime, however apparently random, belonged to that order, and might, through proper observances, benefit from alignment with it. Everyone's lives might benefit: the cults were uncommonly democratic; one did not need to belong to a certain family, or to a certain nation to participate in the mysteries. One did need to commit one's self to the obligatory purifications and initiations, and one did need to keep the secret.

The cults enjoyed a widespread popularity in the Mediterranean, especially in the centuries after Alexander, and were only extinguished by the rise of Christianity, which insisted that its Mystery was a jealous Mystery. The last cult tolerated by the Christianized Empire was that of Isis, which had emerged very early (c. 2400 BC) and whose temple at Philae in Upper Egypt was finally closed by Justinian in AD 536. Something of the peculiar beliefs and practices of the mysteries of Isis are known, because Apuleius ended his novel, *The Golden Ass*, with his protagonist's initiation into the cult (with rites of purification and initiation), and because Plutarch published a critical summary of its core myth, which actually reads something rather like a murder mystery: Two Egyptian brothers, Osiris and Seth ("Python" in Plutarch's version), marry their two sisters, Isis and Nephthys (or Nepthys). Seth, suspecting that Osiris has seduced Nephthys, murders his brother by trapping him in a specially designed coffin. The coffin is released onto the Nile, and floats to the Mediterranean Sea. Isis engages in a long and ultimately successful search for the body, interrogating everyone she meets. She finally locates it in Lebanon, and returns to Egypt with it. Seth then seizes the body, dismembers it, and scatters the fourteen pieces around the countryside. Isis recovers all the pieces (but one) and reconstructs her husband's body. Their son, Horus, punishes Seth. Osiris descends to the underworld, where he serves as the justice before whom the dead must demonstrate their innocence.

Christianity, as it evolved from Galilee to Rome may have absorbed some iconography, and even some theology, from the mystery cults (images of Isis's devotion to her son Horus, for example, have been thought to have influenced the Christian view of Mary and her Son), but it was distinguished in at least two important respects. First, it answered the timeless questions with a time-bound event, not immemorial rites: the mystery of the Incarnation polarized all of history into a definite, progressive revelation, from Eden to the Crucifixion to the Apocalypse. And second, it made the repetition of its own rituals public. Initiates were not bound to silence; they were commanded to evangelize, and to impose them everywhere. The sacraments were open to all who with a right will wished to participate; in a catholic church, only perverse reprobates decline the universally available communion of God's saints. Christianity's synthesis of timeless repetition of ritual and creed with a timely allowance for progressive revelation which permitted a Council or a Pope (or a Luther or a Calvin) to innovate in the name of tradition enabled it to assure congregations for more than a millennium that there were final answers. People might be puzzled by the happenings in their lives for six days; quotidian affairs might seem a plotless succession of occurrences—tales told by an idiot, signifying nothing,—but on every seventh day, the Christian was reassured that there was an Author writing the tales, that He knew what every event signified, and that in history's last chapter, He would explain what He had known all along, and all would make sense.

But by the eighteenth century, some Europeans began to reject the mysterious dogma that required a second coming for what was knowable to be known. Western thinkers were increasingly knowing things for themselves, here and now: the system of the planets, the circulation of the blood, the laws of gravitation and optics. The Christian system had relied upon incomprehensible realities such as incarnation, three-in-oneness, and transubstantiation to show that there was no hope of grasping the true structure of reality, at least not prior to the revelations of the apocalypse. The new system relied upon what it proclaimed to be entirely comprehensible principles to show that there is a knowable structure of reality. Even in its early formulations, the principles of the new, scientific system were not quite as comprehensible in fact as they were in theory—Newton's equations remained caviar to the general, and there have surely always been a majority of people who benefit from technological advances without understanding their operative principles. But the benefits are real, and they constitute persuasive evidence that science does know, with the further implication that what science doesn't know is unknowable. In 1869, Thomas Huxley would coin "agnostic" to express the scientific method's banishment of unempirical matters to the realm of intrinsic unknowability. There are, to the scientist, no ultimate mysteries—no concession that there may be meaningful questions to which the answers can be definitely known, but not by us. There are, of course, questions which science has yet to answer; technologies will continue to improve; but questions that science cannot answer are, ipso facto, unanswerable, meaningless questions. Science can press toward ever more precise answers to questions about the first and last moments of the universe; it may even predict the number of weeks of life remaining to a man, and may construct a reliable scale to measure the pain the man will experience. And it can do much to alleviate the pain.

But what if we concede much to science's ability to know, yet still want a solution to the mystery that surrounds our own first and last moments, still want our sense that our individual fates are knowable and known? What if we want a scientist who knows about more than regularities in the physical world? What if we want, in a scientific age, the mysterious assurance that someone knows—knows infallibly—what has happened to us? Then, perhaps, we want a detective in a mystery story.

I

When, in 1848–49, the last year of his life, Edgar Allan Poe collected his ideas about his world, and especially about its end, in a prose poem, *Eureka*, he naturally thought in a scientific vein. He began with the physical principles of Kepler, Newton, and LaPlace; indeed, LaPlace's nebular hypothesis, published in 1796, was a central element in Poe's vision of the course of the universe's past and future. In the end, Poe concluded with his own idiosyncratic cosmology, suggesting that "the processes we have here ventured to contemplate will be renewed forever, and forever, and forever; a novel Universe swelling into existence, and then subsiding into nothingness, at every throb of the Heart Divine" (*PT*, 1356). In this rhapsody, Poe clearly moved beyond science, but not until he had built a firmly scientific foundation for his revelation. Science, Poe well knew, had become the measure of reality in the nineteenth century, and Poe was an intelligent and interested reader in the fields of science (which for Poe included phrenology and mesmerism as well as astronomy and psychology and electricity and aeronautics). More than a dozen of his short stories can be classified as science fiction, though in all there is a measure of ambivalence. Science knew much and would know more, but it could not know everything. It could hypothesize nebulae, but not a Heart Divine.

And so in his short stories as in *Eureka*, Poe tried to penetrate to truths beyond those accessible to scientific investigation. His horror tales begin in strange places—in castles and in catacombs and in the minds of men who are sure (*quite sure*) they are not mad—and move into stranger places: places where science knows nothing. Poe exploits the frisson of unknowability. But he also, in 1841, devised a form of story in which a scientific analyst knows, and knows precisely, what the mysteries once claimed that divinity knew. The scientific analyst knows what happens inside a person's mind (this is M. Dupin's first achievement in his debut story), and he knows, through scientific reasoning, what a man's—or, as it happens, a woman's—final fate is. He cannot, like Isis, revive the victim whose end he has reconstructed; he cannot claim to know what happens after death. But he can make scientific sense of death; he can take a scene of bizarre carnage—a locked room, a throttled body thrust upside down in a chimney, bags of gold coins left behind—and discover the sequence of causes and effects which must have led to this result. And the sequence will constitute scientific knowledge, not opinion: one need not trust the detective; he is no priest. His conclusions will be empirically verifiable; they will be verified. And as a result, the community will be restored: if he cannot reconstruct the corpse, he can regenerate the society. The world makes sense again, and life's sane rhythms can resume. M. Dupin performs this scientific mystery in "The Murders in the Rue Morgue," and the feat resonated so well with the popular audience, that Poe encored his detective twice. Within a couple of decades, Emile Gaboriau adapted Poe's invention in a series of popular novels, and in 1881, Arthur Conan Doyle inaugurated his version of the scientific mystery in *A Study in Scarlet,* and the knowing investigator became one of the fixtures of modern fiction.

But while the knowing investigator is the defining figure in the formula of the mystery, the baffled bystander is decisive: he is why the story works. He is the surrogate for the reader: he perceives a confused world in which there seem to be no clear answers to the crucial questions, and no clear way to reach answers. In the tales of Poe and Conan Doyle and of most of the mystery writers in the Classical tradition, he is the narrator; his is the voice with which the reader is invited to identify. Conan Doyle deliberately opened *A Study in Scarlet* with an autobiographical chapter in which Dr. Watson establishes his bona fides as a common Englishman. With his medical degree and his experiences in the British army, Watson may even claim to be a bit above the common in intelligence and experience. He is a man who assumes that his civilization's sciences have mastered the problems that beset it. Like the citizen of Rome, the citizen of imperial England inhabits a world that seems to be well ordered by the order of his own culture. An Englishman's common sense in the late nineteenth century might well appear to an Englishman to have genuinely common—universal—application.

But then there is Jack the Ripper, or, a bit less melodramatically, the apparition of a yellow face in a window, or a missing three-quarter, or a stolen carbuncle: occurrences civilized order cannot account for, which defeat the systematic sciences of investigation. Unsolved murders are especially troubling, because they echo thoughts of our own mortality. They remind us that there are patches of experience—important, crucial patches—that defy scientific solution. Watson's dismay at the bloody scene at Lauriston Gardens, like the narrator's dismay at the carnage in the Rue Morgue, is ours. We are horrified by the scene because it is bloody, and because the blood makes no sense. The detective, however, is challenged by it. We want to know what happened; he sets out, with magnifying lens, to find out—scientifically—what happened. And when he finally knows, he explains. His auditors (Watson, Lestrade, the reader), now sharing his knowledge, can resume their routines, secure in the knowledge that human fatality can be comprehended. Having been there, been baffled, and been enlightened, they—like the mustai in the temples of Isis—can resume their normal confidence that their common sense is common, that the order of their lives is the order of life.

II

The modern mystery is a short or long work of fiction defined by plot, in which the last section or last chapter explains all that has been experienced and misunderstood in the narrative. There is always misunderstanding in experience, and always understanding in the last chapter exposition. The narrative transpires in a world like ours—circumstantial realism is a prerequisite of the genre; and all the empirical laws of physics, chemistry, biology, and psychology apply (well, most of the laws of psychology). The characters behave rather as we do, though they are, presumably, a bit more frequently venal and lecherous and mendacious and homicidal than we are; this is, after all, an artful narrative which simplifies a bit, and exaggerates a bit. And the characters find themselves in a world in which the Standard Science of Knowing seems to lack the power necessary to know the fates of individuals. The police force usually represents the current state of society's scientific knowledge; it commands all of the resources of the new technologies, and, when it really matters, it always gets things wrong. It recruits minds like those of Inspectors Lestrade, Gregson, and Japp, or District Attorney Hamilton Burger: intelligent, but pedestrian; models of common sense and, in a crisis, invariably incompetent. Society has authorized them as its official investigators, but their systematic science is unequal to the special challenges which special malefactors have posed. In "The Murders in the Rue Morgue," confronted with a chaotic scene of women's corpses and bags of gold inside a locked room, the police, needing to arrest someone, arrest the bank clerk who brought the gold to the women's room, though they are unable to account for how he escaped the room, why he left behind the gold, or why witnesses affirm variously that he or his accomplice spoke Spanish, Russian, English, or German. Even more clearly, in the third Dupin tale, "The Purloined Letter," the policeman, Inspector G——, is the epitome of the normal scientist. Charged with recovering a stolen letter, Inspector G—— supervises his men as they search the suspect's rooms with systematic exactness, measuring spaces with precision, using probes and "a most powerful microscope,"—and discovering nothing.

Not all policemen are as ineffectual as Inspector G——, and even Dupin concedes that G——'s system is not always at a loss. "The Parisian police," he says, "are exceedingly able in their way. They are persevering, ingenious, cunning, and thoroughly versed in the knowledge which their duties seem chiefly to demand. . . . Had the letter been deposited within the range of their search, these fellows would, beyond a question, have found it" (*PT*, 688). This view becomes axiomatic in the Classical detective story: the police, with their Standard Science of Knowing, are excellent at comprehending ordinary crime scenes and apprehending ordinary criminals. But their systematic science is invariably frustrated by the extraordinary crime and the extraordinary criminal. In these cases—these cases of peculiar circumstance, peculiar motive, peculiar means—science fails to find the answer. When it comes to the very individual instance, only a specialist in mysteries can provide the answer. The standard scientific specialist is at a loss: his knowledge, like all scientific knowledge, is of uniformities. Our deaths, once we have abandoned the assorted mysterious sacraments that did establish a certain and significant uniformity, are, from our points of view, very concrete, very private matters.

So Poe, who more than most people was obsessed with the meaning of the dissolution of individuals, invented the detective as a sort of Scientist of the Individual Fate, joining the engagement of the priest to the discipline of the scientist. Located somewhere between the irrationalism of the old cults and the rationalism of the new science, the detective uses the modern method to achieve the old end. Poe presents Dupin as a brilliant analyst with a touch of the poet. As an analyst, Dupin comprehends science, and much space in the three stories in which he appears is devoted to his exposition of his ratiocinative method to a narrator (and a reader) who is almost as impressed with the methodological dissertation as he is with the final chapter exposition. Dupin's discourses on method certify him as a systematic, scientific thinker, though his model science is mathematics, and since Pythagoras at least, mathematics has served as the tool of mystics as well as of empiricists. But Dupin is imaginative as well as rational; as a poet, he comprehends human individuality and can apply his abstract methodology to the concrete problems of time-bound human affairs. Science knows what force is required to thrust a woman's body upside down up a chimney; Dupin applies this knowledge imaginatively to the fate of Mlle. L'Espanaye. Only a creature with a bestial mind and bestial strength could have committed the atrocity: it must have been a beast. (The tuft of orangutan's hair clutched in the hand of one of the corpses is also helpful in drawing this conclusion, though Dupin mentions it belatedly.)

Dupin's success at demonstrating that, with a touch of poetic genius, a scientific analyst can reconstruct a person's life and explain his or her fate was a milestone. He became the only one of Poe's protagonists to make repeat performances, and Poe received letters complimenting him on the ingenuity of his new form of fiction. Dupin's return in two later tales also has another significance. Even when they do not end a story as "a nearly liquid mass of loathsome—of detestable putridity," Poe's protagonists rarely conclude their experiences in a condition that invites further adventures. Dupin, the detective, is himself nearly untouched by his experiences. He may rescue a benefactor or avenge an insult, but neither of these motives is emphasized. Rather, he reconstructs lives (and deaths) because he can. He possesses a power which he uses, and it is the power (the method) that is heroic, not the person. Dupin himself is a willful eccentric, marking his distance from his fellow citizens by residing in a time-eaten and isolated mansion and perambulating Paris at night. These qualities mark the priestlike quality of the detective: he is separated from the laity of his city; he is invested with a power that enables him to see through the obscurities of phenomena to the noumenal lines of individual fates. His role is similar to that of the Guardians in Plato's *Republic*, whom E. R. Dodds has described "as a kind of rationalized shamans" (210). Werner Jaeger summarizes the qualities that came to be associated with the Platonic hero: "the philosopher is the great eccentric, an uncanny but lovable character, who deliberately isolates himself from the society of men in order to live for his studies. He is childishly naive, awkward and impractical; he lives in eternity, not time and space" (151). Dupin, the first detective, was certainly eccentric and uncanny; not, perhaps lovable; childish, at least, in his love of games and pranks; awkward and impractical; and surely out of time and space. Sherlock Holmes quickly added the element of lovability, perhaps with some loss of uncanniness. The detective's special character—whether it is a matter of native genius, training, dedication, or toughness—places him in the role once filled by priests (or priestesses); he is the designated protector of his community. But he must work through rationalized, explicable investigations, not through magical rituals. The detective's grunts and cryptic queries and close examination of apparently irrelevant details may appear bizarre, but every apparently bizarre gesture will eventually prove to supply a link in the final explanation. And unlike the augurers who eyed with equal closeness the entrails of a sacrificed goat, the detective must lay out irrefutable (i.e., unrefuted) inferences that lead from the objects he examines to the ordered narrative of causes and effects which he asserts constitute the reality behind the apparent chaos of experience. The detective's fundamental obligation—even more fundamental than apprehending the criminal—is to end every narrative with a credible account of how and why every obscure deed was done. He may, in fact, not catch the murderer, or catching the murderer, may let him go; he may never refuse the reader a cogent explanation of what has happened.

And so the crucial premise of the genre is: life is always explicable; more specifically, the end of life is always explicable. This is a more modest premise than that of the mystery cults; the detective cannot explain what happens after death; he certainly cannot promise to facilitate or predetermine that transition. When Isis had uncovered the hidden remains of the victim, she could reunite them into the resurrected Osiris. This power is beyond the detective; but his fable does, after a fashion, imitate several of the motifs in the Isis–Osiris–Horus–Seth mystery: carefully plotted murder, search, reconstruction, vengeance and punishment, final justice. In the myth, the narrative is the answer to the mystery; the rituals of the cult simply introduce or imitate that narrative. In the mystery novel, the narrative is the mystery that the detective solves. Unlike the myth, which speaks through its actions, the mystery novel empowers a single human voice, to which it assigns infallible authority. One individual expounds the truth of what has happened to a group of individual characters linked by a crucial event—a murder. And he does so by reciting a credible sequence of causes and effects, a sequence that will, in a successful mystery, be both surprising and entirely plausible.

Working entirely within the limits of human experience, he achieves more-than-human (though less-than-divine) authority. He cannot intuit the future, but starting from the present moment, he can always recover what has happened from what remains. He can make the past yield secrets to the present. Nothing important is ephemeral in the world of the detective; no code is unreadable. And this is some consolation. It is, evidently, a very great consolation. It took Arthur Conan Doyle fully to institutionalize the figure of the detective, but his presence in Western culture since *A Study in Scarlet* was published in 1881 has been ubiquitous. The insatiability of our appetite for narratives with someone explaining everything in the last chapter is manifest in the size of the "Crime and Mystery" section of any bookstore.

And because each of these narratives enacts precisely the same plot, there is obviously a ritual element to the mystery story. It is clear that we distinctly prefer more repetition to less. There are hundreds of mystery writers and hundreds of detectives. But the tendency is for the initiate to pursue a single writer and a single detective, reading all of the slight variations that that one source can produce before moving on to another writer and another detective, usually of a similar variety. This impulse to exhaust a particular instance—to read dozens of Holmes stories, dozens of Poirot stories, dozens of Ellery Queen or Perry Mason or Lew Archer stories—is remarkable. It results in two contrary effects, one expansive and one reductive: the detective's world acquires texture and breadth, and that broad world is shown again (and again and again) to be subject to the detective's singular technique of knowing.

Just as a priest performs his essential function by virtue of his investment in his office—bad men may, in theory, serve as good priests—so the detective performs his essential function by virtue of his execution of a narrative convention—the Final Explanation, not by any intrinsic qualities of his character. He may, in fact, have virtually no character; a more insubstantial creature than Perry Mason is hardly imaginable, and he was for several decades by far the most popular detective in American popular culture. Mason exists almost entirely as a moving force for the defense; his life as a man is invisible. More ambitious writers than Erle Stanley Gardner have, for different reasons, also downplayed their detective's individualities: Father Brown and Hercule Poirot, Philip Marlowe and Lew Archer are all thinly defined as persons. Father Brown and Poirot are distinguished by a few habits; they barely seem to exist in any biographical/historical time. Marlowe has many personal opinions, but very little personal history; Lew Archer, as Ross Macdonald has written, was intended more as "a consciousness in which the meaning of other lives emerges" (185–86), than as a fully incarnated individual himself.

Of course, other mystery writers have cloaked their rationalized shamans in a wealth of biographical detail: Sherlock Holmes and Lord Peter Wimsey, Nero Wolfe and Travis McGee acquire substantial personal histories (and the trend since the 1970s has been toward a proliferation of these "thick" detectives). But even thick detectives must detect; they must show that they know how to know, and that in the end they can explain the end.

As a result, the reader of mystery stories achieves through the artifice of fiction what the initiate of the mystery cults achieved through the artifice of ritual: a sense that life is explicable. The detective cannot, as the priest can, provide an answer to the timeless question: after death, what happens? But—admitting that timelessness is beyond his capacity—he can answer the temporal question: death, what happened? It is a different question—a profoundly different question—but it is still a question about Last Things, the last things that matter to a Darwinian age which accepts that knowable reality is time-bound. He cannot offer either of the first two solaces which Burckhardt said that the original mysteries provided— a remedy against misfortunes in earthly life or against an unhappy existence in the beyond; but he can provide a version of the third: he can demonstrate that annihilation is not total, that the traces of one's existence are never entirely extinguished.

Repetition was essential in the mystery cults. The general practice seems to have required three defined experiences: *myesis*, a preliminary initiation; *telete*, the initiation into the mystery (those thus initiated being designated *mystai*); and *epopteia*, a second experience of the ritual, undertaken one year later. The last two stages were apparently the crucial ones, universally mandated. And they have a peculiar parallel in the detective story. The telete experience, in which the person repeats as a knower a ritual previously experienced as frightening novelty, corresponds to the reader's reviewing, through the detective's enlightening summation, the true plot of the novel's action. It is only then that the reader has fully comprehended "The Mystery of Marie Rogêt" or *The Mysteri-*

ous Affair at Styles. But there is another sort of ritual of repetition to the mystery story. Cultic ceremonies are repeated exactly; the mystery story is repeated with a difference: always the same essential plot of confusion and clarity, always the figure of the detective, always the recovery of what appeared to be a vanished past, but always with new settings, new victims, new suspects. A mystery story, having been read as a mystai and then, through the detective's reconstruction, as an epoptai, is exhausted. But mystery stories are not exhausted. The reader is encouraged to open a new volume, read through the new narrative as a new mystai and the new reconstruction as a new epoptai. The ceremony is thus unending. One reads a series of narratives, each with the same sequence of action (crime—investigation—resolution), but an original cast of characters and an original scene. Every person and thing is different; every sequence is the same.

Finally, and here the analogy is exact, the mystery story, like the mystery cult, imposes silence upon its enthusiasts. Initiates and readers are both enjoined not to tell others what happens in the end. That would ruin it.

4

"All men by nature desire to know": The Metaphysics of the Detective Story

> "He appears to have a passion for definite and exact knowledge."
> —Young Stamford, in A. Conan Doyle's *A Study in Scarlet*

> "The story is his adventure in search of a hidden truth."
> —Raymond Chandler, "The Simple Art of Murder"

> "I like to get at the truth."
> —Detective Chief Inspector Alan Banks,
> in Peter Robinson's *Cold Is the Grave*

THE WORLDS OF THE DETECTIVE MAY BE SEEN TO FALL IN A SPECtrum ranging from Arcadian Great Good Places to Hardboiled Mean Streets, with few stories located entirely at the extremes. Most at least intimate an awareness of the other world: World War I is not entirely suppressed in *The Mysterious Affair at Styles*, and Mike Hammer does drive to a college on an Arcadian hill in *I, the Jury*. But there is another sense—a metaphysical sense—in which the detective story presents itself as a two-world phenomenon: whatever its superficial scene, the deep structure of all detective stories implies a dualism: there is always a world of reality beneath a world of appearance. These two worlds ordinarily coincide: what you see is what there is. The detective story is about those moments when they diverge, when appearances prove to be deceiving, and reality seems inaccessible. The citizens of the world suddenly realize that they don't know what has happened, and that they don't know each other, and sometimes even that they don't know themselves. And they realize that not knowing matters.

The world of appearances which the crime discloses is the world of everyone except the villain, who has constructed the false appearances, and thus dissociated what seems to be from what is; and the detective, who deconstructs the false appearances and realigns seeming with being. The world of appearance is, in the Classical tradition, above all, the world of the narrator (Watson, Brett, Hatch, Jameson, Hastings, Van Dine, et al.). It is, indeed, a *raison d'être* for the Classical narrator: his dull submission to and inevitable bafflement by appearances serves as the shadow that heightens the brilliance of the detective's insights into the truth of reality. The narrator's world is one of happy normalcy, with normal explanations for all that normally happens. But the crime—the crime without a normal explanation—shatters this normalcy. Because the crime is inexplicable—how could this have happened? why? how could he (or she) have done this?—the safe, familiar world cracks, and chaos and old night threaten to descend. But then the detective intervenes and restores the light; he assimilates the anomalies into a reasonable, irrefutable narrative of quotidian causes and effects. He does not alter objects, but he reinterprets them, assimilating them back into a narrative of normalcy. He picks up fragments (bits of testimony as well as things), examines them closely, and uses them as touchstones to expose false narratives and as foundation stones for his own, true narrative, a narrative that restores the cosmos.

The detective's logos, then, has an almost divine quality to it. But it does not quite function as God's initial creative utterance. It does not speak things—light, firmaments, fishes, and fowls—into existence; it speaks a narrative of connections into existence. The detective's logos does, indeed, name the villain, and by naming him, in a sense it creates him: he was the butler; now he is the murderer. But the real re-creation of the detective is the chain of causes and effects that make the butler the murderer; merely naming the killer would be inadequate in any form of the detective story. The naming must be persuasive; it must be conclusive, and that derives from the indubitable moral logic that the words of the detective's exposition carry. And unlike God's logos, that of the detective appears only at the end of the book, not at the beginning; it is a revelation, not a genesis. The villain's words and actions provided the genesis: by killing and by constructing a false narrative which conceals the true identity of the killer, the villain generated the world of appearances in which no one can be sure of anything; all judgments must be held in suspense. It is an unhappy world: unhappy, of course, for all those associated with the world of the crime. This is the main point that Agatha Christie makes in her brief discussion of the genre in her *Autobiography*: "The important thing is still the innocent. . . . *They* are the ones that matter" (530). But it is also an unhappy world for the readers. The world is one full of morally significant things and actions, but the readers know that, until the final chapter, they don't know which things and actions are significant, or what they signify. They can never quite be sure that the perky young girl or the handsome lover or even the horse-faced maid isn't really a greedy or a jealous or a psychopathic killer (or that the suspected jealous killer isn't really a misunderstood young girl). Nor will there be the highbrow luxury of terminal ambiguity. The reader knows that generic conventions stipulate that everyone be one or the other, a sheep or a goat: in the end, every character's virtues and vices will be itemized and valued. The characters *will* be judged, but for nine-tenths of the narrative, they *cannot* be judged. Classical mysteries—beginning with the locked room of "Murders in the Rue Morgue"—often add an additional irritation: we not only know we don't know who did it; we don't even know how it was done.

But our ignorance is always temporary. Appearances always yield to that final revelation. The detective's retrospective narration seizes upon those items and those actions that have upset the community's sense of physical and moral reality and employs them as the proofs in his incontrovertible account of what *really* happened. It is a matter of storytelling, of supplying credible causal links—by convention, the *only* credible causal links—between dismayingly discontinuous phenomena: strangely mutilated corpses, broken furniture, scattered coins, shrill cries, blood-smeared razors. The detective proves that methodical investigation can educe the story that brought these anomalies to the place and the state in which they have been found, and, further, can link these causes and effects into a narrative that explains definitively how and why the crime occurred. The detective's lesson is that *all* appearances, even the most abnormal, can be understood if read correctly by the right method. There are no mysteries impenetrable by human inquiry; man is the comprehender of all things.

This is, of course, an optimistic and secular worldview; it is an optimism and secularism that has appealed steadily to Western audiences since the middle of the nineteenth century. It is an optimism about the power of men (and women) to understand the world, unaided by divinity, or by authority of any sort. It is also an optimism about the nature of the world men and women find themselves in. The detective story implies, as part of its essential generic contract with the reader, that in the world of the narrative there will be baffling appearances, and that, in the end, these bafflements will be exorcised. We do not need to see through glasses darkly. All effects will be shown to have sufficient causes, and normalcy, if not paradise, will be restored. The detective story is, thus, at one level an endlessly repeated fable that argues that objectivity is still possible; there is, after all, a complete and absolute and demonstrable account of what has really happened. There is one, and only one, narrative that correctly assigns causes to effects, murderers to their victims.[1]

II

"It is clear," he said, "We have been misled by appearances.
> —Investigating magistrate, in Emile Gaboriau's
> "The Little Old Man of Batignolles"

The detective story's premise that behind shifting and deceptive appearances lies a permanent and true reality echoes a premise that has held a central place in the Western worldview since the ancient Greeks. It is a "two-world" premise that can be contrasted with the "one-world" (or "this world") premise that most other world cultures seem to have embraced. In the one-world model, the universe of material and immaterial things and powers simply exists, evolving in an organic process through time. There is no absolute, objective other world against which man can measure the accuracy of his understanding of this or that portion of the process; there is no fixed, external point from which to view the whole.[2] The two-world impulse of the Greeks insisted that there was such a point, and that it was possible, through an analysis of the ephemeral material things of the universe of experience, to reach—perhaps through incremental steps—a sharper view of the unchanging ultimate reality which this point provided. The project the pre-Socratic philosophers set for themselves centered on this question: What is objectively real? What can be *known*? What is real and true, and therefore knowable, must be real and true for all time, not for a moment.

Plato developed this premise into a philosophic edifice to which, it has been said, all Western philosophy is a footnote. In *The Republic*, Socrates uses the Allegory of the Cave to illustrate what he means by knowable truth. He depicts average minds as chained to a wall in a cave, able to see only the shadows cast against the opposite cave wall by a flickering firelight from behind them. This is timebound illusion (opinion). The exceptional mind is released from its chains, turns and sees the fire and the images which cast the shadows (belief); it may then, with great effort and with the aid of other enlightened minds, rise out of the cave to see the shadows of things cast by the Sun and, finally, to see the real things by sunlight (the archetypal Forms). The climax of the progression occurs when the exceptional mind can bear to see the Sun (the Good) itself. This is knowledge.

Aristotle followed Plato, beginning his *Metaphysics* with the assertion: "All men by nature desire to know" (243), also meaning, by "know," objective, unchanging knowledge. Insofar as Aristotle's text, by the accident of its being bound after (*meta*) his *Physics*, gives metaphysics its name, this desire to know can be fairly described as the most fundamental of Western metaphysical principles. Aristotle's map of the path that leads to knowledge differed from Plato's—he was disinclined to accept Plato's Forms; but he too saw the direction as moving from ephemeral appearances to permanent realities.[3]

Christianity (influenced by the Greek spirit through Platonic and Neoplatonic thought) adapted the two-world paradigm, with a temporal Creation existing in some relation to the eternal Creator. It insisted that the Creation is both real and knowable; that it is, in fact, known by God, though centuries of dispute could not resolve how a changeless divinity could *know* a world of contingency without collapsing that contingency and the freedom it permits into a pre-known, pre-determined nature. This remains a mystery: the timeless City of God (where things are known) somehow both includes and succeeds the temporal City of Man (where things must be believed). Knowledge was attainable by man: nearly attainable through rational analysis, though ultimately secured only by faith.

When faith's warranty began to expire for many in the eighteenth century, and the miracles of science began to convert first the intellectuals and then the masses to the materialist doctrines of empirical verifiability, the possibility of knowledge seemed threatened. Hume proposed his celebrated denial that anything could be known; the sensible world of appearances, which was the only world, offered only probabilities. Kant replied with his supersensory noumena, restoring the second world of certainties. The Romantic philosophers reclaimed a mystical unity by viewing the evolving Creation as the embodiment of a dynamic Creator realizing Himself (Itself) in history. Hegel rationalized this historical development as the necessary unfolding of the Absolute's self-knowledge. The American version of this Romantic solution was prominently articulated by the Emersonian Transcendentalists who proposed a unitary vision of an Oversoul that embraced all particular realities in a progressive revelation through history.

Edgar Allan Poe professed to despise Emerson and his dynamic metaphysic (and, as well, Plato and his dualistic metaphysic: "if the question be put to-day, what is the value of the Platonian philosophy, the proper answer is—'exactly nothing at all,'" [*Writings*, 154]). Poe advocated a peculiar metaphysics of his own, one that was both dynamic and dualistic. He most fully defined it in his final major work, *Eureka* (1848). There he describes reality as an endlessly repeated process of the universe expanding into particularity and diversity and contracting into unity, using the image of the diastole and sys-

tole of a singular divine heart, with the dispersion into isolated entities constituting unhappy appearances (the Cave?)
and the collapse to unity constituting the reality for which the
entities long (Sunlight, Oversoul?). The two realms are thus
sequential, not coincidental. A person existing as a particular
individual may intuit the unity (an intuition that can be based
on an analysis) and may yearn for it, but the person's very
particularity excludes him (or her) from it: it is fully attainable only *after* the annihilation of individuality.

In his nonfictional exposition of this vision, Poe actually
cites a principle enunciated by his fictional detective, Dupin.
Reason, Poe writes in *Eureka*, can perceive the underlying
unity which is the source and the goal of the diversity with
which Reason is confronted by noticing "peculiarities,"
"roughnesses," "protuberances" (*PT*, 1293) in appearances.
Poe notes that he has already made this point in an earlier
publication. He actually says, "I have elsewhere observed . . . ,"
but a footnote refers us to "Murders in the Rue Morgue," and
the "I" who makes the observation in that story is, in fact,
C. Auguste Dupin. That the detective, especially in the Classical mode, infers truth from peculiarities, roughnesses, and
protuberances (ferrades, tufts of hair, misunderstood ejacu-
lations) is clear enough. And that the poet, in *Eureka*, is
following a similar method at a much higher level of abstrac-
tion—his peculiarities, roughnesses, and protuberances include the laws of gravity and radiation—is also clear enough.

But there is also an interesting implication to the two appli-
cations of the analytic method. *Eureka* proposes a universe
which pulses toward and from Unity; it is this recurrent
achievement of Unity which, Poe believes, all souls—but especially sensitive, poetic souls—passionately aspire to reach.
But that unity is always temporary (and thus, as experienced
in time, tragic). The unceasing and unvarying rhythm of the
pulse from dispersion to unity and from unity to dispersion is
the true eternal identity of Poe's universe:

Guiding our imaginations by that omniprevalent law of laws, the
law of periodicity, are we not, indeed, more than justified in entertaining a belief—let us say, rather, in indulging a hope—that
the processes we have here ventured to contemplate will be re-

newed forever, and forever, and forever; a novel Universe swelling into existence, and then subsiding into nothingness, at every
throb of the Heart Divine? (*PT*, 1356)

Poe's celestial Jerusalem, like that of Chaucer's Parson, is a
pilgrimage. The end, paradoxically, is the process; the unchanging unity is an unchanging pattern of change.

This would appear to relate both to the timeless Arcadian
rhythm of the Classical detective story, which uses the same-
ness of cyclical routines as a figure of timelessness, and as
well to W. H. Auden's interpretation of the detective story's
ritualistic effect upon its readers. The devoted reader of Arcadian detective stories, Auden declares in "The Guilty Vicarage," experiences (and desires to experience) an endless
repetition of a movement of Losing the Great Good Place and
Regaining the Great Good Place. Losing is Poe's diastole; Regaining his systole. Just as in each universal pulse, the dispersion into particulars will yield unique separate fates (in
Poe's grotesque fiction—think Berenice, Usher, Ligeia—bizarre
fates), so each enactment of the detective story introduces a
new crime, new suspects; but every detective story contracts
with a predictable rhythm to its uniform ending: the detective
explains all. The genre came quickly to value novelty in the
opening of the narrative precisely because the end of the narrative was so narrowly prescribed. This rigid prescription
was so emphatic that it became the object of parody and ridi-
cule before the end of the nineteenth century, and yet that
very consistency appears to be the source of the genre's undiminished popularity.

The two rhythms—Arcadian cycles and of reiterated readings—are, however, analogous, not identical. The individual
Golden Age mystery evokes the timeless, cyclical routines
of the Great Good Place as a premise against which to pose
the particular wrong of the crime and of the suspicion that
attends the crime. The story ends with the restoration of
Goodness's timeless cycles, a restoration that is felt to be
permanent. Those novels that recount a sequence of crimes
only prove the point: the increasing tension and terror created by the sequence emphasizes the pressure of time upon
the detective and his dislocated community, but this serves

merely to accentuate the finality with which the detective turns the world back to its natural, timeless cycles. On the other hand, Auden's description of the devoted reader's experience is precisely that of Poe's throbbing heart: a novel mystery swelling into existence, and then subsiding into clarity,—a reading experience that can be renewed forever, and forever, and forever. Though Auden may be mistaken about the motive for the devotion to this experience—"the driving force behind this daydream is the feeling of guilt, the cause of which is unknown to the dreamer" (24)—he is surely correct about the effect. Even readers of Hard-boiled detective fiction participate in this pulsating pattern of normalcy-mystery-normalcy, normalcy-mystery-normalcy, normalcy-mystery-normalcy; though for the Hard-boiled, there is nothing edenic about "normalcy."

II

"But there must be something!" she protested aloud. "It's all so—nebulous. Nobody's guilty, and nobody's really innocent. Something must be provable."
          —Charlotte Pitt, in Anne Perry's *Paragon Walk*

"The not knowing—all the not knowing in this fucking life, you know? It gets to you. Makes you crazy. You just want to know."
          —Tony Traverna, in Dennis Lehane's *Prayer for Rain*

Because the detective story always ends with knowledge dissolving the troubles caused by the inexplicability of the violence, the genre tends to underplay the magnitude of the initial crisis. The reader picks up the narrative, knowing that there will be an upset, and that the upset will be set right. That the upset is usually a fatal one means that it must be taken seriously: taken seriously, but not *felt* seriously. The consequent confusions may, therefore, especially in the initial, Classical phases, be experienced more as puzzles, than as crises. Things certainly seem to be falling apart, but the murder of Roger Ackroyd hardly portends some rough beast slouching toward Bethlehem. Nonetheless, that is the implication: if the crime cannot be explained and guilt assigned, then the present world—the Enlightenment world of rational progress toward disciplined knowledge of the universe—is rocked. John Buchan, who wrote his thrillers at the moment the Classical form was entering the Golden Age, provides a clearer statement of the stakes. (Like the detective story, the popular thriller also makes a generic guarantee that the narrative will end in a happy resolution, but the instrument is different: things will work out, but pluck, decent values, and chance, not an embodied methodical knower, achieve the result.) In an early novel, *The Power-House* (1916; serialized in 1913), Buchan has his villain, Andrew Lumley, expound upon the notion that the violence that erupts into the everyday world amounts to more than an intellectual puzzle. Over cigars after dinner, Lumley challenges the novel's hero, Leithen: "Did you ever reflect, Mr. Leithen, how precarious is the tenure of the civilisation we boast about? . . . You think that a wall as solid as the earth separates civilisation from barbarism. I tell you the division is a thread, a sheet of glass. A touch here, a push there, and you bring back the reign of Saturn" (35). Lumley continues the argument for several pages, making the case that "as life grows more complex, the machinery grows more intricate, and therefore more vulnerable. Your so-called sanctions become so infinitely numerous that each in itself is frail. In the Dark Ages you had one great power—the terror of God and His Church. Now you have a multiplicity of small things, all delicate and fragile, and strong only by our tacit agreement not to question them" (36–37). Lumley is a megalomaniac, but the benign Dr. Greenslade says much the same thing in Buchan's *The Three Hostages*, and similar sentiments can be found in other of Buchan's thrillers. This uneasy sense that the membrane that separates civilized routine from barbaric chaos is thin indeed haunts popular literature in the nineteenth and early twentieth centuries, and lies behind the appeal of the detective story, though the detective story concentrates upon domestic manifestations of the threat. (And with figures such as Dr. Moriarty, even the detective story alludes directly to this dread of a world turned upside down.) If order can be restored through knowledge in a disturbed microcosm on the

Rue Morgue, it can, surely, be restored in the macrocosm by the same means. Dupin's narrator, Watson, Hastings, and all the common citizens of all detective novels skate upon thin ice. Were it not for Dupin, Parisians would live in a world where a mild bank clerk surnamed The Good (Adolphe LeBon) could, with no motive at all, savagely mutilate two women and ransack their room, yet steal nothing.

But there is Dupin, and The Good didn't do it. Poe can describe a shattering of the glass between the civilized appearances and barbaric appearances because he has imagined a mind that can reconstitute the pane, restoring the bank clerk to civilization, and assigning the barbaric crime to its bestial perpetrator. The irrational barbarism was illusion after all; there was a reason (an apish reason to be sure) why the gold was left behind, why Mlle L'Esplanaye was stuffed upside down up the chimney, why the witnesses all heard the different things they claim to have heard. (Poe could, of course, and did also describe shatterings of the glass without reconstitution. Those stories led popular fiction toward a different genre.) The detective is, in a detective's world, precisely the secular equivalent of what Lumley called "the terror of God and His Church"; he is the modern, scientific authority, the great power who holds the world together when the nefarious actions of a mysterious villain threaten to dissolve it in disorder.

III

"You have not observed. And yet you have seen."
—Sherlock Holmes, in A. Conan Doyle's "A Scandal in Bohemia"

The two worlds of the detective story are separated by perception. Watson and Holmes inhabit the same gaslit London. And the two men share many habits and values. But, as Holmes remarks in the first short story, "A Scandal in Bohemia," where Holmes observes the world, and can know it, Watson merely sees the world, and (to use Plato's analysis) naively believes it. Holmes offers a trivial example. Watson has climbed the stairs to 221B Baker Street hundreds of times, but cannot tell the number of steps. Holmes can: "I know that there are seventeen steps, because I have both seen and observed" (*ASH I*, 349). The division between the world of those who see and that of those who see and observe is emphatic throughout the first phase of the detective story. Dupin's narrator, Holmes's Watson, Craig Kennedy's Jameson, Thorndyke's Jervis, Poirot's Hastings, Vance's Van Dine all are seers. They, like the reader, see steps and clues, but do not "observe" them, and do not know how to observe them. They see effects, but because the causes cannot be seen, they do not know them. They are confined to an experience of fleeting impressions, and do not concern themselves to examine the causes behind the impressions.

Sight works most of the time. The narrators are competent men of the world; they are excellent reporters. They are, indeed, excellent journalists: they record quotidian experience with accuracy and with an engaging style. (They also rely with implicit faith in the comprehensive accuracy of newspaper accounts of crime.) They have the worldview of a good journalist; they are current in general matters of arts, sciences, and politics. Watson's dismay at Holmes's ignorance of Literature, Philosophy, Astronomy (knowledge "nil"), Politics ("feeble"), Gardening ("nothing"), and Geology ("practical, but limited") is a journalist's dismay. And yet, "knowing" all these things, when the journalist is confronted with a true mystery, he is lost. The crime scene is, for him, a baffling collocation of detritus and testimonies; he can enumerate and record, but he cannot connect and make sense. He is not a fool, not, at least, in the best stories. But he is constitutionally unable to observe, to know; and his constitution is ours.

Watson's world of effects is a real world, often minutely transcribed. Like the reader, he participates in the usual domestic chores of life—taking his breakfast, reading the paper, visiting his patients, playing the horses. He "knows" these routines, and readily recognizes them in the establishments that he visits. They are like the stairs to 221B Baker Street: they are the données of life in a realistic world. They are the obvious and necessary means of getting from the street to the first floor; their function is their reality, and one need not inquire into their precise dimensions, or the materials of which

they are composed, or the means by which they were constructed,—or their number. Watson's experience of his own
stairway is, most of the time, sufficient. The tread is always
there when his foot descends upon it. But in a crisis, when an
act of violence interrupts the routine world, seeing is not
enough. Then one must *know* the stairs; then the dimensions,
the materials, the construction, the number may matter; then
the mind that observes and knows is required. Then we need
the detective. Watson's world flows happily in the usual
streams of daily life. Only when there is an abrupt interrup-
tion of the flow does the problem of knowing arise. Then intelligence must puzzle out the aberration and identify the cause
of each odd eddy.

The world of appearances is characterized by a normalcy
of familiar routines. Watson's distinctive yet unexceptionable
career—medical degree, army service in Afghanistan, medical practice—warrants him as an exponent of normalcy; in
accepting him as narrator, the reader accepts that the world
with which the narrative begins is a normal world. (The abnormal inclination for isolation and night which Dupin's companion evidently shared with Dupin was more problematic;
post-Watson companions all share Watson's preference for
daylight and gentility). But Watson's normal world is a fragile
thing. It can be shattered by an inexplicable act of violence.
Watson naturally reacts to the violence, but it is the inexplicability that matters. A step on his daily stairway seems unac-
countably to have vanished, and as a result, the day no longer
makes sense. His routines cannot comprehend the violence
and its consequences. The normal guardians of normalcy are
at a loss. The observant eye of the detective is not. Even the
most bizarre effects, properly understood, can be traced to
mundane causes. And if one understands how and why the
stairway lost its step, one can once again trust the stairway,
and once again travel between floors with one's usual un-
thinking confidence. The detective can show that all of the detritus of the moment of violence can be entirely accounted for
by normal physics and normal psychology. Murder does not,
after all, obligate us to anxiously examine every stairway we
come across, in the fear that steps may randomly vanish at
any moment; it does not contradict the comfortable world the

community had happily assumed that it knew, and that, unhappily, it had feared it had lost. By showing that the causes of aberration can be actually and certainly known, Holmes restores the knowable world to the mystified Watson.

IV

> "Then I have to bustle about and see things with my own eyes."
> —Sherlock Holmes, in A. Conan Doyle's *A Study in Scarlet*

> "What the detective story is about is not murder but the restoration of order."
> —P. D. James

The scene of the crime is the visible challenge to the narrator's eye: it presents him with unaccountable facts. What he sees shocks his intelligence as well as his sensibilities. The sight of mutilated corpses of the L'Espanaye women is certainly horrid, but the story's interest necessarily lies in the baffling (to the narrator), telling (to Dupin) circumstances that surround it: the apartment that is "in the wildest disorder" (*PT*, 405). The chaos consists of a clutter of objects and sounds—broken furniture, scattered coins, shrill cries, bloodsmeared razor, above all, those peculiarly mutilated corpses—all reported in the *Gazette des Tribunaux*, with no credible explanation as to why these objects and sounds appear when and where they do. The world of appearances is thus a world in which effects are clear, but their causes are unimaginable. As a result, for those introduced to the scene, either by reading the *Gazette des Tribunaux* or "The Murders in the Rue Morgue," the world suddenly seems a frighteningly random place. Anything—even, given the locked room, impossible things—can happen, and there are no intelligible, judgable motives. The world of reality, which the detective discovers and expounds at the narrative's conclusion, is, by contrast, a world of necessary and recoverable causes, knowable causes to which culpability can be assigned.

The scene of the crime appears to be a world in which a sort of moral entropy seems abruptly to have manifested itself.

"The wildest disorder" that is visible in the clutter of the murder scene signifies a potentially fatal collapse of the social energies that keep things in their place, that "wall as solid as the earth separates civilisation from barbarism" which Lumley mocked Leithen for believing in. In the world evoked by an unexplained crime, things have fallen apart: human relations as well as furniture and coins and razors. Thomas Pitt, in Anne Perry's *Paragon Walk*, summarizes the invariable effect of murder: "Everyone had been afraid, looking with new eyes at friends, even at family; suspicions had been born that could otherwise have lain silent all life long. Old relationships had faltered and broken under the weight" (10). The cohesion of the entire social universe threatens to dissipate into heated accusations and unfounded suspicions.

By discovering a morally coherent narrative of the events that led to the apparent chaos, the detective reverses the entropy: by casting light, he realigns the relationships that the crime had inflamed and distorted. Both hatred and love can now confidently be directed toward their true, deserving objects. In demonstrating that there is an intelligible cause for every bit of detritus, for every suspicious action, he makes what had appeared to be a story of collapse and disintegration into a story of plot and intention. Things happened not because control was being lost, but because willful, energetic malignity had been exercised, a malignity that can now be identified and exorcised. Order, the detective proves, remains the natural state; the disorder was aberrational. Dr. Watson's world, in which violence seems horribly random, is replaced by Sherlock Holmes's world, in which every detail is fixed in a narrative of effects and causes.

The Classical detective asserts that intellect—human intellect—can reverse the entropy, and so he often affects a pose of indolence. Dupin with his analysis, Holmes with his science of deduction, Poirot with his grey cells, Vance with his drawl: all profess that mind properly applied can derive real order from apparent disorder. Sherlock Holmes's languor, which he combated with his seven-per-cent solution, embodies the extreme. But it is an extreme offset by Holmes's uncommon physical vigor when actually investigating a case. In this as in other respects, Conan Doyle artfully balanced the vivid colors of his character to unite in him significant contraries. The balance is significant: the Classical detective is an empiricist; he must have matter to exercise his mind upon, and even when he has a factotum, as Dr. Thorndyke has Polton, he himself is always an active collector of data. Dupin's initial dissertation on the autonomous authority of the analyst's mind remains the trademark of the Classical detective, and to highlight this principle, he may be presented as an alienated intellectual, a fop, a spinster, or an immobile fat man. His naturally ordered cosmos has been disordered by a malignant intellect; it will be reordered by a benign one.

But, of course, the evildoer has had to act upon persons and with things, and it is only through observing the physical consequences of those actions that the detective can recover the true plot. For all his affectation of indolence and immobility, the detective's work is always strenuous. The Classical mode, following Poe, would have it that the main arena of struggle is the grey-celled mind of the detective. But Poe's followers, beginning with Gaboriau, recognized that the detective's physical activity is not merely a decorative enhancement of the drama. The detective's visual, auditory, tactile, at times even olfactory encounters with the scene of the crime are essential. He must *work* his way to his solution; he must *do* things to restore Arcadia. The dialectic between mind and world is crucial. And direct and indirect signs of this necessity are evident in the Classical tradition. Lecoq and Holmes will imitate Dupin's search of the L'Esplanaye house in the Rue Morgue in their own adventures, but with increasing energy. Holmes examines his first corpse: "His nimble fingers were flying here, there, and everywhere, feeling, pressing, unbuttoning, examining, . . . So swiftly was the examination made, that one would hardly have guessed the minuteness with which it was conducted. Finally he sniffed the dead man's lips, and then glanced at the soles of his patent leather boots" (*ASH I*, 168). Dupin adopts green spectacles; Lecoq and Holmes will be much more ostentatious in their use of disguises. "You would have made an actor, and a rare one" (*ASH I*, 661) exclaims a Scotland Yard inspector after being duped by Holmes's impersonation of an aged sailor. Dupin makes a flamboyant gesture of returning the purloined letter;

Lecoq and Holmes will make a career of flamboyant gestures. After returning a purloined document in "The Naval Treaty," Holmes declares, "Watson here will tell you that I never can resist a touch of the dramatic" (*ASH II*, 189). Dupin engages in a crucial struggle with his great antagonist Minister D———; Holmes will struggle with Moriarty, Wolfe with Zeck. All of these conventions argue that detective heroism involves more than analytic thought. Thought is primary in the Classical tradition, but active, strenuous, physical engagement with the world is also essential.[4]

This physical engagement is not insignificant. It is, of course, a desideratum in popular literature. There is obviously more excitement generated by accounts of bodies in motion than by accounts of minds in thought. Dupin's purely mental exercise, "The Mystery of Marie Rogêt," has always been regarded as the least of his triumphs. But the detective's activity is more than a concession to popular tastes; it asserts that necessary and sufficient access to permanent and important knowledge can be obtained by interrogating the lingering effects of past events. These may even be distantly past events: detectives of all sorts are called upon to solve decades old, and sometimes even centuries old, crimes. Alan Grant's 1951 investigation into the 1483 murder of the princes in the Tower of London in Josephine Tey's *The Daughter of Time* is the classic example. These bravura performances underline the detective story's fundamental claim that no event is irretrievable; the past can always be reordered; no error is eternal.

And the interrogations of even the most cerebral of detectives require contact with the tangible world: the signs that he reads—whether things or words—will be physical. It is by touching the world that the world is understood; it is by manipulating the present with one's hands as well as with one's mind that one accesses the past. In this respect, even the Classical detective is not a Platonist. In the *Phaedo*, Plato has Socrates disparage physical action as an avenue to reality:

> Now take the acquisition of knowledge; is the body a hindrance or not, if one takes it into partnership to share an investigation? . . . Surely the soul can best reflect when it is free of all distrac-

tions such as hearing or sight or pain or pleasure of any kind—
that is, when it ignores the body and becomes as far as possible
independent, avoiding all physical contacts and associations as
much as it can, in its search for reality. (Plato, *The Last Days of
Socrates*, 109–10)

Socrates decides that "the unaided intellect" applying "pure
and unadulterated thought to the pure and unadulterated object" (110) constitutes the path to knowledge. "We are in fact
convinced that if we are ever to have pure knowledge of anything, we must get rid of the body" (111). The detective, even
the most ratiocinative of detectives, is always engaged in a dialectic with the physical world. He cannot escape the cave;
but if he cannot rise to the light of the ideal sun, he can make
the firelight within the cave yield a useful certainty. By exer-
cising a method of investigation, he can overcome the flickering
appearances, or, rather, he can *use* the flickering appearances. Observation, to use Holmes's term, is not a bodiless,
Platonic alternative to Watson's seeing; it is a more intense
engagement—a more intelligent application—of the body's
faculties. The Classical detective celebrates his reason, but
he is nonetheless profoundly an empiricist, as Plato was not,
and as the "scientist," who was emerging as an identifiable
character at the moment Poe invented the genre, was. The detective is not trying to "get rid of the body"; he is, in fact, committed to using the body (his concrete apprehension of
concrete clues) to explain the body (the corpse). The knowledge he reaches is pure in its ultimate certainty, but not, in
Plato's sense, pure in its ideal origins.

V

"Then we sailed forth into the streets."
—C. Auguste Dupin, in Edgar Allan Poe's
"The Murders in the Rue Morgue"

The Classical detective, with his emphasis upon ratiocination and analysis, may appear to undervalue this essential
physical engagement that is required to recover the order of
events; the Hard-boiled detective, if anything, appears to

overvalue it. For him, active, strenuous, physical engagement is primary as well as essential. He too must think, but where the Classical detective claims that thought should precede action, the Hard-boiled detective claims that action must precede thought. His world has more irregularities than regularities. There are decencies in the Great Wrong Place—Effie Perrines, Red Norgaards, Anne Riordans—but they are exceptional. The balance is tilted toward selfish individualism, and the private eye's own experience is consistently that the weak yield the wall to the strong. But through persistent and energetic effort, he can establish a small space of order; he can bring one falcon to hand as everywhere around him the gyres widen.

His task, as a result, requires energy and will. He struggles harder to achieve more limited success: he always arrives at knowledge; he always orders a piece of his city; but there are barbarians at all the gates. *Inside* all the gates. Moral entropy *can* be stopped, but only as long as the detective strains against it; it will resume when the case is closed. This is why exhaustion is the Hard-boiled equivalent of the Classical detective's indolence. And it is why the Hard-boiled extreme of exhaustion, in the first phase especially, is that signature moment when the private eye is beaten into unconsciousness. With an Olympian view, the Classical detective often finds his world stale and unprofitable; Holmes and Poirot both complain about the poverty of evildoing in their time. The private eye, subject to all the shocks that flesh is heir to (fists, saps, guns), finds that it nearly—temporarily—overwhelms him. Even when the sap passed out of fashion, and the Engaged private eye retains consciousness throughout the novel, he (or she) still suffers a world-weariness and a cynicism that reflects an acknowledgment that the world will wear a man (or a woman) down.

The private eye's world, then, is one in which effects are normally incommensurate with their causes: the contrasting rewards society bestows upon the work of the poor and of the rich usually make the point. This is true in both the tough, early phase of the paradigm and in the later, more sensitive phase. But the detective's intensity and toughness enable him to defy the general drift toward moral chaos. He can force order in an island of experience—the island of his current case. There, at least, the causes of effects can be known, and judged.

VI

"There are thirty-two ways to write a story, and I've used every one, but there is only one plot—things are not as they seem."
—Jim Thompson, qtd. in Polito

Thompson's observation may well apply to all fiction, but it has a special validity in crime fiction. That things are not as they seem may be a consolation to a pious believer who disdains the all-too-apparent snares of the flesh, but it is an ominous, disquieting thought in the world Thompson depicts in his novels. It suggests that things *are* worse than they appear to be, and that reality may be catching up to us. When it does, it will hurt. In the world of Thompson's alienated and sociopathic protagonists, the way things actually *are* can be frightening; perhaps it is best not to know, best to stick with belief.

The generic contract of the detective story insists upon a more optimistic interpretation of Thompson's line. It promises that things will *seem* bad (disordered, confused), but will turn out to *be* good (properly ordered, just). And in order to emphasize this typical movement, both the initial confusion and the concluding clarity take exaggerated, improbable forms: the detective encounters more crimes, and especially more homicides, than are provided by nature to any actual man in any actual community. And these crimes are accompanied by remarkable circumstances—the most remarkable being the obscurity of the perpetrator: after all, most actual murderers, if they are ever identified, are identified immediately, or at least quickly. Most actual murders are not mysteries. And most actual mysteries are not solved. Fictional detectives not only solve all of their cases, they do so with an exposition that accounts for everything, that answers every question that has been raised. As a result, what, in the beginning, seems to have happened, and what, in the end, is realized to have happened are both designed to draw attention to themselves. The reader must be conscious of the excessive disarrangements caused by the crime, and the excessive neatness of the detective's recovery of the true plot. No other genre of literature makes this absolute commitment to depicting a good (or, at least, better) world of *is* replacing a bad world of *seems*. It is only when the detective story approaches the condition of postmodernism that the commitment dissolves into ambiguity and ends without an exposition of a definite reality. These dissolutions are fascinating and provocative, but they are, in intention and in result, aberrational. The detective story in all of its authentic modes moves from unhappy, realistic chaos to happy (happier), realistic (Real) clarity.

In the Classical mode the chaos is unnatural, caused by the murder and by the necessary concealment of the identity and the method of the murderer. Chesterton's Father Brown story, "The Sign of the Broken Sword," provides an example. General St. Clare is a maniacal Puritan who, having gone bad, goes worse. When, on a campaign in Brazil, a subaltern, Major Murray, threatens to expose his treason, the general murders him, and then orders his troops to make a suicidal charge, littering the field with corpses, among which that of the murdered officer might lie undetected. Thus an Arcadian field in Brazil—St. Clare murders Murray "there by the singing river and the sunlit palms" (154)—is turned by one man's villainy and need for concealment into a field of carnage and chaos—an exact image of the worst imaginable state of disorder. The general's perfidy is punished by his surviving officers and men, but, for reasons of policy, the public record is allowed to memorialize the general as a valiant hero. It takes a detective to go behind the false narrative of the public record and recover the true story that correctly explains the battlefield's corpses and permits an accurate judgment upon the actual behavior of all the principals. In the Hard-boiled mode, no maniacal general—no singular cause—is required: the world is naturally a battlefield. The detective's task is to remain focused upon clarifying the identities of the combatants in one field of action in the midst of a world at war. But again, he must recover a singular story that accounts for the corpses and explains the actions of the main characters.

The detective uses things and actions to discover the plot—the Classical detective tends to use things and actions; the Hard-boiled to use actions and things; but the story—the narrative of moral causes and effects—is what "All men by nature desire to know." The detective must reorder time and space, but he does so to reorder motives. He breaks down alibis; he demonstrates how the murder must have been done *here*, at *this* time, by *this* means, and for *this* reason. General St. Clare broke his sword before the cavalry charge; Major Murray was murdered before the battle; the tip of the general's broken sword is embedded in his private enemy, not in the nation's, and these observations lead Father Brown to the crucial knowledge: the general who did this was a maniac, a traitor, and a murderer; the major was an honorable man; the Brazilian general, Oliver, was *not* a vindictive victor. There is "the story of what appeared to happen," the story of heroic General St. Clare, which was promulgated for political reasons, and there is "the story of what happened," which Father Brown discloses. The disorder of the battlefield permitted both stories to be told; it matters that the detective be able to tell the true story.

And this suggests the emphasis that precipitates the detective story from suspense fiction in general. Thompson's universal plot—"things are not as they seem"—can be narrowed to: the apparent *story* of events is not the true *story* of events. In "Casual Notes on the Mystery Novel" (1949), Raymond Chandler wrote, "Mary Roberts Rinehart, I think it was, once remarked that the point of a mystery story was that it was two stories in one: the story of what happened and the story of what appeared to happen" (*Raymond Chandler Speaking*, 68). The Hard-boiled Chandler is citing the Classical Rinehart. This is the common premise of all detective fiction. The true things that matter are true stories, true plots. Ultimate truth is not, as it was for Plato, a timeless, unchanging Form or an Idea; it is a temporal sequence of causally related actions—a story. The other, noumenal world consists of narratives, and narratives are, inherently, time-bound. This world of phenomena—of disconnected effects, of corpses and litter—is made intelligible by the detective's ability to access those noumenal narratives. And the point is that those narratives are always retrievable. Phenomena may vanish, but the narrative can be reconstructed, even after decades, even after centuries. The true story can always be told.

VII

"Simple and odd," said Dupin.
—C. Auguste Dupin, in Edgar Allan Poe's "The Purloined Letter"

The detective is the one who can tell. He protects the innocent, but more importantly, by demonstrating that the story is never lost, he demonstrates that moral causes and effects are, in a sense, eternal and immutable. There is something permanent and absolute. Plato's Guardians are otherworldly; they are, explicitly, possible only in an ideal republic. The detective does not perceive Forms in a realm beyond the world of mutability. His knowledge is, from the first, rooted in the particularities of the tangible world, the "peculiarities," "roughnesses," "protuberances," and it is a knowledge of causes that brought those "peculiarities," "roughnesses," and "protuberances" to where they have been found. He understands that change is real as well as apparent, and the narrative of real change is necessary for moral judgment. If one has a method and the will to apply it, one can always move from the present baffling world of mutilated corpses and scattered rubbish to an irrefutable account of morally responsible causes. Although he is, like a Platonic guardian, an outsider, he does not bring outside truths to a cavern-bound community. Rather, he brings an outside method and will, and so is able to observe what others only see. He knows how to know the truth; the truth is in the world—in the web that has been woven for him to unweave.

The detective thus draws a true past from the factitious falsehoods of the present. The critical moment is the one in which the detective realizes the true story. Ross Macdonald's Lew Archer habitually uses the Jungian term "gestalt" to emphasize this point at which the detective suddenly realizes how to arrange the pieces of the puzzle in a new and unexpected way. Tony Hillerman's Navajo detective, Joe Leaphorn, describes the moment in a way that echoes dozens of his English and American predecessors: "Abruptly, he saw the connections, how it had happened, and why it had happened" (*Sacred Clowns*, 342). It is at this moment that the second world—the world of certainty, of the true story—is called into existence by the detective. It may take a chapter or two before he shares the certainty with the suspects and with the reader, but the reader is now assured that the confusions are illusory and that sense will be restored. The detective has connected what was apparently unconnected or misconnected; the universe is not dissipating into random heat.[5] That is the heart of the detective story: a hero in a world that resembles the reader's world knows how to know what has happened in the world. If Galileo whispered against the Church, "e pueve muevo," the detective whispers against Agnosticism, "we still can know."

These, then, are the two worlds posited by the detective story: a visible, ephemeral world of present experience, which is unstable and unknowable—a battlefield littered with meaningless or misunderstood corpses and broken swords, and an archived world of the unchangeable and thus knowable past, which the detective can infallibly retrieve in all of its crucial dimensions by practicing his method of investigation. The tangible first world is infused with traces of the intangible (past) second world. It is the intangible past world that is objectively real; it cannot change and it can, therefore, be known. It *must* be known if there is to be order in the tangible present. And the detective knows how to know it.

VIII

"Eureka!"

—Archimedes

The detective's moment of insight—a moment enjoyed by effetest amateur and by the toughest dick—is, of course, a conventional narrative strategy. It is a challenge to the reader, who, if the novelist has succeeded, has *not* had a gestalt, has *not* seen the connections, does *not* know how it had happened, and why it had happened. It is, in this respect, a supplement to the element of surprise the detective story always requires in the end. The plot of what really happened which replaces the plot of what seemed to have happened must contain connections that have never been thought of, yet which, when thought of, appear to be inevitable. The most obvious element of surprise is the identity of the villain, but methods and accessories and motives also contribute to the unexpectedness of the ending.

The significance of this surprise aspect may relate to the metaphysical roots of the genre. The Chinese detective story traditionally identifies the villain in the first chapter; surprising identities, methods, accessories, and motives are not evoked (see chap. 3, note 7). The Western detective's habit of asserting that he alone has seen the connections reflects the essentially egoistic pursuit of truth in the West: "I knew it first" is the claim of a knower in competition with other knowers. This eureka moment implies that the heroic investigator not only reaches the truth, he or she reaches it before everyone else. The reader is thus struck twice: first, when the detective announces he sees what the reader has not, and second, when what the detective has seen proves to be so unlike what the reader had anticipated. Thus the detective endlessly repeats the "Master of Truth" strategy of the Greeks: it is as important that he refute the views of others (with the reader as the chief among the others) as that his own view be certainly true. The certainty is achieved by convention: the generic suspension of disbelief enables readers to accept as fair solutions what, in other fictions, would be unacceptable improbabilities. (The imposition of too great a suspension is one of the cardinal sins of the detective story writer.) The refutation of others is achieved above all through the surprise element. The Classical form emphasized the refutation by frequently presenting a fully developed, coherent, wrong solution, which the detective can demolish before he presents his own fully developed, coherent, correct solution. Thus Lestrade and Gregson industriously construct misguided plots for Holmes to explode. Hamilton Burger and Lieutenant Tragg invariably construct complicated plots that implicate Perry Mason's clients and that account for all the circumstances of the case (all but one or two unnoticed details). Often it is the very clever villain who manufactures an elaborate scenario supported by deceptive clues which lead everyone (except the detective) to a false conclusion. But even when alternative theories are not elaborated, the mere befuddlement of Watson and the reader constitutes an "other" view which the detective's clarity can defeat.

IX

"Time present and time past."
—T. S. Eliot, "Burnt Norton"

"Nothing, I thought, was ever entirely lost."
—Sid Hally, in Dick Francis's Come to Grief

The detective story usually starts with an individual for whom time has dramatically ended: the victim of a murder. The victim may be in an afterlife of pure knowing or, if the sound and fury actually signify nothing, of pure unknowing; but the detective story has no interest at all in the afterlives. The story is interested in the lives of individuals upon whom time presses. These survivors are not, as they might have been, moved by the victim's elimination from the tangible world to thoughts of their own mortality; they are rather moved by the troublesome suspicions and inconveniences that the death has introduced into their present lives. The villain's action has made them conscious of time. They are aware that they are not seeing things clearly, and even more aware that they are not being seen clearly by others. They realize that they do not know and that they are not known.

Even in those forensic detective stories in which the corpse plays a major role (cf. the discussions of postmortem lividity in the Perry Mason novels, or, much more graphically, the autopsies in the Kay Scarpetta novels), it appears as a present object of analysis rather than as a memento mori. Philip Marlowe's elegiac thoughts about Rusty Regan sleeping the big sleep in a dirty sump at the end of The Big Sleep are exceptional. But if the corpse does not inspire the survivors with graveyard meditations, it does embody the inertness of the past. Death moves a person from the fluid realm of knowers into the unalterable realm of the objects of knowledge. But the corpse is *not* known; that is the point. One familiar formula involves the misidentification of the body, but even when it is correctly identified, it is a problem: its very corpseness—how it became a corpse—is the central mystery which must be solved.

The solution often explicitly involves play with time. In the Classical mode especially, the villain frequently times the crime precisely to obscure his role as its cause. Alibis (or absences of alibi) are standard features in most detective stories. In the Classical mode, these alibis may be calculated to the minute, and documented in tables. They remain important in the Hard-boiled form, though the calculations are usually less nice. Where the Classical detective may need to determine everyone's location in the house during a crucial interval of minutes, the Hard-boiled detective surveys a wider city scene, where everyone's location during a crucial morning, afternoon, or evening matters.

Time often presses upon the detective's investigation: he or she must solve the crime urgently to prevent another crime or to save an endangered person. Both Classical and Hard-boiled detectives encounter serial killers; both must rescue kidnapped or trapped victims. Occasionally in the Classical mode and often in the Hard-boiled, the detective himself is endangered and races to ward off threats to his or her own person. This time-pressure is, of course, a familiar element in all popular literature that uses suspense to captivate readers.

And time comes to a conventional end at the close of every detective story. Though some artful writers add a coda of sorts—Marlowe's "big sleep" meditation is an example—every reader knows that the story is over when the detective recites the final unrefuted, irrefutable narrative of what really happened. When the true story of the past, intangible world is told, the detective story is over. Objective reality, in the form of a cause-and-effect narrative, has been expressed; order has been reestablished, and the possibility of knowing order has been demonstrated. The genre's work has been done.

And the worker has been a man or woman peculiarly placed

in time. Until the 1970s, he himself has tended to be more or less exempt from time: not exactly immortal—even Sherlock Holmes eventually retires (and, a few decades earlier, had died at Reichenbach Falls), even Poirot died (sixty years after his retirement in 1916)—but the detective is not significantly aged or significantly affected by any of his cases. Time touches others—the victim, of course; but also those who experience a time of suspicion and then a time of relief from suspicion, and the villain for whom, at the story's end, time runs out. Watson might marry Mary Morstan, or Hastings his Cinderella, but Holmes and Poirot (and Marlowe and Mason) remain inhumanly untouched by the persons and the events they undertake to know in the course of their investigations. The marriages and other renewed bonds that occur at the end of the time of suspicion serve to emphasize the timeliness of the detective's work. By making the past known, he saves the present and secures a fruitful future. But he rarely alters his own present. He leaves the story as he entered it, unmoved by the changes that he has wrought. At the end of *The Case of the Velvet Claws*, Perry Mason takes the grateful young woman whom he has just saved to an open file drawer in his office. "When I get all done with your case you're going to have a jacket in there, just about the same size as all of the other jackets, and it's going to be of just about the same importance. . . . I'm telling you just where you stand in this office. You're a case and nothing but a case. There are hundreds of cases in that file, and there are going to be hundreds of other cases" (213–14). Eva Belter and her crisis of identity (unfaithful wife? liar? blackmail victim? blackmailer? murderer?) are everything during the time of the investigation, and nothing afterward. As a Hard-boiled hero, Perry Mason makes much of his total personal commitment to his clients, but in the end, having succeeded through commitment, he is just as indifferent to their further personal fates as the languid Philo Vance presents himself to be throughout the investigation itself. The detective enters his case as a tabula rasa, and he exits it wiping the slate clean again. He will not be altered by what he has learned or what he has done or what he has felt. He begins every case with an identical freshness. He rescues people by recovering their true pasts—by proving what they have done, he demonstrates who they truly are, but his own past has no impact upon who he is. His unique nature in this respect marks him as a sort of shaman.

He is marked like Plato's exceptional individual; because he perceives more clearly, he is radically alienated from the community of cave dwellers, for whom shadows suffice. He has not, to be sure, "seen the truth about things admirable and just and good" in the universal sense that Plato contemplated. His vision is more particular, but it is equally inerrant. And as Plato realized, the seer will be a stranger in the cave. The detective may possess a household, but aside from a fixed circle of intimates and routines, he is estranged from his contemporaries whose lives develop (and end).

The detective's timelessness must, however, be qualified in some respects. A minor point is that many of the Golden Age narrators favored footnotes referring the reader to the detective's prior cases. These are clearly consumer alerts, not efforts to give the detective a past; they provide the readers with an additional title to purchase upon their next visit to the bookshop. More serious are the notable exceptions prior to 1970, such as Peter Wimsey's uneven progress toward union with Harriet Vane, or Nero Wolfe's acquisition of a personal and professional past. But Wimsey's growth as a man doomed his career as a detective, and Rex Stout balanced Nero Wolfe's increasing awareness of his own past with other shamanistic traits: his fantastic weight and immobility and rituals. Wolfe and Wimsey only emphasize the detective's essential untimeliness.

The most serious qualification of the detective-as-shaman appears with the post-1970 proliferation of Engaged detectives who acquire more personal past than they know what to do with. The seeds of the new nature lie in the Hard-boiled revolt, which made the detective's character—his *will* to know—a key part of his technique, and thus a source of his authority. The Classical detective achieves objective knowledge through detached manipulation of data. The private eye achieves it by committing himself to a sequence of revelatory confrontations, and the self which he commits—Chandler's "complete man," "common man," "yet . . . unusual man"— becomes crucial. As a result, in the Hard-boiled phase, the detective's social views, and eventually his social relations, function in part as his credentials. They make him the reliable knower that he must be. By 1970, this necessary interest in his extra-curricular convictions was becoming a comprehensive exhibition of his (or her) full humanity—the detective's upbringing, ethnicity, pieties were all being explored. The Engaged detectives are as articulate in recounting developments in their ongoing personal relationships as they are recounting developments in their ongoing investigations. Nor are the two aspects of their narratives separated: through their investigations they acquire lasting acquaintances, friends, lovers, children (and, as well, lasting memories and traumas). They have ceased to be blank slates, entering every case without bias. They are no longer The Detective; they are the Man Detecting, or the Woman Detecting.

By entering the temporal world of changing relationships, the detective certainly gains in humanity, but also enters into a new tension with the world he or she inhabits. Hitherto the detective's plotless life was easily and conventionally injected into the conventionally overplotted lives of the victims, suspects, and villains. Now that the detectives' own lives are plotted over a series of novels, their engagements threaten to compete with their pursuit of the truth. Do readers of Anne Perry's Thomas Pitt series purchase the next novel to see once again how Pitt proves that crime can be reconstructed, or to see how Thomas and Charlotte negotiate the challenges of their marriage and their times? The element of personality was always there, but now it has emerged as a nearly autonomous source of narrative appeal. Readers want to know the knower, as well as what the knower knows.

X

"There's a reason for everything."
—Sheriff Brandon, in Erle Stanley Gardner's
The D.A. Calls It Murder

Entering time does not alter the certainty of the knowledge the detective attains, but it does significantly affect its quality. It is less comprehensive. In the Great Good Place, the detective's knowledge of Good and Evil is sufficient to regain paradise: at the story's end, all that needs to be known is known, and so all is once again right with the world. The Hard-boiled private eye's knowledge is never enough to reform the Great Wrong Place, but it suffices to clarify all the moral relations in the pocket of society which the investigation explored. Sam Spade accepts that his world limits what he can know far more than Sherlock Holmes's world limited him; Spade cannot, for example, know whether Brigid O'Shaughnessy loves him, or even whether he loves her. That knowledge is inaccessible in the world he has been given. But he can know that Brigid killed his partner Miles Archer; he can know how to judge Brigid and Joel and Wilmer and Casper Guttman. And that knowledge, like the knowledge of Dupin or Holmes, is final.

The Engaged detective enjoys the same access to final knowledge as regards the case under investigation. But now knowledge about the reality of the crime is not the only necessary knowledge. The detective needs to know himself (herself); the reader is encouraged to ask, Who is the detective? as well as Who done it? And while the second question continues, by convention, to be answered objectively and absolutely, the first is, also by convention, unanswerable. The detective's identity is now a work in progress; each novel adds (or subtracts) friends and lovers, associates and spouses. Because the Engaged detective story has become a story about an investigator as well as a story about an investigation, there is always this faint—and sometimes strong—suggestion that each novel is an installment, not an accomplishment, that the important story is not the one in which reality is separated from appearances once and for all, but the one in which the detective matures in an unending temporal process of understanding himself or herself and his or her society.

This complicates the fable by adding a fundamental tension between the novel, which dedicates itself to finality, and the series of novels, which dedicates itself to provisionality. The case is always closed; the life is always open. The objectivity and impersonality of the Classical detective's technique gave the detective a simple and unquestioned power over time

present and time past. His own immunity to time was a cor-
relative of this power. The life of everyone else in his world
was vividly subject to change; the narrative was *about* the
transformations they undergo. But his own life consisted of
changeless customs—nocturnal peregrinations, tobacco in
the Turkish slipper, orchids 9:00 to 11:00 and 4:00 to 6:00.
Nothing important changed. And consequently, he never suffered. Because he *was* a rational technique, he was a stranger
to all emotions; he felt nothing—nothing except temporary intellectual frustration and ultimate intellectual satisfaction.
Or, to avoid an easy objection, almost nothing. Dupin enter-
tains an urge to exact revenge, surely a private emotion. But
characteristically, the urge emerges from a void: "D———, at
Vienna, once did me an evil turn" (*PT*, 698). What evil turn?
when? why? Even when the Classical Detective did begin to
acquire a biography, it was, for the most part, a simple story
of success—of difficulties surmounted, of marriages made.
The Classical detective story presented a clear fable: ignorance brings suffering; knowledge brings relief.

The Hard-boiled shift to character-as-technique took a crucial step toward a more somber view, which is why the Hard-
boiled novelists always enjoyed a better press among critics.
The private eye performs the same knowledge-brings-relief
ritual as the Classical detective, and with the same uniformity
of result. But he does suffer, and his suffering is essential. He
suffers in obvious degrees—he is threatened and bound and
beaten, insulted and humiliated, shot at and shot. He also suffers in other ways. He loses comrades and friends; he is betrayed by clients, and by cops, and over and over by women.
He suffers from desire: Spade really wants Brigid. It is
through his endurance of this physical and emotional suffering that the private eye works his way to knowledge. He must
be a man as well as a thinker, and the addition of manliness
alters the formula. But not much, for it is manliness, not
Spade-ness or Marlowe-ness, that enables the detective. That
is, it is not Sam Spade's biography that qualifies him as an investigator; he has no biography (the nameless Continental Op
is prototypical in this respect). What matters is the man
Spade is now, faced with Miss Wonderly and her desire to rescue her sister from Floyd Thursby. It is what Spade does in

the course of the novel that makes him the hero, and in this respect he is closer to Holmes than to Spenser or V. I. Warshawski. Because he suffers, Spade's identity is more complex than Holmes's, but Hammett and Conan Doyle are both interested only in who he is and what he does, not in who he has been, and who he will become. Philip Marlowe suffers a great deal in every novel, but he recovers remarkably well from each trial, and he resumes his next investigation with undiminished diligence. The knowledge he acquires, like that acquired by his Classical counterpart, continues to be about other people.

The Engaged detectives continue the tradition of resilience, but their elasticity is more human—they have less of it. They acquire and retain scars, and, however slowly, they visibly grow older. There begins to be room for suffering to teach them not only about the systemic vices of their cultures, but also about their own human conditions. Detectives will never put out their own eyes and exile themselves when they discover the truth. They will never discover that they are the solution to the problem (stories such as Will Hjorstborg's *Falling Angel* which do develop this possibility are, necessarily, singular tours de force). But even the suggestion that the detective must know himself as well as his world adds a dimension to his quest. The Continental Op worried about having gone "blood simple" in *Red Harvest* (1929), and Philip Marlowe indulged in pages of self-examination and self-reproach in *The Long Good-bye* (1956). Many of the post-1970 detectives are almost puritanical in their scrupulous self-examinations (and, like the Puritans, often, as well, self-righteous to the point of priggishness). But there does appear to be a tendency to supplement the detective's search for truth in the lives of others with a search for truth in his or her own. The first search fits into a single story, and satisfies the need to believe that reality can be precipitated from appearances; the second search occupies a series of novels, and implies that inconclusiveness is also valuable.

This means that the essence of the detective is no longer defined by the web. He or she has become a hero of learning, as well as of knowing. They still know; they still prove on every occasion that objective truth can be established. Present effects are always the result of recoverable past causes, and responsibility for what has been done can always be determined. This is the reassuring metaphysic of the detective story. History—the history of individuals; the history of *us*—is never lost. In "The Boscombe Valley Mystery," Sherlock Holmes, in a generous gesture, declines to expose the murderer, consigning him to "a higher court than the Assizes" (*ASH II*, 151). It is precisely because confidence in the purview of that higher court was becoming less tenable that the achievement of the detective became so attractive. Even if there is no higher court, no Last Judgment, there is the Detective's Judgment, which is also certain and objective. The detective repeatedly demonstrates that the world of things that have happened is real and knowable. It is a web, every thread of which can be traced. There are no mysteries. There are always conclusions.

Unless the detective himself becomes a mystery. If the detective needs to know himself, he engages in an unendable quest. It is a quest that can stop—the author may die, or lose interest, or lose an audience; it cannot conclude. (The exceptions, such as Nicholas Freeling's Van der Valk, who dies, and Sjöwall and Wahlöö's Martin Beck, whose life follows a programmatic trajectory, prove the rule. They are anomalies, and, in any event, although the authors may have preconceived their detectives' ends, those ends remain undetermined for readers; there is no generically prescribed conclusion to a detective's life.) It does not appear that the addition of contingency (I wonder how Joe Leaphorn will deal with the death of Emma, his wife of thirty years) to a fable of certainty (I know Lt. Leaphorn will find out what happened to Dr. Friedman-Bernal) has diminished the appeal of the fable. It has, perhaps, enriched it.

XI

"Seldom, very seldom, does complete truth belong to any human disclosure."
—Jane Austen, *Emma*

In most fiction, especially highbrow fiction, and in life, complete truth is at best an approachable ideal. There are always equivocations, doubts, uncertainties. Detective fiction proposes that complete truth does belong to human disclosure—to the disclosures of the detective in the final chapter. And these disclosures are far from seldom; they are mandated. Having defined everything that matters as the circumstances of a crime—who, how, when, where, why—the detective's disclosures are "complete." And they are human. The detective discovers what he discloses without access to supernatural powers; his method may be difficult—it may require uncommon intelligence, or uncommon will—but it is not inhuman.

The prose of few detective story writers comes close, or even tries to come close, to the excellence of Austen's, but it might be observed that Austen's plots come close to being as formulaic as those of the detective story writers. Marriageable individuals engage in minuets of sense, sensibility, pride, and prejudice and, in the end, marry. But marriage is an indefinite terminus, as is the maturity with which a bildungsroman must end. Even the protagonist's death, which concludes many novels, is an event open to interpretation. Readers are always invited to think about what has happened in novels. In detective novels, they are coerced into accepting what a character tells them to think about what has happened. They must, if they accept the genre's contract, believe what the detective eventually tells them has occurred. They may not permit themselves to judge that final explanation. If they do judge it—if the response to the detective's exposition is one of doubt or disbelief—then the novel is a bad detective novel.

The reward of surrendering disbelief is a reading experience that, in addition to the incidental pleasures of interesting scenes, exciting actions, cerebral or racy dialogue, promises the principal pleasure of ending with a satisfying, complete, and true account of what happened. There will always be troubling deceptions and misunderstandings, and there will always be absolute clarity and comprehension. The novel offers a vision of the world that is like the world which we experience, only more articulate. The detective novel adds: and is entirely explicable. For some readers, like Edmund Wilson, the price of explicability is too high. Only very artificial webs can be unraveled, and the artifice requires un-natural contortions of character and event. But it is clear that, for more than a century, millions of readers and dozens of very talented writers have been willing to pay the price, and to pay it over and over again. We want to know that we can be known.

Notes

CHAPTER 1. THE DEVELOPMENT OF THE DETECTIVE STORY, 1841–2004

1. *The Place of Dickens, Collins, Green, and Rinehart.* A trend in recent criticism has been to highlight the contributions of Dickens, Collins, Green, and Rinehart. The first two writers produced novels with depths that clearly reward study and, as a result, lend gravitas to a popular genre whose shallowness has embarrassed some readers; the second two writers were not the shallowest writers and were, as well, women. Some explanation of their marginalization here may be in order.

Bleak House and *Edwin Drood, The Moonstone* and *The Woman in White* are certainly great novels, and detectives and detection are key elements in their narratives. Dickens corresponded with Poe, and Collins was certainly influenced by Poe. But it is hard to see any of these novels as being in the commercial line of detective fiction which Poe inaugurated. Sgt. Cuff and Inspector Bucket cast interesting sidelights on the image of the detective in nineteenth-century fiction, but Procrustean critics must amputate far too much of their novels to fit them to the form of the detective story in its first (or any) phase. Of course, as great and popular novelists, both Dickens and Collins could not but influence all fiction writers, including detective fiction writers, who followed them. There is, for example, a Dickensian touch to many of the minor characters in the stories of R. Austin Freeman, and one Thorndyke novel, *The Mystery of Angelina Frood* (1924), plays directly on the title (and plot) of Dickens's last novel.

Anna Katherine Green (1846–1935)—"The Mother of the Detective Story"—and Mary Roberts Rinehart (1876–1958) were certainly eminent practitioners in the genre in their time. Mary Elizabeth Braddon (1835–1915)—"Queen of the Circulating Libraries"—might fairly be added to the roll. Braddon was a versatile and popular writer; Green and Rinehart, though they wrote in other veins as well, declared themselves writers of mystery fiction, and saw themselves as working in a tradition. Mary Roberts Rinehart, who published *The Circular Staircase* in 1908 and remained for several decades one of the most popular detective novel writers, was aware that she was shifting the genre by giving more body to character and setting. Because she, like Anna Katherine Green, remained a bit quaintly Victorian in her sense of what appropriate characters and settings were—Mrs. Rinehart declared that she could not write anything that might "depress" her children—Rinehart lapsed into irrelevance, as in the 1920s the mainstream of detective fiction moved toward the cleverness of the Golden Age and the realism of the Hard-boiled. Though more often studied than read today, the novels of these women were very popular in their time, and they remain rewarding reading. They are being studied for their depictions of the female condition as embodied in the victims of crime, the suspects, and the investigators, and the results of these studies are often provocative.

But who, in the four corners of the world, remembers any of their detectives? To call Anna Katherine Green "the mother of the detective story" may accurately describe her importance in keeping an expanded form of the detective story in the public eye between Gaboriau (1866–69; in English 1871–91) and Conan Doyle (Holmes, 1887–1927). Anna Katherine Green's twelve Ebenezer Gryce novels were published between 1878 and 1917, three of them prior to the debut of Sherlock Holmes in 1887. Mary Roberts Rinehart did become the mistress of the "had-I-but-known" subgenre of mystery fiction. Perhaps because they were women, perhaps because they were novelists, perhaps because the particular conventions they exploited became obsolete, the forms of narrative and the types of detective that they developed remained on the sideline of the tradition. Sherlock Holmes refers to Dupin and Lecoq as his predecessors; he does not mention Green's Ebenezer Gryce or Braddon's Robert Audley. Everyone after Holmes refers to Holmes. In a 1904 poem on the detective story, before she published *The Circular Staircase* (and after Anna Katherine Green had published twenty-two genre novels), Mary Roberts Rinehart herself listed Poe, Gaboriau, and Conan Doyle as the representative detective story writers.

A small, but perhaps telling, indication of the status of the early female novelists appears in a late novel by Agatha Christie. Hercule Poirot is obviously enough a scion of Holmes. But in chapter 14 of *The Clocks* (1964), Christie has Poirot pause to reflect upon fictional detectives. His commentary ends with praise for Sherlock Holmes, but it opens with an extended compliment to Anna Katherine

Green's *The Leavenworth Case*: "It is admirable. . . . One savours its period atmosphere, its studied and deliberate melodrama. . . ." (116). But it is significant that what Poirot praises is the beauty of the sisters, Mary and Eleanor, and the psychology of the maid, Hannah. Green's detective novel is noteworthy for its portraits; Conan Doyle's detective stories for their detective. The detective who exists to detect is the hero of the first phase.

2. *Lecoq*. The only other important detective of the first phase who acquires a significant character, Gaboriau's Lecoq, proves the point. Lecoq is a creature of novels, not of short stories, and so there is a pressure to fill in his character. Gaboriau chose the novel because, with Balzac as his model, he wanted the space to represent a more complex depiction of the social relations that prevailed in France in the 1860s. Though he made conscious use of Poe's paradigm, he saw himself as a novelist and a social critic. He preferred to label his project *le roman judiciaire*. It was the social relations of the individuals and families involved in the action of the crime, not those of the detective involved in the investigation of the crime, that interested him most. Still, the detective-in-a-novel inevitably acquired more dimensions than the detective-in-a-short-story. But Lecoq's dimensions were, for Gaboriau, insufficiently important to impose even a basic consistency. In *L'Affaire Lerouge* (1866) Lecoq is the secondary detective. He is a reformed criminal (in the vein of Vidocq), in an uneasy relation with his superior, Gevrol; in *Monsieur Lecoq* (1869), where he is the primary hero, he is the altogether admirable scion of aristocrats. Lecoq, as a methodical detective, is a constant as he grows from the one novel to the next; it is this that matters. His personal history does not matter, and so was subject to rewriting.

3. *Inspector Maigret*. Inspector Maigret, who first appeared in ten novels published by Georges Simenon in 1931, offers a contrast to the isolation of both the Classical and the Hard-boiled detective in Anglo-American literature. Although he is, like all detectives, essentially an individualist in his inquiries, Maigret is, from the first, a man among men (and, married to Mme Maigret, among women). He works with colleagues, and his approach to investigation fundamentally requires him to relate to people—to witnesses and to suspects. The Classical and Hard-boiled detectives attempt to determine what has happened; they focus on actions and judgment. The Maigret novels are almost entirely about social observation and sympathy; they focus on character. Maigret employs neither elite analytical intellect nor proletarian will; rather he uses fellow feeling and an eye for nuances of language and behavior to detect the

sources of antisocial action. All detectives study the reactions of suspects. Classical detectives tend to provoke reactions according to an experimental plan; they are seeking confirmation of a hypothesis that they have derived from the examination of physical evidence. Hard-boiled detectives tend to provoke reactions without a plan; they are seeking an hypothesis, and they are, as well, asserting their masculine identities. Maigret also provokes reactions, but without a plan and without aggression. He is curious, and not just about whodunit. For both the British and American detectives, the Classical and the Hard-boiled, the end is knowledge of innocence and guilt; all understanding of character is subservient to that end. The detective must identify and eliminate the innocent so that what remains must be the guilty. Maigret achieves the same end, but it is clear in most of his novels that he—and Simenon—are genuinely more interested in the characters of the persons he meets, both innocent and guilty, than in their innocence or their guilt.

But if Maigret is more human than his Classical or Hard-boiled peers, he is noticeably less willfully self-involved than the detectives who share some of his sensitivities in the Anglo-American tradition after 1970. Maigret does evolve a personal history; he does age slowly in the decades between 1931 and 1972, and he moves into retirement. But he is not as militantly and as articulately introspective as the Engaged detectives; Simenon never makes Maigret's inner life (as a man, a husband, or a citizen) a principal source of interest; the victim, the villain, the bystanders: these are primary objects of study. Maigret, like the Classical and Hard-boiled detectives, begins each case fresh. His sympathies, like the Great Detective's intellect and the Private Eye's will, are undiminished by his prior experiences.

4. *The Underworld*. The emergence in American cities of an organized criminal "Underworld" in the Prohibition decade of the 1920s was an important factor in the development of the ethos of the Hard-boiled mode. The Hard-boiled Underworld is the antithesis not only of the Golden Age's Great Good Place, but also of the early Classical detective's more heterogeneous London (and New York). Gaslit London had its squalid tenements and its high-crime districts such as the East End and Limehouse, but these were balanced by districts of affluence and culture. Holmes visits opium dens, but he also attends recitals and concerts. Similarly, Dupin visits the Rue Morgue and, in "The Mystery of Marie Rogêt," betrays a familiarity with the milieus frequented by proletarians and criminals, but he also treats with ministers of state and pronounces upon neoclassical tragedy. And there was, above all, a sense of the me-

tropolis as an imperial capital: it might be the cesspool into which "all the loungers and idlers of the Empire" were drained, but it was also the director of the empire's course and the repository for its wealth.

The big American city in the 1920s was, to be sure, home to powerful industrial imperialists, but there was a widespread sense—an especially American sense which claims Thomas Jefferson as its prophet—that the cities themselves were intrinsically immoral places, that the power of industrial wealth was inevitably the source of corruption. The crime syndicates, which emerged partly in response to Prohibition (1920–32), came to embody the essence of this uncivil urban world. They crystallized what noncriminal syndicates tried to disguise. The mobs ran comprehensive anti-cities, with their own anti-economies and their own rigorously enforced anti-systems of control. The notorious gangsters such as Al Capone in history and Little Caesar in literature were portrayed as Captains of Anti-Industry. As a result, the wrongness of the Hard-boiled place appears not as accidental or local or intermittent, but as inherent and pervasive and institutional. The venality and the violence of the gangster are merely unmasked renditions of the techniques of the politician or the capitalist. (See Robert Warshow's "The Gangster as Tragic Hero.")

5. *The Dime Novel Detective.* The pulp magazines which emerged in the early twentieth century—*Argosy, Top-Notch, Detective Story, Western Story, Sea Stories, Sport Story,* and dozens of successors, including *Black Mask*—were the heirs of the dime novels which had begun to appear at the time of the Civil War. Both forms appealed largely to a male audience, presenting young heroes encountering adventure in cities and in various wildernesses (the American West, the Klondike, the sea). The heroes proved their moral worth in action. The moral standards were conventional, but the actions were various and exciting; it was this variety and this excitement that sustained the form.

Western and frontier stories were, in fact, the first dominant genre among the dime novels, but by the late 1880s, mystery and detective fiction had become preeminent. Names such as Old Sleuth (first in 1872), Old King Brady (1885), and Nick Carter (1886) reappeared in hundreds of dime novel adventures. These detectives were in many respects more closely related to their frontier/western cousins than to Sherlock Holmes and the other late nineteenth-century descendants of M. Dupin. They were what Gary Hoppenstand has called Avenger Detectives. The protagonists were "detectives," but, as Hoppenstand's label suggests, detection was not their primary activity. The avenger detective was "a steamroller, which, like a juggernaut, propelled over clues and criminal alike. Classical Detective fiction, on the one hand, would keep the reader in doubt about the solution of the crime or the capture of the criminal until the end of the story, while dime novel detective fiction, on the other hand, *never* kept the reader in doubt" (Hoppenstand, 136).

The detectives featured in the pulp magazines which supplanted the dime novels after World War I drove their juggernauts with a bit more finesse. They found themselves in a world that, in the end, needed to make sense. As a result, while a Race Williams could still punch and shoot his way to a solution, Carrol John Daly found himself under some obligation to give Race reasons for shooting at the targets he shot at, and for reaching the conclusions he reached. The web of deceit in which the Hard-boiled detective found himself might be less byzantine than that encountered by Ellery Queen or Gideon Fell (though *The Dain Curse* demonstrates that it might not), but even in his pulpiest avatars, he faced the detective's generic task of unraveling a plot that had been raveled for him by the author.

6. *Natty Bumppo.* James Fenimore Cooper's Natty Bumppo, with his eye for the broken twig, has sometimes been cited as a precursor of the detective hero. And the connection between the popular genre of the Western and that of the detective story—especially the Hard-boiled detective story—has been noted. Westerns and Hard-boiled stories often cohabited in the pulp magazines, and the isolated, violent, and very masculine hero was common to both. Self-sufficiency was a radical virtue in both traditions, the private eye's privative lifestyle serving as an urban version of the Western hero's camp or cabin. But it is an urban version; there is no really clean, uncontaminated space in the city. Spade cannot bar his door against the cops, or against Brigid, or against Guttman, Cairo, and Wilmer. Marlowe cannot keep Carmen from his bed. Natty Bumppo can retreat from Templeton to the cabin he shares with Chingachgook, and when he can't—when Judge Temple's laws entangle him—he can head west to the prairie. The Hard-boiled detective, so often based in Los Angeles or San Francisco, can't head west; there are no territories to light out for.

7. *The Police Procedural and the State.* The police procedural highlights the detective's problematic relationship to the state. In its essential form, the detective story sets a man who knows in a community that does not know. It is the community's bondage to appearances that makes the detective's acuity valuable and dramatic. The drama is often intensified by juxtaposing the individual detec-

tive to the embodied officers of the community's intelligence; that is, by setting the person of the isolated detective against the person or persons of the police force: Dupin vs. Inspector G———; Holmes vs. Lestrade, Gregson, Hopkins, et al.; Poirot vs. Japp, Perry Mason vs. Sgt. Holcomb, Lt. Tragg, and, in his final decades, Hamilton Burger make the same point. It is precisely the failure of the state's system of investigation that necessitates the intervention of the detective. Whether an amateur, a consulting detective, a lawyer, or a private eye, the detective alone solves the puzzle that baffles the minions of officialdom. And even when the detective, as a Scotland Yard Inspector, is himself a minion, his success is implicitly assigned to his personal virtues, rather than to his professional. But the detectives of the police procedural succeed because they are professionals, because they follow, with detailed precision, the official procedures that govern state-of-the-art police science. In its normal forms, the detective story argues for individual perception of truth; in the police procedural, it appears to argue for collective perception. The community is still baffled, but it has constituted a representative body of its members who, by working according to a prescribed system of investigation, uncover the truth. The police are common men; their commonness is insisted upon: they have blind spots and prejudices, they have wives and husbands and children and aging parents, they have taxes and mortgages to pay. They succeed, therefore, apparently not as a result of their own excellence, but as a result of the excellence of the system they serve, the machine of which they are the parts.

But while the triumph of a system may stimulate the admiration of a philosopher, or even of a scientist, it has limited appeal in popular fiction. There is an audience for stories of technological fables. The vogue of Arthur B. Reeve at the beginning of the century, or, at a somewhat more sophisticated level, that of Tom Clancy at the end of the century illustrates the possibility. But while readers may be awed by the machinery, they identify with the individual who presses the levers—Craig Kennedy or Jack Ryan. In the police procedural, the individuals are the levers; it is Steve Carella's cop-ness, not his grey cells or his Carella-ness, that empowers him.

Of course it isn't. His intelligence matters, and, in the fairly hard-boiled city of Isola, his Carella-ness very much matters; it contributes to his success as an investigator, as well as to his interest as a character. Similarly, Martin Beck's Beck-ness is crucial. The central conceit of the Beck series lies, indeed, in the competition between Beck's cop-ness and his Beck-ness. In the course of the ten novels he develops from a proficient state investigator and inadequate family man to an alienated public man and a happy private man. Most police procedurals do not advance such a program of alienation, but they do, inevitably, set the person against the procedure. The investigator's success, in his job and in his life, is determined by his character as much as by the state system which he enforces, and this is what holds the form inside the detective story paradigm.

The detective story's general view of the police has evolved. In the Classical mode, they often appeared as ineffectual functionaries, implying that the state was good-willed, and competent enough in common cases to recognize the truth and secure justice. There were also detective-heroes who operated with state sanction: Lecoq, and then Hanaud and Bencolin of the Paris police; and a legion of Scotland Yard Inspectors including, prominently, French, Alleyn, Appleby, Gideon, Wexford, and Dalgleish. These were men who represented the state as both highly competent and wisely just. But although their state sanction is significant, it is not decisive. They do not succeed because they are agents of the state; they succeed because they, like Dupin, Holmes, and Poirot, possess the individual genius to observe and to conclude. They might draw upon the resources of their organization, and might even be regularly accompanied by subordinates, but they accomplish the work of detection through their own singular intelligence and dedication. Their victories reflect to the credit of the state which employs them, but the state remains at a benevolent distance from the action of perceiving reality.

The successful police detective, even in his Romantic embodiment as individualist investigator, was a European creature. The American tradition was always more suspicious of the state, and less willing even to grant nominal victory to an official body. If the detective must be state-sanctioned, it would be as the authorized antagonist of the state's prosecutor: lawyer detectives such as Ebenezer Gryce, Randolph Mason, Ephraim Tutt (in the series of novels by Arthur Train), Gil Henry (in the series of novels by C. W. Grafton). The Hard-boiled revolt, with its assertion that American society is fundamentally corrupt, only reinforced this native suspicion of the society's government. The quintessential Hard-boiled attorney is, of course, Perry Mason. The state is not necessarily evil even in the Hard-boiled tradition, but it is Leviathan—a vast machine that responds to the needs of those whose fingers press the switches. And these are usually the fingers of the legitimate or illegitimate rich: in *Red Harvest*, those of the industrialist Elihu Willsson and of the gangsters Pete the Finn, Lew Yard, and Max Thaler.

The state, including its frequently corrupt police force (Police Chief Noonan in *Red Harvest*), is generally an obscurer of truth and an obstacle to justice.

Engaged detective story writers, children of the social welfare state which had matured in Europe and been inaugurated by Franklin Roosevelt in the United States, are inclined to restore a view of the state as at least potentially benevolent. They grant it an authority that can counteract the rapacious proclivities of capitalist excess, but concede that it has often been hijacked by bad men—capitalists, racists, militarists, developers, homophobes. Outside the U.S., engaged detectives are frequently enrolled in official ranks; in the U.S. they remain usually private agents. In either case, they remain in practice individualist investigators.

8. *Homosexuality and the Hard-boiled*. One need not subscribe to trends in literary criticism to see that homosexuality poses a special problem for the Hard-boiled style, with its emphasis upon successful inquiry through what the culture regarded as the peculiarly manly qualities of toughness and willfulness. The effeminacy of the homosexual is an obvious and useful shadow against which the private eye can assert his manliness. Holmes advertises his intellect by interrogating a walking stick or a hat; the private eye advertises his masculinity by deprecating homosexuality.

In the more sophisticated Hard-boiled, this deprecation is verbal, as in Marlowe's dismissal of pansies, or it takes the form of pertinent action, as Spade easily disarms the threats posed by Joel Cairo and Wilmer. In less sophisticated Hard-boiled novels, the author contrives occasions for gratuitous violence against homosexuals, as in *I, the Jury*, when Mike Hammer pours a pitcher of water over the heads of "a couple of pansies" who are pulling at each other's hair below his window. The point is always that the detective is the real man.

But the point is never quite settled. Marlowe refers to the "stealthy nastiness" of a "fag party" (*SEN*, 636) in *The Big Sleep*, but, as many readers have noticed, in the next novel he is himself uncommonly attentive to the violet eyes ("Eyes like a girl, a lovely girl") and "soft," "delicate" skin of Red Norgaard (*SEN*, 950). Two novels after *I, the Jury*, Mike Hammer falls in love with Juno Reeve, a statuesque blonde with "creamy" skin—and, as he discovers just before he shoots her on the last page, with male genitalia. The argument can be made that these peculiar attractions, as well as the gratuitous sneers at homosexuals, imply that the private dick is, at heart, himself a homosexual. A less extreme conclusion might be that these writers—the lowbrow Spillane as well as the higher-brow

Chandler—were dramatizing the ambivalence at the core of the Hard-boiled detective. As a detective, the private eye *is* his manliness, but in this as in everything, he is vulnerable. His heroism lies not in his easy and automatic repudiation of unmanliness. The repudiation is right and proper, but it is not easy. Even in the matter of sexual identity, knowledge—self-knowledge—is achieved only through dangerous encounters.

Homosexuality is much less of a problem in the Engaged detective story. There are, of course, a number of Engaged stories featuring homosexual detectives. But even when the detective is heterosexual, one of the easiest ways of aligning him or her with the angels is to assign him a homosexual best friend (see the Alex Delaware series by Jonathan Kellerman, the Sharon McCone series by Marcia Muller, the Sunny Randall or Jesse Stone series by Robert B. Parker). An aversion to homosexuality is, without exception, a hallmark of villainy (though not necessarily a proof of homicidal behavior). There is no ambivalence here.

9. *Didacticism*. The didactic impulse lies in the genes of the detective story. The first paragraphs of "Murders in the Rue Morgue" make up an extended disquisition on "the mental features discoursed of as the analytical," and the story itself is presented as an illustrative pendant to the disquisition. Poe would, of course, have been appalled to see himself cited as a precedent for didacticism in any form of fiction. And the educational element in "Murders in the Rue Morgue" is limited to these erudite discourses on method. The Dupin stories may teach readers about the power of analysis to derive order from disorder, but they cannot be accused of teaching much about how a man should live his life, which was the sort of moral didacticism Poe anathematized. They certainly do not teach anything about Paris, other than the names of a few streets and districts and the kind of shutters called by Parisian carpenters *ferrades*.

Later writers in the Classical mode inevitably added individual measures of moral vision and of more or less esoteric information, but while the reader could pick up a bit of Egyptology or pharmacology, encounter brief lectures on the thought of Nietzsche or Freud, learn the workings of a seismograph or a selenium light switch, these were secondary attractions. The Golden Age writers tended to reduce them to a minimum, though again Dorothy Sayers represents the contrary impulse, with her determination to educate readers about the operations of an advertising agency or the theory and practice of change-ringing church bells.

The Hard-boiled paradigm's allegiance to realism necessarily implied an increased measure of didacticism. The Hard-boiled writers proposed to teach their readers about the ways things really work in the big city. The detective doesn't just know how to solve the crime; he knows all the milieus of his world—he can confront with equal poise the millionaire in his mansion and the bindlestiff in his flophouse. He can describe the sociology of a neighborhood, or report on how Hollywood controls publicity, or advise readers on effective techniques for tailing a suspect. These knowing demonstrations of the private eye's street-smarts are the Hard-boiled equivalent of Sherlockhomitos. He shows he is powerful by showing how well he knows the real world.

There is less machismo in the didacticism of the Engaged detective, and more moralism. There is still the device of asserting the hero's knowingness: the detective knows the ways of cops and businessmen and con-men. John D. MacDonald was one of the first (and the best) at empowering his investigators by showing their command of the technologies of running a hotel, building a condominium, or operating a stock-trading scam. MacDonald evidently knew a great deal of this from experience; he supplemented his experience with research. Later writers, with less experience, rely on more research. Elmore Leonard, an admirer of MacDonald's work, is scrupulous in his study of milieus and technologies, and employs a research assistant to ensure accuracy. Many novels are now prefaced by acknowledgments to the experts (police, doctors, locals) who have supplied the writer with the inside information and perspectives that provide the reader an incentive to read the novel: the acknowledgment is a warranty stating that the world that the reader is about to enter is a true one, as well as an entertaining and/ or provocative one.

This emphasis upon enlightening the reader not just about whodunit, but also about the workings of the world and the proper political and moral judgments about those workings has evidently become a significant part of the appeal of the genre. It is, perhaps, interesting that the spy story, especially as reconceived by Ian Fleming in his James Bond novels, offers the identical supplemental attractions: the detective knows how things work, his adventures take place in accurately described exotic locales, and he usually embodies an explicit political and moral perspective on the world. The immense popularity of James Bond and his facsimiles anticipated slightly the rise of the Engaged detective; it also evaporated abruptly in the 1980s with the end of the Cold War, while the detective keeps on detecting. And this suggests that while readers may find the incidental tuition offered by both the spy novel and the detective novel to be attractive, the lasting appeal of a popular genre resides in archetypal plot: it is because he or she detects that the detective retains readers. A detective who can also provide informed instruction on a technology (fire-fighting, forensic medicine, running a business) or on the customs of a region or on a historical era—for example, ancient Rome or ancient China, medieval or Elizabethan or Victorian England—certainly adds to the didactic satisfaction of the detective story, but the satisfaction derived from knowing a technology, a region, or an era is cognate to, not identical with, the essential satisfaction of knowing whodunit. Knowing that there will be a hero who knows how to separate the guilty from the innocent gives the genre its thus far endlessly appealing center.

Nonetheless, this secondary didacticism—this impulse to lecture soberly on extraneous matters—helps to distinguish between the American and the English approach to the genre. Americans seem always to have been more likely to prefer a pill of instruction beneath the sugar of detection. Dupin's extended lectures were followed in the early twentieth century by Craig Kennedy's professorial expositions of the scientific principles behind technological innovations. Given the minimal attention Arthur B. Reeve devoted to characterization, scene, and plot in the Kennedy series, it seems that its immense popularity can only be attributed to these expositions. This American predilection grows only more pronounced in the last quarter of the twentieth century. Dick Francis's English narrators are often generous in their explanations of how things work, but it is the American writers who so earnestly seek new technologies, regions, and eras about which they might inform their public. This earnestness raises a second distinctive aspect of the American approach to didacticism, especially in the Engaged phase. Not only are American writers careful to get their facts right, they are careful to get their morality right. They tend to be more insistent and explicit than their British counterparts. They do not, for example, merely deplore intolerance; they appear to be irritated by it. They seize the reader's lapels and demand his or her sympathy. Because they expect American society to live up to the spirit and the letter of its egalitarian principles, they see imperfections not as an inevitable element in human nature, but as the visible signs of a willful intolerance that obstructs the achievement of a beloved community.

English writers may desire to convey a regional flavor, and may even explore issues of ethnic difference, or sexual exploitation, but they achieve their effects without the militance that American writers adopt. English writers probably also have morals, but they are less inclined to have their detectives expound them, or their saints and sinners so simply embody them. The point is not that Colin Watson is a vaguely racist snob, or that Sara Paretsky is a parochial and puritanical harridan; both writers create sensitive detectives, set them in carefully observed locations, and confront them with morally complicated problems. The writers and their detectives are Engaged in ways that their predecessors were not. But the American writers and detectives always seem to want everyone to know just how Engaged they are.

10. *The Detective's Remembrance of Things Past.* Actually, Marlowe does have a few moments of recollection. In *The Lady in the Lake* (1943), two novels after *The Big Sleep*, Marlowe does briefly recall Ann Riordan and Red Norgaard, and in Chandler's final short story, variously titled "Wrong Pigeon" and "The Pencil," Ann Riordan returns again to play a small role. But the rareness of these moments makes the point. The backward references in *The Lady in the Lake* are conventional gestures, comparable to the footnote references to prior cases in S. S. Van Dine or Ellery Queen novels, or to the occasional backward allusions in the Sherlock Holmes saga. These are merely devices to encourage the reader to read the earlier novels; they do not create a depth of memory for the detective. "Wrong Pigeon" *is* late (1958), following *Playback*, the final novel, in which Marlowe agrees to marry Linda Loring. By the 1950s, the first signs of the transition toward the Engaged model were already appearing, and these signs of Marlowe's acquisition of memory of a personal past are only tentative steps toward the development of the detective's life as a generic attraction.

The continuities in Kinsey Millhone's life are qualitatively different. Her evolving relations with her octogenarian landlord, Henry Pitts, and with the tavern owner, Rosie (and Henry's evolving relations with Rosie), are discussed in every novel. She meets Jonah Robb in the second novel, reencounters him in the third, starts to sleep with him in the fourth, and ends the relationship in the seventh. She hears Robert Dietz's voice in the first novel, becomes intimate with him in the seventh, loses touch with him, and then regains him in the thirteenth. She rediscovers her second husband in the fifth novel, and her first husband in the fifteenth. By careful reading, one can ascertain that Kinsey was born on 5 May 1950, her parents died on Memorial Day weekend 1955, she met her first husband in November 1970, married him in August 1971, left him on 1 April 1972, and witnessed his death on 1 June 1986. The Baker Street Irregulars have spent decades debating chronology in the Holmes saga without approaching this precision.

And that, of course, is because Conan Doyle was careless in such matters. He gave Sherlock Holmes more substance than most Classical detectives, but the substance was functional, not an end in itself. He aimed to stimulate the reader's interest in the detective, but he did not ever conceive of that interest as primary. Kinsey Millhone's growth as a person is an essential element in Grafton's novels, and maintaining consistency and continuity in depicting this growth becomes very important. This emphasis is a key element in the conception of all Engaged detectives.

Chapter 2. The World of the Detective Story

1. *Backward Construction.* The detective's world must be constructed in a peculiar way. An 1845 review of Poe's *Tales*, probably written by Poe himself, makes the point that the tales of ratiocination are "written backwards" (*ER*, 872). The author starts with plot, and with the end of the plot, not the beginning. The plot is a structure of action involving a murder (or other criminal enterprise) which, as it transpires, leaves behind physical effects upon objects and mental effects upon persons. It is this plot—this structure—that must be reconstructed by the detective. The author, therefore, begins by imagining the physical and mental effects that might persist in the world after the action has been completed and that might lead a detective (but not a reader) to infer the causes of those effects. These chains of effects and causes, then, become the threads of the web which will be unraveled.

Poe's views on "writing backwards" were not consistently favorable. His response to William Godwin's *Caleb Williams* (1794) illustrates his ambivalence. Godwin's novel is sometimes seen as a precursor of the detective story, though it is a tale of crime and pursuit, rather than one of crime and detection. At the conclusion of an 1842 essay on *Barnaby Rudge*, Poe wrote: "'Caleb Williams' is a far less noble work than 'The Old Curiosity-Shop'; but Mr. Dickens could no more have constructed the one than Mr. Godwin could have dreamed of the other" (*ER*, 244). Poe thus seemed to recognize the greater achievement of Dickens's art; but acknowledged that in forms of fiction where "construction" matters, Godwin's idiosyncratic art of backward composition was preferable. But in an 1845 note on the novel, Poe was more completely dismissive. He observes that Godwin "says that the novel was *written backwards*" (Poe's italics), and remarks, "This mode cannot surely be recommended, but evinces the idiosyncrasy of Godwin's mind" (*ER*,

1294). Finally, Poe opens "The Philosophy of Composition" (1846), by reciting Dickens's comment that "Godwin wrote his 'Caleb Williams' backwards" (*ER*, 13) and adding: "Nothing is more clear than that every plot, worth the name, must be elaborated to its *dénouement* before any thing be attempted with the pen" (*ER*, 13).

2. *The Romantic Detective.* It was natural for Poe, who matured in the decades when Byron was a name to conjure with and to castigate, to dress his detective hero in a costume of alienated genius, bestowing upon him an aristocratic genealogy, a disdain for vulgar minds and vulgar motives, a preference for solitude and for the night. He did not, notably, give his detective the carnal appetites that frequently pressed upon both Byron and his heroes. This may be partly due to Poe's peculiar response to the attractions of the flesh, but it also ensured that the detective could be entirely self-sufficient; he does not need the world, or anything (or anyone) in it. Gaboriau would experiment with a worldly detective, but Conan Doyle's decision to revert to an anticarnal figure sealed the Classical type. Sherlock Holmes would indulge a few exotic appetites—tobacco, cocaine, violin. But Holmes would not need a lover; he would not need a chef or a wine cellar. Later Classical detectives might have a chef (Wolfe), or appreciate wine (Wimsey), or consume quantities of beer (Fell, Wolfe), and these do further flesh out the detective. But he remains, to a significant degree, a withdrawn, superior person.

Dupin's egoism, it must be admitted, lacks the titanism of that of Byron's heroes. In a semirealistic district of Paris, Dupin is recherché; in the neighborhood of Mont Blanc, he would be a paltry thing. But even in their watered-down form, the signs of the detective's Romantic genius are functional as well as emblematic. His poses dazzle the reader's eye, and facilitate the essential sleight-of-hand by encouraging that tendency "to confound the ingenuity of the suppositious Dupin with that of the writer of the story." It is the plot that actually creates the detective's authority, but it is his remarkable character that captures the attention. Gaboriau's evolving sense of Lecoq's potential as a dominating figure plays to the same end, but Gaboriau was inclined more to assign the Romantic postures to the aristocratic heroes of the social melodramas which constituted the backgrounds of the detective narratives, and to make Lecoq, with his dedication to his profession, more a commonplace man with a singular talent (though Lecoq himself acknowledges personal motives in *Le Dossier no. 113*). Conan Doyle assigned Sherlock Holmes an eccentric and somewhat wayward character in *A Study in Scarlet*, and developed that waywardness considerably in *The Sign of Four*, making the Bohemian Holmes as Romantic a hero as a high Victorian audience could embrace.

The Golden Age, perhaps as a response to the First World War, revived the Romantic taste in heroes. The willful waywardness of Dupin and Holmes declines into the neatness and the fine mustaches of M Hercule Poirot, or the aristocratic persiflage of Sir Peter Wimsey, or the weighty immobility of Nero Wolfe. Still, the same effect is aimed at: the writer attaches bells and whistles to the character of the detective to encourage the reader to ignore the fact that it is plot, not character, that drives the narrative and defines the detective's deep appeal.

The Hard-boiled detective forgoes this deceptive plumage: his character is militantly undistinguished. He is anti-Romantic. Chandler calls him a knight, but then Chandler had to: chivalry is not the self-evident quality of the private eye. It takes an authorial intervention to provoke the thought that the working detective might, in fact, be the modern, ironic, proletarian knight-errant. In place of genius and eccentricity, therefore, the Hard-boiled mode employs violence and sex as the magician's assistants. The impulses and the actions of the dick and of the thugs and vamps whom he encounters occupy the reader's attention as the plot moves toward its surprising vindication of his power as knower.

3. *Poe and Verisimilitude.* In a review of *Robinson Crusoe* published early in Poe's career (1836), Poe specifically celebrated its "potent magic of verisimilitude" (*EQ*, 202). He also made the observation that few readers ("not one person in five hundred," 201) correctly attributed the excellence of the novel to the artfulness of the author, a comment curiously parallel to his observation that detective story readers are also inclined to overlook the ingenuity of the writer. Poe had imitated Defoe's circumstantial verisimilitude in his adventure stories, such as "Descent into the Maelstrom" and *The Narrative of A. Gordon Pym*, and to much the same purpose as Defoe; the concrete details anchor the narrative and make the fantastic events credible.

It might also be observed that the verisimilitude of the three hats, one cap, "and two Shoes that were not Fellows" in *Robinson Crusoe* is also juxtaposed to a search for meaning and design. Crusoe, as much as Dupin, is looking for an explanation for disaster. Why has a providential God cast him up on this barren island? He finds the answer not in things (tufts of hair, slit throats, untouched gold), but in patterns of action: he suffers shipwreck when he defies counsels of authority; he enjoys success when he responds to "hints" from the spirit world. It takes a number of wrecks and a number of successes before he recognizes the pattern and declares his submission to providential authority (and, as part two of the Crusoe saga suggests, his submission is not irrevocable). The detective is also seeking a pattern, but it is a singular pattern leading to a singular conclusion: he seeks to know what was done, not what to do. And, especially in the Classical form, he seeks his knowledge from things. Crusoe never imagines that the three hats, one cap, "and two Shoes that were not Fellows" can teach him how to live his life. They are purely happenstances. Such concrete things might be happenstances in the detective story, but they might not be. The three large silver spoons discovered on the floor of the L'Espanaye apartment happen to be the number, size, and metal of the spoons the L'Espanayes happen to have possessed. The razor and the untouched bags of gold are telling.

Gold tells nothing to Robinson Crusoe, though his recovery of gold from his wrecked ship is a famous incident: scrapping together fragments to shore against his ruin, he finds some gold and silver in a drawer. In his desperate situation, he is moved to declaim on the vanity of money—"O Drug! Said I aloud, what art thou good for, Thou are not worth to me, no not the taking off of the Ground, one of those Knives is worth all this Heap. . . ." (Defoe, 57). And then, "upon Second Thoughts," he gathers up the heavy coin and conveys it to the uninhabited island. The declamation and the second thought tell the reader, and perhaps Crusoe, something about the character of man. And this—the pattern of a man's responses to the things and the events of the world—is what interests Defoe as a novelist and Crusoe as a retrospective narrator. It is an interest that originates in a habit of spiritual autobiography which the English Puritans cultivated: pious persons kept journals of their lives so that they could review at a distance of months or even years the lessons that the providential world could teach them about their successes and failures.

This puritanical tradition may even have contributed in a way to the Hard-boiled style. The private eye also sees little intrinsic value to things (see note 6); he rarely attempts to draw inferences from distinctive shutters or tufts of hair. He does look for patterns of action and reaction, though always the actions and reactions of others. It is the meaning of their story, not his own, that he must elicit. And it is an entirely secular meaning. It is not God who has wrecked the ship, and spared the voyager, and disclosed the gold, all to teach a wayward Yorkshireman the merit of accepting his middle station in life. The Hard-boiled detective simply assumes that a chain of natural causes and effects—physical and psychological—will always be recoverable and will always link a misdoer to his misdeeds. (The Engaged detective, though it would shock his or her emancipated spirit to hear it, takes another step toward the puritanical model. Though in each novel they still work primarily on discerning the patterns in the stories of others, their growing autobiographical impulses move them a bit further in the direction of men like Jonathan Edwards or Benjamin Franklin.)

4. *Disguise.* Perhaps the most significant sign of the detective's genetic disposition to action is his early addiction to disguise as a method for investigating the truth. Detectives may ratiocinate in an armchair, but they use disguise on expeditions. Disguise is the tool of the extrovert; cogitation of the introvert; and the early detectives were, in this regard, well-rounded individuals. Even Dupin, who aspired to purely stationary detection in "The Mystery of Marie Rogêt," dons green spectacles when he goes to visit Minister D———'s rooms in "The Purloined Letter." Lecoq's mastery of disguise is as remarkable as his mastery of inference. Old Sleuth, Cap Collier, and Nick Carter are considerably more remarkable for their disguises than for their inferences. Sherlock Holmes employs disguises in at least thirteen of his adventures. (Disguise is the principal device of Allan Pinkerton's agents in the semifactual detective narratives of his cases which were popular in the late nineteenth century.)

It was the Golden Age's exclusive emphasis upon intellectual puzzle-solving that permanently devalued disguise. It preferred detectives who were so thoroughly themselves that masks were unthinkable. It was the Poirotness of Poirot, the Vanceness of Vance, the Wolfeness of Wolfe, the Fellness of Fell that empowered the detective, and it would be a diminishment of Poirotness, Vanceness, Wolfeness, or Fellness to have the hero put on the costume of a proletarian or "an amiable and simple-minded Nonconformist clergyman" (*ASHI*, 363). It would also have been ridiculous: Poirot as anyone but Poirot? Of course, the dramatic uses of disguise were not completely abandoned. Peter Wimsey plays the role of Death Bredon through most of *Murder Must Advertise.* But the real recovery of action came with the Hard-boiled revolt, and there the action was so furious that the additional incentive of disguise was largely superfluous. (Though it is noteworthy how often the private eye must impersonate someone else; he is not a master of disguise, but he is so common—so physically undistinguished—that he does not need disguise to appear to be someone else.)

5. *Arcadia?* It may be objected that "Arcadian," with its reference to the simple hillside life of the shepherd, is an inappropriate

designation for Golden Age locales that include theatrical troupes, railway cars, and New York City mansions. Country houses may evoke a suggestion of the pastoral world, but theaters, trains, and brownstones are unlikely to yield the lazy murmur of bees in the flower-borders, the gentle cooing of pigeons in the tops of the elms, or the whir of mowing-machines coming from distant lawns. Philo Vance's first case takes place in the Benson mansion on Manhattan's West 48th Street. Yet as he stares at the corpse, the narrator, S. S. Van Dine, can make the same conventional Golden Age observation regarding the anomalous character of the crime. He recalls his experience at the front during World War I in order to make a contrast: "In France death had seemed an inevitable part of my daily routine, but here all the organisms of environment were opposed to the idea of fatal violence." The "organisms of environment" here can hardly be called bucolic. They must include "the din of the city's noises." Yet even in the Manhattan mansion, Van Dine makes pointed gestures toward recalling the look and the meaning of Arcadia: "The bright sunshine was pouring into the room [the look of Arcadia], and through the open windows came the continuous din of the city's noises [the urban reality], which, for all their cacophony are associated with peace and serenity and the orderly social processes of life [the meaning of Arcadia]" (*The Benson Murder Case*, 24).

"The orderly social processes of life" in *The Benson Murder Case* are those of a sophisticated social set. Its rhythms are not those of the shepherd, but they are insistent rhythms, and they represent the regular operation of a natural and benign cosmos. Golden Age novels, even when they take place entirely in such anti-Arcadian settings, still imply worlds characterized by "peace and serenity and the orderly social processes of life," not by the vicissitudes of empire and war (the trenches of France).

And this contrast between an ahistorical place where the context of action will endlessly renew itself and a history-burdened place where every action creates a new context is the point of the pastoral. The love of Strephon for Chloe is singular, but the hillside on which he sings of it will be the same when his grandson sings to his Chloe. Aeneas's love for Dido is singular, but so is the razed Troy whence he came, and so is the Dido-less Carthage which his pious debt to as yet unfounded Rome compels him to leave. The Orient Express, with all its cars and conductors and attendants, ran its regular route every day before and every day after the remarkable winter day in which twelve individuals murdered the villain Rachett. The regularities of the Golden Age detective story are naturally, given the century in which they were written and the generic commitment to realism, not always those of the Classical, or even of the Renaissance, poet, but they are regularities that serve the identical aesthetic function. The principal difference, indeed, lies not in the quality of the regularity, but in that of the singularity: the detective story is a pastoral about death, not love.

Cycle and repetition are the keynote. If it is not a green cycle of bees and doves and mowers, it is still a cycle: of theatrical seasons, or train schedules, or household routines, or village customs. (With its unaltered detective hero performing the same action again and again, the mystery story is itself a cyclical experience; *reading* mysteries is an Arcadian experience about Arcadian experiences.) Murder violates the cycle: it asserts a permanence against the repetition. The detective does not, as Auden would have it, restore paradise; he ends the suspense between tick-tock and tick-tock. At the end of the novel, the rhythm resumes its immemorial beat.

A note on *otium*: this is a significant term. It occurs with surprising frequency in Latin pastoral poetry (Rosenmeyer, 67), and constitutes a value that is peculiarly appropriate to the bucolic tradition and to the detective story. It is originally a military term meaning "leave from active duty," and it came to signify "vacation, freedom, escape from pressing business, particularly a business with overtones of death" (Rosenmeyer, 67). The Golden Age detective, and the earlier methodical detectives as well, were amateurs. Even Holmes, who sometimes wears the mask of a professional "consulting detective," is clearly engaged in a nonmercenary pursuit of malefactors. He is no more motivated by pecuniary reward than is Dupin when he collects his 50,000 francs. The Classical detective, when he detects (and however energetic the detection may be), is at leisure. The business—whodunit—is genuinely a pressing matter for the suspects, and, insofar as it involves murder, the business possesses overtones of death (no more than overtones: the death is rarely an intensely felt crisis for anyone). But for the detective (and for the reader) the business is a vacation. It engages the intellect in a delightful puzzle, providing a vacation from dull realities. It posits a naturally rhythmic, happy world which has been violently disturbed and which will, through analysis not violence, be restored to its rhythmic happiness. It is a place of otium.

It might finally be noted that the phrase *"Et in Arcadia ego"* (Also in Arcadia I am) comes not from Virgil or Theocritus, but from Renaissance painters: first in a painting by Giovanni Francesco Guercino (ca. 1618–23), then in two paintings by Nicholas Poussin (c. 1630 and c. 1646). The paintings depict green pastoral landscapes, with the shepherds discovering skulls and the motto. The point is precisely Auden's: the skull and motto are, to the shepherds, baffling discoveries: like the corpse in the detective story, the skull is "shockingly out of place, as when a dog makes a mess on a drawing room carpet," and like the clues, the motto must be read and understood.

6. *Hard-boiled Trifles.* Of course, Hard-boiled detectives do not entirely overlook physical evidence. Fingerprints and ballistics and handwriting analysis are all part of the context of the detective's investigation, but they are precisely the details left to the technologies of the police. What Holmes and Thorndyke gathered for themselves, the private eye—or the defense attorney—allows the government to collect and interpret. The government can reliably tell what finger touched which object, what gun fired which bullet, and what hand wrote which message; what the government cannot do is draw the correct inferences from these findings. Perry Mason or Philip Marlowe can.

Occasionally, a Hard-boiled story does turn on a physical clue; it is noteworthy when it does. In *Farewell, My Lovely*, Marlowe gives one of his cards to the alcoholic Mrs. Florian, and she sets an empty glass on it (chapter 5). Later, he is informed that Lindsay Marriott, a client in an apparently unrelated case, has one of his cards with "a round smear across one corner" (chapter 12; *SEN*, 823). A reader trained in Golden Age detection will make the connection, or will reproach himself for failing to make the connection when Marlowe finally expounds it (chapter 40). But this is an unusual phenomenon in Marlowe's experience.

Sam Spade's technique in *The Maltese Falcon* illustrates the usual value of trifles in the Hard-boiled world. Spade correctly infers the identity of the murderer of Miles Archer by combining two trifles observed by a policeman—that the shot that killed Archer burnt his coat and that his own gun was still tucked on his hip—with his own knowledge of the sort of man Archer was: not dumb enough to let anyone but an attractive female client get so close to him in such a remote location without having drawn his own weapon. The trifles are necessary, but what is essential is knowledge of how a man behaves.

There are two significant functions of physical detail in the Hard-boiled world. The first is to contribute to the Hard-boiled equivalent of the *ferrades* effect. In *The Long Goodbye*, Philip Marlowe drives to Roger Wade's house in exclusive Idle Valley. He notices the landscape just before turning into the manicured estates of the valley:

The stretch of broken-paved road from the highway to the curve of the hill was dancing in the noon heat and the scrub that dotted the parched land on both sides of it was flour-white with granite dust by this time. The weedy smell was almost nauseating. A thin hot acrid breeze was blowing. I had my coat off and my sleeves rolled up, but the door was too hot to rest an arm on. A tethered horse dozed wearily under a clump of live oaks. A brown Mexican sat on the ground and ate something out of a newspaper. A tumbleweed rolled lazily across the road and came to rest against a piece of granite outcrop, and a lizard that had been there an instant before disappeared without seeming to move at all. (*LN*, 618)

In a Classical detective story, there would always be the possibility that the granite dust, or the acrid breeze, or the tethered horse, or the brown Mexican might be a significant thread in the web. In *The Long Goodbye* they are not threads, nor is the reader expected to carefully note and recollect them. The details are purely aesthetic: to make the scene real and to set a mode of lassitude. The Mexican is there because he was there, and perhaps because he faintly echoes the Wades' brown servant, Candy, and the brown gangster, Mendy Menendez, and Marlowe's brown visitor, Señor Maioranos. He is not there because he explains anything.

The other important function of Hard-boiled detail is to provide an equivalent to Sherlockholmitos. Instead of using moments of incisive but irrelevant inference to empower their detectives, the Hard-boiled writers used the detective's precisely described processes to demonstrate his command of his world. Sam Spade's artful rolling of his cigarettes in chapter 2 of *The Maltese Falcon* is a minor example. The private eye knows the way things are done— how to jimmy a door, or flirt with the hat check girl, or impersonate an insurance salesman. And by doing these things, he demonstrates a proletarian savoir faire that implies the same degree, if not the same type, of mastery of his world.

7. *Hard-boiled Arcadia*. Of course, even Hard-boiled detectives occasionally find themselves in Great Good Places. Sometimes, as in Mike Hammer's brief excursion to Packsdale in *I, the Jury* (1946), the point is the simple one that the corruption of mean streets of the big city can infect a small college on a hill in a small town, and that the toughness that works with the hardened denizens of Gotham also works with the deans and students of the ivory tower. Sometimes, as in many of Ross Macdonald's Lew Archer novels, there is a genuine Arcadian note in the background. Archer's world is Hard-boiled, but it is haunted by an Arcadia Lost. Many of his cases take him to college campuses, and, especially in the later novels, into the natural world—the seas and forests of

southern California. In no case does the entire case appear to be contained within such a scene; Archer is at home in his car, and, like all Hard-boiled detectives, he must continuously move in order to learn. But Macdonald's unrelenting theme is that the origins of crime lie in the Oedipal past, and intimations of Arcadia seem to be part of that past.

Philip Marlowe's Arcadia is perhaps the most interesting. Chandler responded to the nature of southern California, as well as to the denatured city. In *Farewell, My Lovely*, Marlowe drives his client to a payoff in the foothills. He notices "the smell of kelp and the smell of wild sage from the hills"; he listens to the crickets (*SEN*, 809). And then he is knocked unconscious, and awakens, nauseous, to find his client murdered. It is not quite a dog-messing-the-carpet moment, but Chandler certainly is contrasting the peaceful natural scene with the acts of violence.

In a more developed contrast in a later novel, *The Long Goodbye*, Chandler sets up Idle Valley as a fabricated Arcadia, where the wealthy can seclude themselves in a green world of live oaks, cottonwoods, and huge undulating lawns. But although death enters Idle Valley, Chandler's principal point is that it never really was an Arcadia. Before the crime and after, it is filled with rich louts who are different from poor louts only in that they have more money. It is another country, but its morals are the same.

The most interesting of Chandler's Arcadias appears in *The Lady in the Lake* (1943), much of which transpires in the bucolic setting of Puma Lake, based on Chandler's vacations at Big Bear Lake. He constructed the novel primarily from two short stories, "Bay City Blues" (1938) and "The Lady in the Lake" (1939), with a few excerpts from a third, "No Crime in the Mountains" (1941). The first of these was entirely a Great Wrong Place story—Bay City is the wrongest of places; the second included two key scenes set at "Little Fawn Lake," and the third transpired almost entirely at the lakeside, and might almost qualify as a Great Good Place story. The very title of the third story—"No Crime in the Mountains"— suggests an Arcadian retreat. The line is repeated by several of the citizens of Point Puma, the little village near Puma Lake which detective John Evans drives to in response to a request for assistance. There is even a tame doe, an icon of pastoral innocence which Chandler retained in *The Lady in the Lake*. There is some description of the flora and fauna of Puma Lake in the story, and more in the novel: "wild irises and white and purple lupine and bugle flowers and columbine and pennyroyal and desert paint brush" (*LN*, 26); granite rocks, waterfalls, blue jays, squirrels, woodpeckers.

But this idyllic world is not, in either the story or the novel, offered as a normative scene. It is not a place whose natural innocence is violated by an expungeable bad man.

In "No Crime in the Mountains," Puma Lake is, in fact, the center of a German and Japanese plot against America: John Evans encounters a Nazi conspirator (who eventually commits suicide with a "Heil Hitler!") who has been working with a couple of Teutonic women and a couple of Teutonic men and a hissing Japanese man. The plot is incredible in nearly all respects, but the point is not just that the mountains are full of crime; it is that the crime—fascism— which threatened the entire world in 1941 also threatened the mountains. The Great Wrong Place could infiltrate even Puma Lake. The last lines of the story belong to the local constable: "'A night like this,' he said, 'and it's got to be full of death'" (429). This may appear to express Auden's sentiment, that the corpse be "shockingly out of place," but the constable is not just referring to the corpse (corpses—there are at least four in the story: two Nazis, a local accomplice, and an innocent native). The death that the night is full of is the mortal combat of the Second World War. The mortal combat of the First World War was what was excluded from Styles Court; there the only death that mattered was that of Mrs. Inglethorp. Puma Point attempts to include what the Classical Great Good Places excluded. That the resulting narrative is an absurd failure demonstrates that neither paradigm of the detective story can plausibly accommodate fables of collective, international evil, but it also shows that Great Good Places are inherently inhospitable to Hard-boiled detectives, and that the effort to plant private eyes in Arcadia will prove fruitless. Anthony Boucher's 1945 anthology, *Great American Detective Stories* suggests that it might produce one result. Chandler had published twenty-one short stories by 1945. Boucher, the eminent reviewer of detective fiction, and himself a celebrated author of Golden Age stories, chose "No Crime in the Mountains" to represent Chandler: surely the worst of Chandler's detective stories, but the closest he would come to the Great Good Place tradition which defined the genre for Boucher.)

The intrusion of the war is less overt in *The Lady in the Lake*, but even in the novel, it is used to provide a context. The government is dismantling rubber sidewalks to supply the war machine, and the dam at Puma Lake is guarded by armed sentries who will play a functional role in the ending of the novel. But the principal evil that infiltrates Puma Point in the novel is definitely domestic: it has reached Puma Point from Bay City, Chandler's very model of the corrupt American city, with disorder imposed by crooked cops who report to crooked politicians who report to the gangsters running the offshore gambling ships. There are fewer deaths in Puma Point in the novel, and Marlowe experiences a degree of genuine relief in the mountains. (The genuineness is undercut by a detail: Puma Lake is held in place by a dam with a mill wheel. There was, however, no mill at Puma Lake: the wheel is a relic of a motion picture set, a bit of Hollywood, even in Arcadia.) But there is not, at the end, any sense that Marlowe has cleansed Puma Point. Puma Point is as clean (and as tawdry) as it was in the beginning. The crime did not belong to Puma Point; it belonged to Bay City, and Bay City is like all Great Wrong Places at the end of the story: an individual fragment of disorder has been removed; the mean streets remain.

CHAPTER 4. "ALL MEN BY NATURE DESIRE TO KNOW"

1. *Detectival Infallibility.*

> "Don't you ever have a failure, Monsieur Poirot?"
> "The last time was twenty-eight years ago," said Poirot with dignity. "And even then there were circumstances."
> —Agatha Christie, *Cards on the Table* (1936)

> "That is Scotland Yard," he said. "Inspector Grant. Never had an unsolved crime to his name."
> "I hope you write my obituary," Grant said.
> —Josephine Tey, *A Shilling for Candles* (1936)

By 1936, at the height of the Golden Age, Agatha Christie and Josephine Tey could joke about the infallibility of their detectives. They could do so because readers already knew that, though they might falter on the way and exclaim that they were dunderheads, the detectives *were* infallible. If they did ever fail, it would not be in this case; it would not be in any narrated case.

This is an obvious point, but it has been challenged, and if the challenge stands, then the thesis that the detective embodies the Western drive for objective certainty is, at the very least, undermined. Michael Cohen puts the challenge strongly in his study *Murder Most Fair*. He argues that no sooner had Poe established the formula of infallibility, it was undercut by his successors.

Poe establishes a convention of the detective who does not fail; other authors challenge it almost immediately. In Wilkie Collins's *The Moonstone*

(1868), the professional detective fails and the amateur detective is himself the thief, although he does not know it. In the first group of twelve Sherlock Holmes short stories, *The Adventures of Sherlock Holmes* (1892), the detective fails to catch the villain four times, lets him go twice, and discovers there is no crime four times. In the first decade of the twentieth century, Robert Barr reversed the convention of the infallible detective in his ironically titled stories about a bumbling detective, *The Triumphs of Eugene Valmont* (1906). E. C. Bentley's detective in *Trent's Last Case* (1913) also fails. (Cohen, 29–30)

Two of Cohen's failures are easily dealt with. *The Moonstone* is a great novel that is plotted around an investigation into a mystery, and Collins was influenced by Poe; but the novel offers the failure of a detective, not of a detective in a detective story. It is not a genre novel; Collins was not proposing that Sgt. Cuff become the hero of a series of novels of inconclusive detection. Nor can the failures of Eugene Valmont be counted against the detective in a detective story. The cases of Eugene Valmont are, after all, parodies. As such, Valmont's failures actually testify to the infallibility of the detective: that is what is being mocked.

The failures of Sherlock Holmes are more problematic. It should be remembered first that *The Adventures of Sherlock Holmes* was preceded by two novels, in both of which Holmes was dramatically successful in discovering the truth. But because readers of *The Strand* may well have missed these publications, they cannot be adduced as establishing a presumption of Holmesian infallibility; Holmes's record in the first twelve stories must make its own case. Cohen argues that in ten of the twelve adventures, Holmes falls short of perfection. Even at first glance, six of the ten argue for infallibility: releasing the culprit and discovering that there is no culprit are not failures. If success for a detective means to discover by some method what really happened, Holmes was successful on each of these occasions.

But "fails to catch the villain four times"? If "catch" means "identify"—does Holmes's method yield certain knowledge of who did the crime and where and when and how and why?—then Holmes is twelve for twelve in *The Adventures*, as he must be. The closest thing to a failure must be "The Five Orange Pips," in which Holmes fails to save the life of his client and, as well, fails to capture the killer. But he does know who the killer is, and the reason he fails to capture him is that the killer's ship goes down in a storm at sea before putting into the port where Holmes has arranged for his arrest. Holmes's method is not a perfect prophylactic (he will lose a second client in "The Adventure of the Dancing Men"), but that is not a necessary quality of the detective's art. The detective looks backward and separates what happened from what seemed to have happened, and this Holmes does. To humanize his detective, Conan Doyle lets him slip; but the slip comes in a nonessential aspect of his performance.

(In "The Five Orange Pips," Conan Doyle has Holmes admit to his client, "I have been beaten four times—three times by men and once by a woman" [*ASHI*, 392]. But this is merely a rhetorical gesture, not a depicted defeat; Conan Doyle doesn't show failure. And even here, the client responds, "But what is that compared with the number of your successes?" Holmes acknowledges: "It is true that I have generally been successful.")

Perhaps Cohen counts "A Scandal in Bohemia" as one of Holmes's failures. Close readers have sometimes guessed that Irene Adler, in "A Scandal in Bohemia," is the woman to whom Holmes was referring in "The Five Orange Pips." But if so, again the failure is not relevant. Holmes actually achieves the end he was employed to achieve: the king of Bohemia safely marries his proper bride; "Nothing could be more successful" (*ASH I*, 367) is the king's final comment. Holmes does fail to secure the photograph that threatened the king's equanimity, and he failed to realize that his disguise had been penetrated. As a result, Irene Adler flees beyond his power to "catch" her. Nonetheless, Holmes has investigated; his methods have enabled him to discover the truth (the location of the photograph); he has done what his client wanted done. In the end, he—and the reader—know what has happened.

Perhaps the most damaging example of Holmesian failure appears not in *The Adventures*, but in the second collection of Holmes stories, *The Memoirs of Sherlock Holmes*. "The Yellow Face" is remembered by enthusiasts precisely as the adventure in which Holmes does fail. It opens on an apologetic note, with Watson announcing, "it is only natural that I should dwell rather upon his successes than upon his failures." This is because, he explains, "where he failed it happened so often that no one else succeeded, and that the tale was left for ever without a conclusion" (*ASH I*, 575). Not only does Holmes sometimes fail, but success is sometimes impossible. Some things cannot be known. There must be some uncertainty. And this does qualify the impression of infallibility.

But Watson's is an abstract concession. Even the concrete example of "failure" that he cites—"The Yellow Face"—ends with Holmes's prowess intact. The narrative opens with a familiar device: the client leaves a personal item in the sitting room of 221B Baker Street; Holmes examines the item, and draws a number of inferences about its owner ("obviously a muscular man, left-handed, with an excellent set of teeth, careless in his habits, and with no need to practise economy" [*ASH I*, 576]). These inferences have nothing to do with the mystery at hand, but everything to do with establishing Holmes's infallible ability to read a significant reality (the shape and habits of Mr. Grant Munro) through an apparently insignificant residue (his pipe). Munro's problem concerns his wife's requests for money and her inexplicable interest in a cottage near their country home in Norbury. Holmes prematurely develops a theory involving blackmail by a former husband, though he concedes that "when new facts come to our knowledge which cannot be covered by it," he will reconsider. As it happens, the client forces the issue. He calls Holmes later the same day, requesting that the detective immediately come to Norbury. When Holmes and Watson arrive, Munro has them accompany him to the cottage and, with Holmes's approval, insists upon entering the cottage, where he finds his wife and her daughter by her first marriage to an African American. There was no blackmail, and the first husband was indeed dead.

It is certainly not one of Holmes's finest moments, but it is not an utter failure either, and not just because in the end the truth is known. Holmes draws inferences from the pipe, and is completely vindicated; he draws inferences from Grant Munro's narrative of events, and he is completely wrong. But his wrong inferences constitute, explicitly, a hypothesis to be tested. ("You have a theory," Watson asks. "Yes, a provisional one," Holmes replies. Later Holmes calls it "a surmise," and claims only that "at least it covers all the facts. When new facts come to our knowledge which cannot be covered by it, it will be time enough to reconsider it." [*ASH I*, 586, 587). It is, to be sure, a rather byzantine hypothesis: Holmes devotes a long paragraph to a reconstruction of what he thinks may have happened, including details such as the first husband possibly suffering from "some loathsome disease" and "an unscrupulous woman" who has possibly attached herself to the leper in order to profit from the blackmail plot. When the face behind the yellow mask turns out to be that of a racially mixed child, Holmes's melodramatic scenario does seem ridiculous. And Holmes's final words in the story are thus in some degree justified: "Watson, . . . if it should ever strike you that I am getting a little over-confident in my powers, or giving less pains to a case than it deserves, kindly whisper 'Norbury' in my ear, and I shall be infinitely obliged to you" (*ASH II*, 589). This uncharacteristic humility in the detective is becoming, but it should not be taken too seriously. It shows Holmes's humanity, but it does not really contradict the rule that the detective must succeed in separating what seems to have happened from what happened. It might be noted that in his further adventures, Holmes resumes his customary pose of superiority, and that Watson never does find occasion to whisper "Norbury."

Agatha Christie deliberately plays upon this Holmesian moment in giving Poirot his failure in "The Chocolate Box" from the first collection of Poirot stories, *Poirot Investigates* (1924). It too ends with Poirot asking his companion, Hastings, to whisper "Chocolate box" should he ever feel Poirot is growing conceited. Christie, however, turns the sign of humanity into a joke, having Poirot, in his next breath, proclaim himself "undoubtedly the finest brain in Europe at present" and then be unable to hear Hastings's murmured "Chocolate box." Christie can afford the joke, because Poirot's "failure" does not, of course, diminish his infallibility. And, it might be noted, Poirot's "failure," like Holmes's, occurs in a short story, collected in a volume with eleven amazing and complete successes to set the tone. Neither Holmes nor Poirot ever fails (or "fails") in a novel.

Last on Cohen's list of failed detectives is Philip Trent, a detective who was designed by his author to be a failed detective. *Trent's Last Case* (1913) was intended to play off what Bentley took to be the tired formula of the infallible, and thus, in Bentley's view, inhuman detective. Philip Trent would, in what was intended to be his first and final narrated case, be presented as a Great Detective who had, in the manner of Dupin and Holmes, established a record of unvarying success, but who would now apply his method and come to the wrong conclusion and, as a result, renounce the role of the detective forever. Trent does apply his method to the murder of the financier Sigsby Manderson; he notes two crucial anomalies overlooked by the police, and upon them builds a detailed reconstruction of the complicated way in which the victim's secretary, John Marlowe, established an alibi for himself. The method works; Trent's reconstruction of *how* the murder was done is exactly right. But Trent's conclusion regarding who committed the murder—he accuses Marlowe—is completely wrong. In fact, up until the moment the actual murderer confesses to the crime, Trent has no idea who did it. On the last page of the novel, therefore, Trent vows, "I will never touch a crime-mystery again. The Manderson affair shall be Philip Trent's last case" (221). In fact, Bentley did bring Trent back for two encores, in a novel co-written with H. Warner Allen (*Trent's Own Case*, 1936) and in a series of short stories (collected in *Trent Intervenes*, 1938). Both the novel and the short stories are carefully set prior to Trent's *Last Case;* and in all, Trent is uniformly successful in his investigations. So even Trent fails at failure, as all detectives must.

In the end, the obvious prevails: the detective must succeed. This is such a fundamental generic requirement that it defines out of the genre any story in which the detective fails—really fails to separate appearances from reality. This definition rules out a number of great stories, and rules in a legion of dreadful ones. But it leaves intact a vast and very popular literature of men and women who repeat with unending success the pursuit of truth.

2. *Two Worlds, One World.* The distinctiveness of the Western two-world, appearance-reality model of the universe can be clarified by contrasting it with a non-Western "one-world" (or "this-world") vision. Scholars report that with the exception of the metaphysic developed in India in the third century AD, the two-world model is peculiarly Western—and the Indian dichotomy applies to spiritual, not physical, reality (Lloyd and Sivin, 203). One of the more sophisticated one-world models emerged in China, which, for several reasons, may serve as a useful foil to the Western approach. The Western partition of the world of appearances from the world of reality provides a theoretical basis for objectivity—the possibility of standing outside and taking a wholly external view of things. Objectivity allows Westerners to decontextualize things as "objects" to be analyzed as entities. By contrast, the "this world" vision of classical China, instead of positing an underlying, unifying, and originating principle, begins from the perceiver's own specific place within the world. Without objectivity, "objects" dissolve into the flux and flow, and existence becomes a continuous, uninterrupted process (Ames, 50).

This Chinese worldview has been called "organismic." Bernard Schwartz, in *The World of Thought in Ancient China*, contrasts the Chinese concept of Tien (Heaven) with the Western (Platonic/Christian) view: for the Chinese, "Heaven is indeed no law-giver God standing outside the system; Heaven is necessarily realized within the system" (369). In this "organismic" philosophy, Heaven does not constitute an external, objective reality. "One cannot speak of heaven's transcendental 'theistic' interventions, since Heaven will act only through the impersonal patterns which manifest its being" (370). There is no radical division between an ontologically superior realm (Forms, God, atoms) and the realm of direct human experience. G. E. R. Lloyd and Nathan Sivin, in *The Way and the Word: Science and Medicine in Early China and Greece*, make the same point: Chinese sages sought to understand the cosmos as a

unity in process, and showed no interest in detecting a reality behind appearances. They claimed to be "Possessors of the Way." Authority in the Greek view was achieved through demonstration, and,
in particular, through a dialectical struggle with competing claim-
ants to truth. The Greek natural philosopher aspired to the status of
"Master of Truth," and so needed to refute the authority of others in
order to establish his own. And he needed to assert the incontro-
vertibility of his interpretations: "to win the argument against your
rivals you needed to claim not just that truth was on your side, but
also certainty" (173). The Chinese, by contrast, tended to place authority in tradition; Chinese natural philosophers aimed to affiliate
their ideas with those of prior sages; their declared purpose was not
original discoveries, but rediscoveries—"recovery of what the ar-
chaic sages already knew" (193). "To that end they took over and
redefined existing concepts, such as ch'i, to produce a synthesis in
which heaven, earth, society, and the human body all interacted to
form a single resonant universe" (241). Where the Greek asserted
the novelty of his theories, the Chinese claimed to speak for age-old
wisdom (156). Both views produced innovation; but it was the
Greeks who made innovation a value in itself: their "fierce competi-
tiveness," perhaps the result of inhabiting an *oikomene* of combat-
ive city-states instead of a celestial empire, made them disparage
the old illusions in order to promote the singular wisdom of their
new insights.

There is also a significant difference in the vocabulary of analysis. The Chinese thinkers spoke of the "five phases" (*wu hsing*) of
things, of the "way" (*tao*) of the world, of yin and yang. The Greeks
spoke of "elements" (*stoicheia*), which might interact and combine,
but which possessed unalterable individual natures. The Greeks
spoke of reality (*ousia*), opposing it to appearances (*phainetai*).
Most significantly, the Greeks spoke of "causes" (*aitia*). "Cause"
(*aiton*) was a term derived from the law courts: "*Aiton* denotes what
is responsible for something. *Aitios*, in the masculine is used of the
guilty party. *Aitia* means 'blame or guilt, its apportionment, or an
accusation imputing blame'" (Lloyd and Sivin, 162). The detective's
essential task of identifying a criminal by tracing the crime's causes
from its effects thus echoes the origins of the Western worldview:
the Greeks used "blame" to develop the crucial concept of "cause";
the detective uses causes to assign blame.

Werner Jaeger uses a contrast between the Chinese and Greek
aesthetics to distinguish a peculiarly Greek bias toward objectivity
even in lyric poetry. Unlike the Chinese, "Greek expressions of personal emotion and thought have nothing purely and exclusively

subjective in them" (*Paideia*, 114). Looking at the Ionic origins of Greek thinking, he finds that "personality, for the Greeks, gains its liberty and its consciousness of selfhood not by abandoning itself to subjective thought and feeling, but by making itself an objective thing" (114). Objectification serves as the preliminary even to self-understanding.

If Western thought has inherited this assumption, it may explain why so many readers respond to a narrative formula which says that the crucial knowledge men need properly to judge their fellows must be derived from objective data: fingerprints, timelines, scribbled scraps of paper. The detective story, with its premise that the modern hero must exert himself to shift the experience of his fellow citizens (and of his reader) from Appearance to Reality, seems to dramatize the Western two-world bias. It is a form of fiction that always presents two narrative worlds, and that always concludes that the second narrative world—the one produced by the detective—constitutes objective truth. Decontextualizing objects and actions is precisely the detective's procedure. It is because Inspector G——, Lestrade (and Watson), Hamilton Burger, and the reader interpret things and events in their obvious (and false) context that they go wrong. This is the burden of Dupin's discourses on method, and it remains true in the world of Spenser and Kinsey Millhone. It is the basis of Lew Archer's use of "Gestalt" for the moment when he realizes that the actual relation of people and events is entirely different from the accepted view; the world suddenly restructures itself. What had seemed random and disordered abruptly reveals its morally meaningful order. The surprise at the end of the detective story lies in this dramatic decontextualization: the presumptions which, unhappily, had been sustained by the conventional reading of appearances are overturned, and another, completely persuasive account of the contexts of the crucial actions is substituted.

The detective story was not unknown in China. Judge Dee (Di Renjie) and Judge Pao (Bao Zheng) were historical figures (of the seventh and eleventh centuries, respectively) who, by Yuan times (1271–1368) had become detective heroes in popular stories and, by the late Ming dynasty (sixteenth century), in popular dramas. By the middle of the nineteenth century, multivolume collections of their cases were being published. It has been noted that Judge Bao's revival in a major narrative, Shih Yukun's *Three Heroes and Five Gallants* (1879), may not be unrelated to the Taiping Rebellion (1851–64): "It is no coincidence that a narrative extolling the virtues of an incorruptible magistrate, serving the empire with fearless impartiality and aided by heroes, gallants, and braves

committed to quelling an incipient rebellion should have been performed by storytellers and published at this time" (*Tales of Magistrate Bao*, xiv). This connection only emphasizes one significant
difference between the Chinese and the Western traditions: Magistrates Dee and Bao operate under the aegis of the emperor, who
himself operates under the Mandate of Heaven. (In both instances,
the Mandate is a favorable one: magistrates serving under malignant emperors do not become famous detectives.) The detective
does not assert the originality of his genius; rather, he affiliates
himself with the traditions of wisdom associated with Emperor and
Heaven. Dupin acts on behalf of the royal house, and Holmes fires
a VR into a wall of 221B Baker Street, but neither of them derives
authority from the person of the ruler, or from any tangible or intangible link to anyone linked to the ruler. They certainly endorse
the official morality of their nation, but there is not the sense that
the detective's cleverness is bestowed upon him by his incorpora-
tion into a virtuous discipline that has descended from Heaven to
Emperor to Magistrate. Judge Bao may have been summoned to
justify submission to a just empire; his contemporary, Sherlock
Holmes, was presented more as a justification of Victorian science.
If Judge Bao reassured those disturbed by rebellion (and by Western and Japanese incursions), Sherlock Holmes reassured those
disturbed by Darwin.

As Robert van Gulik, the champion (and translator) of Judge
Dee stories, points out, the Chinese tradition of detective fiction dif-
fers from the Western in several other respects, and some of these
differences bear upon the two-world character of the Western version. The Chinese do not, for example, emphasize the surprise ending with its overturning of the prior narrative. The villain is
formally identified at the beginning of the story. "The Chinese want
to derive from the reading of a detective novel the same purely intellectual enjoyment as from watching a game of chess; with all the
factors known, the excitement lies in following every move of the
detective and the counter measures taken by the criminal, until the
game ends in the unavoidable check-mate of the latter" (ii). "With
all the factors known": discovery of reality is not the point; the reality is known at the start; the enjoyment lies in the depiction of the
criminal's vain attempts to render the reality unknowable. (And, in
some respects, "intellectual" may not even be the correct adjective
for the enjoyment. George A. Hayden writes of the Judge Bao
[Judge Pao] plays which enjoyed a vogue during the Yuan dynasty:
"The playwright sparks the audience's desire for solution purely on
ethical and emotional and not on intellectual grounds" [4]).

As a result, when the Chinese detective realigns appearances with reality, the element of surprise is absent. The appearances were known to be unreal: known by the reader or auditor. There is no Dr. Watson's world of troubled bafflement; there is no doubt that reality is knowable. The Western detective story, even when there is no Dr. Watson, always climaxes with a shock of recognition: the abrupt realization of whodunit—"so *this* is reality!"—enforces the implicit lesson: there *is* a reality behind appearances. There is no shock built into the Chinese detective story. More importantly, "ghosts and goblins roam about freely in most Chinese detective novels; animals and kitchen utensils deliver testimony in court and the detective indulges occasionally in little escapades to the Nether World, to compare notes with the judges of the Chinese Inferno" (van Gulik, ii–iii). These intrusions of the supernatural into the narrative of investigation signify the inclusiveness of the "this world" vision. There is no hint of a decontextualized, external, objective reality. Even dreams have evidentiary value. The detective possesses "extraordinary powers of perception that enable him to see ghosts or to have revelatory dreams" (Hayden, 6). Again, it is not his genius for analysis, nor his will for confrontation which empowers the detective; rather, it is his correct alignment with the way of his world, a world that extends from Heaven to Emperor to heroes, gallants, and braves to Hell. This comprehensive world has been disturbed by the malefactions of the villain; the agents of order in this world—specifically, the agents of the Emperor—engage in an even competition with the villain, and in the end, the way of the world favors order over disorder, and the villain is expunged (and, van Gulik reports, expunged graphically; another Chinese distinction). Virtue triumphs in the Eastern as in the Western form; the moral is the same, but the metaphysic is different.

3. *Greek Two-World Metaphysics.* It may be helpful to present a slightly less superficial account of the Greek roots of the two-world metaphysic.

W. K. C. Guthrie summarizes the Greek view:

[The Greeks were looking] for something permanent, persisting through the chaos of apparent change; and they thought that they would find it by asking the question: "What is the world made of?" The world as our senses perceive it seems restless and unstable. It exhibits natural and apparently haphazard change. Natural growth may proceed or may be thwarted by blind external forces. In any case it is followed by decay and nothing lasts forever. Moreover we observe an apparently infinite plurality of unrelated objects. Philosophy started in the faith that beneath this apparent chaos there exists a hidden permanence and unity, discernible, if not by sense, then by the mind. (Guthrie, 23–24)

Western philosophy begins with the sense that things *are* not what they *seem*.

In the second chapter of his *Metaphysics*, Aristotle reviews the history of Greek attempts to know what things really are. Initially, Greek thinkers sought the unifying reality principle in an underlying physical entity. Things seem diverse, said Thales, but at base, things all originate in water: water is the way things are. The unlimited, said Anaximander; air, said Anaximenes; earth and water, said Xenophanes. (Poe's vision of a pulsing universal reality was, perhaps, anticipated by Anaximander's suggestion that reality consisted of a continual succession of worlds created and then destroyed by an all-enfolding "Indefinite" [*apeiron*]). Heraclitus moved the debate in a new direction. He looked at the movement of things in the world and concluded that the underlying reality was that the things of the world always move. In his dialogue, *Cratylus*, Plato records: "Heraclitus somewhere says that all things are in process and nothing stays still, and likening existing things to the stream of a river he says that you would not step twice into the same river" (Kirk and Raven, 197). Things *are* in process; they don't just seem to be in process. You cannot know the river; you can experience its flow. The cosmos is, essentially, a strife of opposites: "It is necessary to know that war is common and right is strife and that all things happen by strife and necessity" (Kirk and Raven, 195).

Heraclitus was followed by Parmenides, who saved knowledge by sacrificing the world: reality, he asserted, never changes. Things *seem* to the senses to move and change, but motion and change are illusions. Because the division between what is and what is not must be absolute, there can be no transition from being to non-being, or from non-being to being. There is, in reality if not in appearance, no movement, and no change. "What is is uncreated and imperishable, for it is entire, immovable and without end. It was not in the past, nor shall it be, since it is now, all at once, one, continuous" (Kirk and Raven, 273). This logic leads Parmenides to a vision, expressed in explicitly visionary poetry, that there is absolute unchanging certainty in an absolute realm beyond the deceptive world of the senses. Things are not the way they seem.

Both Heraclitus and Parmenides are working within the Ionic tradition of speculation about the external world, but, as Werner Jaeger notes, this initial effort to comprehend what is knowable in the physical world served as the pattern for the succeeding effort to comprehend what is knowable in the mental world: "the Greek spirit, trained to think of the external cosmos as governed by fixed laws, searches for the inner laws that govern the soul, and at last discovers an objective view of the internal cosmos" (150–51). Objectivity, cosmos (an ordered universe of physical and moral experience), knowledge, and reality thus came to be linked.

This set the stage for Plato, who wanted to reconcile the two worlds, or, rather, to establish a method by which citizens, not just visionaries, could pass from appearance to reality, from the disorder of experience to order of knowledge. According to Aristotle, Plato began with a Heraclitean view: "having in his youth first become familiar with Cratylus and with the Heraclitean doctrines (that all sensible things are ever in a state of flux and there is no knowledge about them), these views he held even in later years" (Aristotle, 258–59). But, Aristotle continues, he came under the influence of Socrates, who "was busying himself about ethical matters and neglecting the world of nature as a whole" (259). The problem of the perceivable unknowable (flux, disorder) vs. the unperceivable knowable (clarity, order) is the same for morals as for nature, but Socrates's focus on morals was crucial for Plato. A world of moral confusion was not acceptable, especially to Plato, who found the moral actions of his fellow Athenians—above all, their execution of Socrates—to be intolerable. As a result, Plato developed his theory of Forms (Ideas). He proposed a two-world model: a Heraclitean world of common experience, and a Parmenidean world of changeless Forms. The world of Forms was completely real (with the Form of the Good being the most completely real), and thus knowable; the world of experience was incompletely real, and thus could only justify opinions and beliefs.

Plato's crystallization of the Greek impulse to seek a basis for certain, objective knowledge becomes a keynote of Western metaphysics. A scientific truth, for Plato, "is exact and definite, it is also true once and for all, and never becomes truer or falser with the lapse of time" (Taylor, 31). This insistence that real, objective Being is utterly independent of temporal change yields that Western impulse to postulate two worlds, one characterized by change over time (and not knowable) and one changeless and timeless and knowable.

4. *Dupin's Activity.* The Classical detective's fetish of indolence traces itself directly to Dupin, who proclaimed his disinclination toward physical action in his first and third stories, and in his second story engaged in a tour de force, solving Marie Rogêt's murder by analyzing newspaper accounts from his armchair. This pose is

deceptive. In his admirable study *The Mystery to a Solution: Poe, Borges, and the Analytic Detective Story*, John T. Irwin, who sees the relevance of Plato to the detective story, writes, "the central topic of this book [*The Mystery to a Solution*] grows out of the allegory of the cave's valorizing of mind at the expense of body, that is out of Poe's sense of his detective Dupin as a kind of Platonic embodiment, a sedentary mastermind whose very lack of physical exertion emphasizes the mastery of mind over the material world" (xvi). "Sedentary mastermind" is not really a fair description of Socrates (whom Alcibiades extolled as the hardiest of the campaigners at the battle of Potidaea), or of Plato ("Plato" = "wrestler," presumably a nickname acquired by the unsedentary young man in the gymnasium), or of the Guardians whom Plato proposes as his ideal in *The Republic* (physical training is, he insists, as important as mental [403c–412a]). Nor is it a fair description of Edgar Allan Poe, who never tired of repeating his account of his epic six-mile swim on the James River, or of, even in middle age, attempting to impress his companions with his facility at leaping great distances. Most importantly, it is not a fair description of the practice of M Dupin.

The very first exercise of Dupin's analytic genius occurs during a nocturnal perambulation of Paris. It is true that Dupin has withdrawn into "a time-eaten and grotesque mansion" where he and his companion spend the daylight hours in sedentary "reading, writing, or conversing"; but at night, "we sallied forth into the streets . . . roaming far and wide" (401). When Dupin undertakes his investigation of the affair in the Rue Morgue, he and his companion proceed to the scene of the crime. Arriving there, they make a detailed physical survey of the neighborhood: "we walked up the street, turned down an alley, and then, again turning, passed the rear of the building—Dupin, meanwhile, examining the whole neighborhood, as well as the house, with a minuteness of attention for which I could see no possible object" (413). The detective then makes a detailed examination of the interior: "Dupin scrutinized everything—not excepting the bodies of the victims" (413). Quitting only when it grows dark, he looks into all the rooms as well as into the yard. At the end of this physical exertion, he places the ad in the paper which will, when the Maltese sailor answers it, verify all of his conclusions.

Certainly the important action has taken place in the detective's mind. Before he takes a step toward the crime scene, he has worked out an *a priori* understanding of the probable actions that led to the results reported by the newspapers. It is because he knows what to look for in his physical examination that he finds what he looks for.

Dupin's survey of the building and the rooms is not violent action of traditional heroism, but it is action, and it is necessary action.

This is true again in "The Purloined Letter," where intellectual analysis is seconded by physical exertion. Dupin adopts a disguise (a pair of green spectacles) and visits the nefarious Minister D———. Having located the stolen letter, he returns home and fabricates a facsimile. He then returns to the Minister's rooms, and when a prearranged tumult in the streets draws the Minister's attention to his window, quickly substitutes the facsimile for the original. Here physical exertion and dexterity are almost as important as mental acuity. (To complete the argument, it might be noted that both of the other two tales which are often taken as Poe's contribution to the detective story, "The Gold-Bug" and "Thou Art the Man," also require considerable physical exertion on the part of the detective.)

5. *Coherence and Correspondence.* There is an interesting aspect to the detective story's essential fable of the derivation of truth (a story) from things ("peculiarities," "roughnesses," "protuberances"). "Truth" is proven through a narrative that convinces through its coherence: it is the narrative that explains (assigns a credible cause to) everything. The usual criterion for truth in the Western tradition is "correspondence." Statements are true if they "correspond" to reality. And this, of course, is precisely the claim made by the detective in the final chapter: his statements of what was done, when and where and how it was done, why it was done, and above all by whom it was done correspond to what actually happened. But readers cannot empirically test any of his statements; they cannot examine the windows, or study the tuft of hair retrieved from Madame L'Espanaye's rigid fingers. What persuades the reader is the neatness of the narrative which the detective expounds in the end. It is the elegance with which the troubling pieces are used to explain each other, and the completeness with which the questions that have been raised are answered. Logic is involved, but also aesthetics, and to the extent that the reader *wants* to believe that the final explanation is coherent and complete, even psychology contributes to the "truth" of the reconstruction.

In a sense, then, the detective's pretense to scientific objectivity is a masquerade. This is obvious enough: how could an immaterial character in a fictional world ever really be a genuine materialist? His materialist credentials ("This Agency stands flat-footed upon the ground, and there it must remain. . . . No ghosts need apply," "Adventure of the Sussex Vampire," [*ASH II*, 463]) are necessarily rhetorical, and will always be justified by narrative considerations. Gross violations of material probabilities will, of course, simply end a fictional detective's career. But good detective stories do more than meet the minimum probabilities; their quality is measured in coherence and completeness.

Bibliography

Abbott, Megan E. *The Street Was Mine: White Masculinity in Hardboiled Fiction and Film Noir.* New York: Palgrave Macmillan, 2002.

Ames, Roger T. Introduction to *Sun-Tzu: The Art of Warfare.* New York: Ballantine, 1993.

Aristotle. *Introduction to Aristotle.* Edited by Richard McKeon. New York: Modern Library, 1947.

Auden, W. H. "The Guilty Vicarage." In *Detective Fiction: A Collection of Critical Essays,* edited by Robin Winks. Englewood Cliffs, N.J.: Prentice-Hall, 1980.

Austen, Jane. *Emma.* New York: Signet Classic, 1964.

Barr, Robert. *Selected Stories of Robert Barr.* Edited by John Parr. Ottawa: University of Ottawa Press, 1977.

Barsham, Diana. *Arthur Conan Doyle and the Meaning of Masculinity.* Aldershot, U.K.: Ashgate, 2000.

Bentley, E. C. *Trent's Last Case.* New York: Avon, 1970.

Bertens, Hans, and Theo d'Haen. *Contemporary American Crime Fiction.* Houndsmill, Hampshire, U.K.: Palgrave, 2001.

Bloch, Ernst. "A Philosophical View of the Detective Novel [1960]." In *The Utopian Function of Art and Literature,* translated by Jack Zipes and Frank Mecklenburg. Cambridge, MA: MIT Press, 1988.

Buchan, John. *The Power-House.* London: Dent, 1984.

Burckhardt, Jacob. *The Age of Constantine.* Translated by Moses Hadas. New York: Doubleday Anchor, 1949.

Caspary, Vera. *Laura.* New York: Avon, 1970 [1942].

Cawelti, John G. "Detecting the Detective." *ANQ* 12.3 (Summer 1999): 44–54.

Chandler, Raymond. *Later Novels and Other Writings.* New York: Library of America, 1999.

———. "No Crime in the Mountains." In *Killer in the Rain.* London: Pan, 1983.

———. *The Raymond Chandler Papers.* Edited by Tom Hiney and Frank MacShane. New York: Atlantic Monthly, 2000.

———. *Raymond Chandler Speaking.* Edited by Dorothy Gardiner and Kathrine Sorley Walker. Boston: Houghton Mifflin, 1962.

——. *Selected Letters of Raymond Chandler.* Edited by Frank MacShane. New York: Columbia University Press, 1981.

——. *Stories and Early Novels. New York: Library of America, 1995.*

Charney, Hanna Kurz. *The Detective Novel of Manners: Hedonism, Morality, and the Life of Reason.* Rutherford, N.J.: Fairleigh Dickinson University Press, 1980.

Chesterton, G. K. "A Defence of Detective Stories." In *The Defendant.* 3rd series. London: Dent, 1908 [1901].

——. "How to Write Detective Stories. In *The Spice of Life,* edited by Dorothy Collins. Philadelphia: Dufour, 1966.

——. "On Detective Novels." In *Generally Speaking.* London: Metheun, 1928.

——. "On Detective Story Writers." In *Come to Think of It.* New York: Dodd, Mead, 1931.

——. "The Domesticity of the Detective." In *The Uses of Diversity.* 5th ed. London: Methuen, 1927.

Christian, Ed, ed. *The Post-Colonial Detective.* Houndmills: Palgrave, 2001.

Christianson, Scott. "Tough Talk and Wisecracks." *Journal of Popular Culture* 23.2 (1989): 151–62.

Christie, Agatha. *An Autobiography.* New York: Ballantine, 1977.

——. *Cards on the Table.* New York: Dell, 1964 [1936].

——. *The Clocks.* New York: Pocket Books, 1965.

——. *Double Sin.* New York: Dell, 1961.

——. *The Mysterious Affair at Styles.* New York: Dodd, Mead, 1958.

Clinton, Kevin. "Stages of Initiation in the Eleusinian and Samothracian Mysteries." In *Greek Mysteries: The Archaelogy and Ritual of Ancient Greek Secret Cults,* edited by Michael B. Cosmopoulos. London: Routledge, 2003.

Cobley, Paul. *The American Thriller: Generic Innovation and Social Change in the 1970s.* New York: Palgrave, 2000.

Cohen, Michael. *Murder Most Fair: The Appeal of Mystery Fiction.* Madison, N.J.: Fairleigh Dickinson University Press, 2000.

Cohn, Jan. *Improbable Fiction: The Life of Mary Roberts Rinehart.* Pittsburgh: University of Pittsburgh Press, 1980.

Comber, Leon, trans. *The Strange Cases of Magistrate Pao: Chinese Tales of Crime and Detection.* Rutland, Vt.: Tuttle, 1964.

Conquest, John. *Trouble Is Their Business: Private Eyes in Fiction, Film, and Television, 1927–1988.* New York: Garland, 1990.

Cosmopoulos, Michael B., ed. *Greek Mysteries: The Archeology and Ritual of Ancient Greek Secret Cults.* London: Routledge, 2003.

Cox, Randolph. *The Dime Novel Companion: A Source Book.* Westport, Conn.: Greenwood Press, 2000.

Defoe, Daniel. *Robinson Crusoe.* Edited by J. Donald Crowley. London: Oxford University Press, 1972.

Delamater, Jerome H., and Ruth Prigozy, eds. *Theory and Practice of Classic Detective Fiction.* Westport, Conn.: Greenwood Press, 1997.

DeMarr, Mary Jean. *In the Beginning: First Novels in Mystery Series.* Bowling Green, Ky.: Bowling Green University Press, 1995.

Dodds, E. R. *The Greeks and the Irrational.* Berkeley and Los Angeles: University of California Press, 1951.

Donaldson, Norman. *In Search of Dr. Thorndyke.* Bowling Green, Ky.: Bowling Green University Popular Press, 1971.

Dove, George N. *The Police Procedural.* Bowling Green, Ky.: Bowling Green University Popular Press, 1982.

Doyle, Arthur Conan. *The Annotated Sherlock Holmes.* 2 vols. Edited by William S. Baring-Gould. New York: Clarkson Potter, 1967.

———. *Memories and Adventures.* London: Hodder and Stoughton, 1924.

Drexler, Peter. "Mapping the Gap: Detectives and Detective Themes in British Novels of the 1870s and 1880s." In *The Art of Murder: New Essays on Detective Fiction,* edited by H. Gustav Klaus and Stephen Knight, 77–89. Tubingen, Germany: Stauffenberg, 1998.

Dubose, Martha Hailey. *Women of Mystery.* New York: St Martin's Minotaur, 2000.

Eames, Hugh. *Sleuths, Inc.: Studies of Problem Solvers: Doule, Simenon, Hammett, Ambler, Chandler.* Philadelphia: Lippincott, 1978.

Forter, Greg. *Murdering Masculinities: Fantasies of Gender and Violence in the American Crime Novel.* New York: New York University Press, 2000.

Francis, Dick. *Come to Grief.* London: Pan, 1995.

Frank, Lawrence. *Victorian Detective Fiction and the Nature of Evidence.* Houndsmill, U.K.: Palgrave Macmillan, 2003.

Gaboriau, Emile. "The Little Old Man of Batignolles." In *Great French Detective Stories.* Ed. T. J. Hale. New York: Vanguard, 1984.

———. *The Mystery of Orcival.* New York: Scribner's, 1904 [1871].

Gaillard, Dawson. *Dorothy L. Sayers.* New York: Ungar, 1981.

Gardner, Erle Stanley. *The Case of the Velvet Claws.* New York: Pocket Books, 1970 [1933].

———. *The D.A. Calls It Murder.* New York: Pocket Books, 1958 [1937].

Geherin, David. *The American Private Eye: The Image in Fiction.* New York: Ungar, 1985.

Gillis, Stacy, and Philippa Gates, eds. *The Devil Himself: Villainy in Detective Fiction.* Westport, Conn.: Greenwood Press, 2002.

Grella, George. "Murder and Manners: The Formal Detective Novel." *Novel* 4 (1970): 30–48.

Guthrie, W. K. C. *A History of Greek Philosophy.* 10 vols. Cambridge: Cambridge University Press, 1962–1981.

Haber, Judith Deborah. *Pastoral and the Poetics of Self-Contradiction.* Cambridge: Cambridge University Press, 1994.

Hadley, Mary. *British Women Mystery Writers.* Jefferson, N.C.: McFarland, 2002.

Hammett, Dashiell. *Complete Novels.* New York: Library of America, 1999.

———. *Crime Stories and Other Writings.* New York: Library of America, 1999.

Haut, Woody. *Pulp Culture: Hardboiled Fiction and the Cold War.* London: Serpent's Tail, 1995.

Haycraft, Howard, ed. *The Art of the Mystery Story: A Collection of Critical Essays.* New York: Simon and Schuster, 1946.

Hayden, George A. *Crime and Punishment in Medieval Chinese Drama: Three Judge Pao Plays.* Cambridge, Mass.: Council on East Asian Studies, Harvard University Press, 1978.

Heilbrun, Carolyn. *When Men Were the Only Models We Had.* Philadelphia: University of Pennsylvania Press, 2002.

Hillerman, Tony. *Sacred Clowns.* New York: HarperPaperbacks, 1993.

Hiney, Tom. *Raymond Chandler: A Biography.* London: Chatto & Windus, 1997.

Hoppenstand, Gary, ed. *The Dime Novel Detective.* Bowling Green, Ky.: Bowling Green University Popular Press, 1982.

Hovey, Kenneth Alan. "Poe's Materialist Metaphysics of Man." In *A Companion to Poe Studies,* edited by Eric W. Carlson. Westport, Conn.: Greenwood Press, 1996.

Irons, Glenwood, ed. *Feminism in Women's Detective Fiction.* Toronto: University of Buffalo Press, 1995.

Irwin, John T. *The Mystery to a Solution: Poe, Borges, and the Analytic Detective Story.* Baltimore: Johns Hopkins University Press, 1994.

Jackson, Christine A. *Myth and Ritual in Women's Detective Fiction.* Jefferson, N.C.: McFarland, 2002.

Jaeger, Werner Wilhelm. *Paideia: The Ideals of Greek Culture.* 3 vols. New York: Oxford University Press, 1939–1945.

Jann, Rosemary. *The Adventures of Sherlock Holmes: Detecting Social Order.* New York: Twayne, 1995.

Kaufman, Natalie Hevener and Carol McGinnis Kay. *"G" Is for Grafton: The World of Kinsey Millhone.* New York: Henry Holt, 2000.

Kayman, Martin A. *From Bow Street to Baker Street: Mystery, Detection and Narrative.* Houndsmill, U.K.: Macmillan, 1992.

Kelly, R. Gordon. *Mystery Fiction and Modern Life.* Jackson: University Press of Mississipi, 1998.

Kestner, Joseph A. *The Edwardian Detective, 1901–1915*. Aldershot, U.K.: Ashgate, 2000.

———. *Sherlock's Men: Masculinity, Conan Doyle, and Cultural History*. Aldershot, U.K.: Ashgate, 1997.

———. *Sherlock's Sisters: The British Female Detective, 1864–1913*. Aldershot, U.K.: Ashgate, 2003.

Kijewski, Karen. *Alley Kat Blues*. New York: Bantam, 1996.

Kirk, G. S., and J. E. Raven. *The PreSocratic Philosophers*. Cambridge: Cambridge University Press, 1964.

Kitchen, C. H. B. *Death of His Uncle*. London: Hogarth Press, 1986 [1939].

Klaus, H. Gustav, and Stephen Knight, eds. *The Art of Murder: New Essays on Detective Fiction*. Tubingen, Germany: Stauffenberg, 1998.

Klein, Kathleen Gregory. *Great Women Mystery Writers*. Westport, Conn.: Greenwood Press, 1994.

———. *The Woman Detective: Gender and Genre*. 2nd ed. Urbana: University of Illinois Press, 1995.

Kuhn, Thomas S. *The Structure of Scientific Revolutions*. 2nd ed. International Encyclopedia of Unified Science 2.2. Chicago: University of Chicago Press, 1970.

Lehane, Dennis. *Prayer for Rain*. New York: HarperTorch, 1999.

Leitch, Thomas M. "The Other Sherlock Holmes." In *Sherlock Holmes: Victorian Sleuth to Modern Hero*, edited by Charles R. Putney et al. Lanham, Md.: Scarecrow Press, *1996*.

Lewis, Margaret. *Ngaio Marsh: A Life*. London: Chatto & Windus, 1991.

Lloyd, G. E. R. *Adversaries and Authorities: Investigations into Ancient Greek and Chinese Science*. New York: Cambridge University Press, 1996.

Lloyd, G. E. R., and Nathan Sivin. *The Way and the Word: Science and Medicine in Early China and Greece*. New Haven, Conn.: Yale University Press, 2002.

Loughery, John. *Alias S.S. Van Dine*. New York: Scribner, 1992.

Macdonald, Ross. "The Writer as Detective Hero." In *Twentieth Century Views of Detective Fiction*, edited by Robin Winks, 179–87. Englewood Cliffs, N.J.: Prentice-Hall, 1980.

MacLeod, Charlotte. *Had She But Known: A Biography of Mary Roberts Rinehart*. New York: Mysterious Press, 1994.

Magistrale, Tony and Sidney Poger. *Poe's Children: Connections Between Tales of Terror and Detection*. New York: Peter Lang, 1999.

Maida, Patricia. *Mother of Detective Fiction: The Life and Works of Anna Katherine Green*. Bowling Green, Ky.: Bowling Green State University Popular Press, 1989.

Malmgren, Carl D. *Anatomy of Murder: Mystery, Detective, and Crime Fiction*. Bowling Green, Ky.: Bowling Green State University Popular Press, 2001.

———. "The Crime of the Sign: Dashiell Hammett's Detective Fiction." *Twentieth Century Literature* 45.3 (1999): 371–84.

Marling, William. *The American Roman Noir: Hammett, Cain, and Chandler*. Athens: University of Georgia Press, 1995.

Martin, Richard. *Ink in Her Blood: The Life and Crime Fiction of Margery Allingham*. Ann Arbor: University of Michigan Press, 1988.

McCann, Sean. *Gumshoe America: Hard-Boiled Crime Fiction and the Rise and Fall of the New Deal*. Durham, N.C.: Duke University Press, 2000.

McCracken, Scott. *Pulp: Reading Popular Fiction*. Manchester, U.K.: Manchester University Press, 1998.

McGregor, Robert Kuhn, and Ethan Lewis. *Conundrums for the Long Week-End: England, Dorothy Sayers, and Lord Peter Wimsey*. Kent, Ohio: Kent State University Press, 2000.

Merivale, Patricia, and Susan Elizabeth Sweeney, eds. *Detecting Texts: The Metaphysical Detective Story from Poe to Postmodernism*. Philadelphia: University of Pennsylvania Press, 1999.

Metress, Christopher. *The Critical Response to Dashiell Hammett*. Westport, Conn.: Greenwood Press, 1994.

Miller, D. A. *The Novel and the Police*. Berkeley and Los Angeles: University of California Press, 1988.

Montaigne, Michel de. *Complete Works*. Translated by Donald Frame. Stanford, Calif.: Stanford University Press, 1957.

Mullen, Anne, and Emer O'Beirne. *Crime Scenes: Detective Narratives in European Culture Since 1945*. Amsterdam: Rodopi, 2000.

Nevins, Francis M., ed. *The Mystery Writer's Art*. Bowling Green, Ohio: Bowling Green State University Popular Press, 1971.

———. *Royal Bloodline: Ellery Queen, Author and Detective*. Bowling Green, Ohio: Bowling Green University Popular Press, 1974.

Nickerson, Catherine. *The Web of Iniquity: Early Detective Fiction by American Women*. Durham, N.C.: Duke University Press, 1998.

Nisbett, Richard E. *The Geography of Thought: How Asians and Westerners Think Differently . . . and Why*. New York: The Free Press, 2003.

Nolan, William F. *The Black Mask Boys*. New York: Morrow, 1985.

Nyman, Jopi. *Hard-Boiled Fiction and Dark Romanticism*. Frankfurt, Germany: Peter Lang, 1998.

———. *Men Alone: Masculinity, Individualism, and Hard-Boiled Fiction*. Amsterdam: Rodopi, 1997.

Orzcy, Emmuska. *Lady Molly of Scotland Yard*. New York: Arno, 1976.

Panek, LeRoy. *An Introduction to the Detective Story*. Bowling Green, Ohio: Bowling Green University Popular Press, 1987.

———. *New Hard-boiled Writers: 1970s–1990s*. Bowling Green, Ohio: Bowling Green University Popular Press, 2000.

————. *Watteau's Shepherds: The Detective Novel in Britain, 1914–1940.* Bowling Green, Ohio: Bowling Green University Popular Press, 1979.

Panofsky, Erwin. "*Et in Arcadio Ego:* Poussin and the Elegiac Tradition." In *Meaning in the Visual Arts.* New York: Doubleday Anchor, 1955.

Parmenides. *Parmenides: A Text with Translation, Commentary, and Critical Essays.* Ed. Leonardo Taran. Princeton, N.J.: Princeton University Press, 1965.

Paul, Raymond. *Who Murdered Mary Rogers?* Englewood Cliffs, N.J.: Prentice-Hall, 1971.

Pepper, Andrew. *The Contemporary American Crime Novel: Race, Ethnicity, Gender, Class.* Chicago: Fitzroy Dearborn, 2000.

Perry, Anne. *Paragon Walk.* New York: Fawcett, 1981.

Phillips, Gene D. *Creatures of Darkness: Raymond Chandler, Detective Fiction, and Film Noir.* Lexington: University Press of Kentucky, 2000.

Plain, Gill. *Twentieth-Century Crime Fiction; Gender, Sexuality and the Body.* Chicago: Fitzroy Dearborn, 2001.

Plato. *The Last Days of Socrates.* Translated by Hugh Tredennick. Harmondsworth, U.K.: Penguin, 1967.

————. *The Republic.* Trans. Desmond Lee. 2nd ed. London: Penguin, 1987.

Poe, Edgar Allan. *Essays and Reviews.* New York: Library of America, 1984.

————. *The Letters of Edgar Allan Poe.* Edited by John Ward Ostrom. Cambridge, Mass.: Harvard University Press, 1948.

————. *Poetry and Tales.* New York: Library of America, 1984.

————. *Writings in the Broadway Journal.* Edited by Burton R. Pollin. New York: Gordian, 1986.

Polito, Robert. *Savage Art: A Biography of Jim Thompson.* New York: Knopf, 1995.

Priestman, Martin. *Detective Fiction and Literature: The Figure on the Carpet.* New York: St. Martin's Press, 1991.

Pyrhonen, Heta. *Mayhem and Murder: Narrative and Moral Problems in the Detective Story.* Toronto: University of Toronto Press, 1999.

Readings, Bill. *Introducing Lyotard: Arts and Politics.* London: Routledge, 1990.

Reddy, Maureen T. *Sisters in Crime: Feminism and the Crime Novel.* New York: Continuum, 1988.

————. *Traces, Codes, and Clues: Reading Race in Crime Fiction.* New Brunswick, N.J.: Rutgers University Press, 2003.

Reynolds, Moira Davison. *Women Authors of Detective Series: Twenty-One American and British Writers, 1900–2000.* Jefferson, N.C.: McFarland, 2001.

Rosenheim, Shawn. *The Cryptographic Imagination: Secret Writing from*

Edgar Poe to the Internet. Baltimore: Johns Hopkins University Press, 1997.

Rosenmeyer, Thomas G. *The Green Cabinet: Theocritus and the European Pastoral Lyric.* Berkeley and Los Angeles: University of California Press, 1969.

Ross, Thomas W. *Good Old Index: The Sherlock Holmes Handbook.* Columbia, S.C.: Camden House, 1997.

Roth, Marty. *Foul and Fair Play: Reading Genre in Classic Detective Fiction.* Athens: University of Georgia Press, 1995.

Rowland, Susan. *From Agatha Christie to Ruth Rendell: British Women Writers in Detective and Crime Fiction.* New York: Palgrave, 2001.

Schwartz, Benjamin I. *The World of Thought in Ancient China.* Cambridge, Mass.: Belknap Press of Harvard University Press, 1985.

Schwartz, Richard B. *Nice and Noir: Contemporary American Crime Fiction.* Columbia: University of Missouri Press, 2002.

Shaw, Marion, and Sabine Vanacker. *Reflecting on Miss Marple.* London: Routledge, 1991.

Smith, Erin A. *Hard-Boiled: Working-Class Readers and Pulp Magazines.* Philadelphia: Temple University Press, 2000.

Speir, Jerry. *Ross Macdonald.* New York: Ungar, 1978.

Stein, Gertrude. *Everybody's Autobiography.* New York: Random House, 1937.

Symons, Julian. *Dashiell Hammett.* San Diego, Calif.: Harcourt Brace, 1985.

Tales of Magistrate Bao and His Valiant Lieutenants: Selections from "Sanxia wuyi." Hong Kong: Chinese University Press, 1998.

Tani, Stephano. *The Doomed Detective: The Contribution of the Detective Novel to Postmodern American and Italian Fiction.* Carbondale: Southern Illinois University Press, 1984.

Taylor, A. E. *Aristotle.* New York: Dover, 1955.

Tey, Josephine. *A Shilling for Candles.* New York: Washington Square, 1980 [1936].

Thomas, Dwight. *The Poe Log.* Boston: Hall, 1987.

Thomas, Ronald R. *Detective Fiction and the Rise of Forensic Science.* Cambridge: Cambridge University Press, 1999.

Thompson, Jim. *The Killer Inside Me.* New York: Vintage, 1991.

Thompson, Jon. *Fiction, Crime, and Empire: Clues to Modernity and Postmodernism.* Urbana: University of Illinois Press, 1993.

Thoms, Peter. *Detection and Its Designs: Narrative and Power in Nineteenth-Century Detective Fiction.* Athens: Ohio University Press, 1998.

Todorov, Tzvetan. *The Poetics of Prose.* Translated by Richard Howard. Ithaca, N.Y.: Cornell University Press, 1977.

Tracy, Jack. *Encyclopedia Sherlockiana.* Garden City, N.Y.: Doubleday, 1977.

Van Dine, S. S. *The Benson Murder Case.* New York: Burt, 1926.

Van Gulik, Robert. *Celebrated Cases of Judge Dee (Dee Goong An).* New York: Dover, 1976.

Walton, Priscilla L. *Detective Agency: Women Rewriting the Hard-Boiled Tradition.* Berkeley and Los Angeles: University of California Press, 1999.

Warshow, Robert. "The Gangster as Tragic Hero." In *The Immediate Experience.* New York: Atheneum, 1975.

Watson, Colin. *Snobbery with Violence: Crime Stories and Their Audience.* London: Eyre and Spottiswoode, 1971.

Wentworth, Patricia. *The Brady Collection.* New York: Pyramid, [1949] 1967.

Whalen, Terence. *Edgar Allan Poe and the Masses.* Princeton, N.J.: Princeton University Press, 1999.

Widdicombe, Toby. *A Reader's Guide to Raymond Chandler.* Westport, Conn.: Greenwood Press, 2001.

Willett, Ralph. *The Naked City: Urban Crime Fiction in the USA.* Manchester, U.K.: Manchester University Press, 1996.

Wynne, Catherine. *The Colonial Conan Doyle: British Imperialism, Irish Nationalism, and the Gothic.* Westport, Conn.: Greenwood Press, 2002.

Index

214

DAT